CREATIVE IMPULSES, CULTURAL ACCENTS: BRIAN BOYDELL'S MUSIC, ADVOCACY, PAINTING AND LEGACY

Brian Boydell *c.* 1955

CREATIVE IMPULSES, CULTURAL ACCENTS:

BRIAN BOYDELL'S MUSIC, ADVOCACY, PAINTING AND LEGACY

EDITED BY
BARBARA DIGNAM AND BARRA BOYDELL

UNIVERSITY COLLEGE DUBLIN PRESS
PREAS CHOLÁISTE OLLSCOILE BHAILE ÁTHA CLIATH
2021

First published 2021
by University College Dublin Press
UCD Humanities Institute, Room H103
Belfield,
Dublin 4
Ireland
www.ucdpress.ie

© the editors and contributors, 2021

ISBN 978-1-910820-94-0 *hb*

All rights reserved. No part of this publication may be
reproduced, stored in a retrieval system, or transmitted in
any form or by any means, electronic, photocopying, recording
or otherwise without the prior permission of the publisher.

CIP data available from the British Library

*The right of the editors to be identified as the
authors of this work has been asserted by them*

Typeset in Scotland in Adobe Caslon and
Bodoni Oldstyle by Ryan Shiels
Printed in Scotland on acid-free paper by
Bell & Bain Ltd, Glasgow G46 7UQ, UK

Contents

Contributors

ix

Acknowledgements

xiii

Abbreviations and Acronyms

xv

Introduction

1

PART I: BOYDELL AS COMPOSER

ONE

Must Not Make His Nationality an Excuse for His Behaviour: Brian Boydell, Creative Impulse and Accent

Joseph J. Ryan

14

TWO

Musical Inscapes: An Appreciation of Brian Boydell's Orchestral Music

Axel Klein

24

THREE

'Avert Thy Smitings': A Study of *Magh Sleacht* (1947)

Shauna Louise Caffrey

58

FOUR

Sounding Irish Landscape and Life: Brian Boydell's Scores for Documentary Films

Laura Anderson

71

FIVE

Brian Boydell's Early Songs for Low Voice
Aylish E. Kerrigan
87

SIX

'White Stag' Embodied: *The Feather of Death*, op. 22 (1943)
Philip Graydon
98

SEVEN

A Pack of Fancies for a Travelling Harper (1970):
Context, Performance and Reception
Clíona Doris
108

EIGHT

Heavenly Harps, Heavenly Cloths: The Musical Collaborations of Brian
Boydell and Gráinne Yeats for Irish Harp
Mary Louise O'Donnell
121

PART II: BOYDELL AS CONTRIBUTOR TO IRISH
MUSICAL AND CULTURAL LIFE

NINE

Music at Trinity College Chapel: The Innovations
and Legacy of Brian Boydell
Kerry Houston
139

TEN

Bringing to Life the Spirit of an Age: Brian Boydell and Musical Life in
Eighteenth-Century Dublin
Ita Beausang
149

ELEVEN
A Voice for Irish Art Music: Brian Boydell and the Music Association of Ireland
Teresa O'Donnell
155

TWELVE
Everyone's Music: The Rhetoric of Advocacy in Brian Boydell's Early Broadcasts for RTÉ Radio
Barbara Dignam
169

THIRTEEN
Racing Demons: Brian Boydell as Painter
Peter Murray
185

FOURTEEN
Listing the Papers of Brian Boydell (TCD MS 11128): An Archivist's Perspective
Ellen O'Flaherty
193

FIFTEEN
Authority, Advocacy and Activism: Music in Irish Life and Culture
Niall Doyle
199

Notes
208

Chronology with Cited Works
233

Discography
237

Bibliography
240

Index
242

Contributors

Barbara Dignam is assistant professor in music at Dublin City University. Her research explores intersections of music, language, technology, and culture. She contributed to *The Encyclopaedia of Music in Ireland* (Dublin, 2013) and has published on contemporary Irish composer Roger Doyle in *Irish Musical Analysis,* Irish Musical Studies 11, Gareth Cox and Julian Horton, eds (Dublin, 2014) and on the emerging DIY aesthetic in Irish contemporary music for *TEMPO*, Christopher Fox, ed. (Cambridge, 2017). Her study of women and electroacoustic music in Ireland will appear in *Women and Music in Ireland,* Irish Musical Studies 13, Jennifer O'Connor-Madsen, Laura Watson and Ita Beausang, eds (Woodbridge, forthcoming).

Barra Boydell is emeritus professor of musicology, Maynooth University, and Brian Boydell's son. Co-editor of *The Encyclopaedia of Music in Ireland* (Dublin, 2013), his other books include *A History of Music at Christ Church Cathedral Dublin* (Woodbridge, 2004) and *Music, Ireland and the Seventeenth Century,* Irish Musical Studies 10 (Dublin, 2009), co-edited with Kerry Houston. A founding member of the Society for Musicology in Ireland, he is a recipient of the society's Harrison Medal. His edition of Brian Boydell's memoir *Rebellious Ferment: A Dublin Musical Memoir and Diary* was published by Cork University Press in 2018.

Laura Anderson is assistant professor in musicology at University College Dublin. Her research interests include film music and sound design, twentieth-century music, digital archiving and culture, and French music. Her publications include articles in *Music and Letters* and *Twentieth-Century Music*, and she is co-author, with David Cooper and Ian Sapiro, of the monograph *The Screen Music of Trevor Jones* (London, 2019). Laura was awarded an Irish Research Council Post-Doctoral Fellowship for her research project at Maynooth University, 'Disruptive Soundscapes: Music and Sound Design in French Post-War Cinema' (2017–19).

Ita Beausang is a music graduate of University College Cork and emeritus lecturer at the DIT Conservatory of Music and Drama (now TU Dublin

Conservatoire). Her book *Anglo-Irish Music 1780–1830* (Cork, 1966) is recognised as a seminal work on the period. She was an advisory editor for *The Encyclopaedia of Music in Ireland* (Dublin, 2013) and was co-author with Séamas de Barra of *Ina Boyle (1889–1967): A Composer's Life* (Cork, 2018). She was awarded honorary life membership of the Society for Musicology in Ireland in 2010 and of the Society for Music Education in Ireland in 2014.

Shauna Louise Caffrey is a PhD student and Irish Research Council Postgraduate Scholar at the Maynooth University Department of Music. Her research focuses on the relationship between witchcraft, magic and music on the seventeenth-century stage, and additionally on film music, creative practice and opera. She was the recipient of the Alison Dunlop Graduate Prize in 2019 for her thesis '"*Come all ye songsters of the Sky": Music and Magic in Purcell's The Fairy Queen*'. Shauna Louise is a founding member of the experimental music group Analog On, and an award-winning performance artist.

Clíona Doris is professor of music at TU Dublin Conservatoire and a member of the board of directors of Music Network and the World Harp Congress. She was formerly chair of the Contemporary Music Centre of Ireland. A graduate of The Queen's University of Belfast and Indiana University, Bloomington, USA, her research interests are in creative and artistic practice, research and the dissemination of historical and contemporary repertoire, in particular the music of Ireland. A concert harpist, her CD recordings include releases for RiverRun Records, RTÉ Lyric fm, Louth Contemporary Music Society, NMC and Diatribe.

Niall Doyle is head of music and opera in the Arts Council. A music graduate of Trinity College Dublin, he began a career in music management as chief executive of Music Network, during which time Music Network commissioned *The Boydell Papers* (Dublin, 1997), a collection of essays on the development of music in Ireland, and also arranged a ceremony in which then president Mary Robinson honoured Brian Boydell's lifetime contribution to music in Ireland. He subsequently worked as director of music in RTÉ, chief executive of Opera Ireland and as an arts management consultant.

Philip Graydon is a lecturer in music at TU Dublin Conservatoire and the Royal Irish Academy of Music. He previously taught at Maynooth University, from which he received the degrees of BA and MA. He received his PhD from The Queen's University of Belfast with a dissertation on Richard Strauss's 1927 opera, *Die ägyptische Helena*. His article 'Modernism in Ireland and its cultural context in the music of Frederick May, Brian Boydell and

Aloys Fleishmann' appeared in *Irish Music in the Twentieth Century*, Irish Musical Studies 7, Gareth Cox and Axel Klein, eds (Dublin, 2003).

Kerry Houston is head of academic studies at TU Dublin Conservatoire and director of the Research Foundation for Music in Ireland (musicresearch.ie). A former president of the Society for Musicology in Ireland, he served on the editorial board of *The Encyclopaedia of Music in Ireland* (Dublin, 2013) and has published widely on Irish cathedral music. His publications also include *Music, Ireland and the Seventeenth Century, in* Irish Musical Studies 10 (Dublin, 2009) co-edited with Barra Boydell, and *Documents of Irish Music History in the Long Nineteenth Century,* in Irish Musical Studies 12 (Dublin, 2019) with Maria McHale and Michael Murphy.

Aylish E. Kerrigan holds a BS and MA in Music from the University of Oregon, a Soloist Diploma in Opera and Lieder from the Musikhochschule Stuttgart and a PhD from the Dundalk Institute of Technology. She has recorded extensively and given first performances of Irish vocal works worldwide in addition to lecture-recitals on contemporary vocal music, Lieder and theatre music. She was a guest professor 1994–2015 at the Wuhan Conservatory of Music, China. Her book *Arnold Schoenberg's Opus 15* Das Buch der hängenden Gärten *in Context: The Singer's Perspective* was published by Peter Lang (Bern, 2011).

Axel Klein is an independent scholar and a research associate of the Research Foundation for Music in Ireland. He studied at Universität Hildesheim and Trinity College Dublin and received a PhD in musicology from Hildesheim in 1995. Specialising in Irish art music of the 19th and 20th centuries, his books include *Die Musik Irlands im 20. Jahrhundert* (Hildesheim, 1996), *Irish Classical Recordings: A Discography of Irish Art Music* (Westport, CT, 2001) and *Bird of Time: The Music of Swan Hennessy* (Mainz, 2019). He is co-editor of *The Life and Music of Brian Boydell* (Dublin, 2004).

Peter Murray is an art historian, curator, and also a practicing artist. Director of the Crawford Art Gallery Cork until his retirement in 2018, his publications include over 20 exhibition catalogues and artists' monographs. In 2014–15 he co-edited *Art and Architecture of Ireland Vol V: 20th Century*, published by the Royal Irish Academy and Yale University Press. He also curated 'The Language of Dreams', a 2015 Crawford Gallery exhibition that explored Surrealism in Irish and British art, highlighting the art of Brian Boydell and Thurloe Conolly. He was conferred with an honorary doctorate by University College Cork in 2018.

Mary Louise O'Donnell holds a doctorate from the University of Limerick and is a former Irish Research Council postgraduate scholar and postdoctoral fellow. Her research interests include the history and performance practice of the Irish harp, her publications including *Ireland's Harp: The Shaping of Irish Identity c.1770 to 1880* (Dublin, 2014). An accomplished Irish and pedal harpist, she has performed throughout Ireland, Europe and the USA and recently recorded a CD of Brian Boydell's music for the Irish harp. She has appeared as a soloist on the BBC, RTÉ, TG4, CNN and NHK (Japan).

Teresa O'Donnell is a harpist and musicologist. She has performed with the Irish Chamber Orchestra and is musician-in-residence with Fingal County Council. Teresa lectured at St. Patrick's College, DCU and received a Foras Feasa fellowship (PhD). Her research has featured in the *Journal of the Society for Musicology in Ireland,* the *Journal of Music Research Online* and the *American Harp Journal.* She co-authored with her sister, Mary Louise O'Donnell, *Sisters of the Revolutionaries: The Story of Margaret and Mary Brigid Pearse.* Teresa was awarded a PhD scholarship from the Irish Institute of Catholic Studies, Mary Immaculate College, Limerick in 2021.

Ellen O'Flaherty is a qualified archivist working in the Manuscripts & Archives Research Library in the Library of Trinity College Dublin since 2007, where her main responsibility is the acquisition, management and preservation of the university archives. She is particularly interested in the topic of the preservation of digital archives (both institutional records and personal papers), and in the notion of materiality and its importance for the establishment of the evidentiality and authenticity of archival records. Ellen holds an MPhil in Digital Humanities & Culture from TCD and also a Higher Diploma in Archival Studies from University College Dublin.

Joseph J. Ryan is chief executive officer of the Technological Higher Education Association and was previously vice-president academic and registrar of Athlone Institute of Technology. The founding chairman of the Forum for Music in Ireland, he has also served as the chair of the Contemporary Music Centre. For many years director of the Army No.1 Band, he is also an experienced choral conductor. He completed his PhD on 'Nationalism and music in Ireland' at NUI Maynooth in 1991, and his research publications reflect his interest in the history and welfare of music in Ireland.

Acknowledgements

Above all we wish to express our thanks to the individual contributors to this collection of essays, many of which had their origins in papers first presented at the Brian Boydell Centenary Conference held in both the Royal Irish Academy of Music and Trinity College Dublin in 2017. In this context we reiterate our thanks to the authorities and individuals at the RIAM and TCD and to all those who contributed to the success of the Centenary Conference. A special thanks also to those contributors who, although not presenting at the conference, so willingly accepted our invitation to submit essays on aspects of Brian Boydell's activities that were not covered in the conference programme; and a heartfelt thanks to all of you for your patience during the lengthy process of bringing this book to publication, a process delayed by the Covid pandemic. We also thank Dr Gareth Cox for his support and encouragement.

Noelle Moran and Conor Graham at UCD Press responded positively to our initial proposal, and have been most supportive and helpful during the process of bringing this book to print. Publication would not have been possible without the generous funding support of Dublin City University, with thanks to the School of Theology, Philosophy, and Music; and of the Contemporary Music Centre, with thanks to its director Evonne Ferguson. The CMC has also provided ongoing support behind the writing of several of the essays in this collection through their library of copies of Brian Boydell's musical scores, and for this and their ongoing support of contemporary music in Ireland, we thank all of the staff at the CMC. The extensive collection of Brian Boydell's papers, which includes the originals of many of his musical scores, is held in the Manuscripts & Archives Research Library in TCD, without access to which the research behind many of the essays in this volume would not have been possible. We thank Ellen O'Flaherty and the TCD Library staff for their support both of contributors and directly of the preparation of this volume: photographs of original scores (Plates 1–7) were provided by Digital Collections who hold copyright of these images, and we acknowledge The Board of Trinity College Dublin and the Boydell Estate for permission to reproduce these images. Our sincere thanks are also due to

Sean Barrett and Maeve O'Brien for the photograph of and permission to reproduce Brian Boydell's painting *Atlas Approached*. Other paintings and the photograph of Brian Boydell are reproduced by permission of the Boydell family. Cover image of Brian Boydell by kind permission of The Board of Trinity College Dublin. We also thank Dr Axel Klein for permission to use his discography of Brian Boydell in *The Life and Music of Brian Boydell* (Dublin 2004) as the basis for our Discography.

BARBARA DIGNAM AND BARRA BOYDELL
Dublin
August, 2021

Abbreviations and Acronyms

a	alto/contralto
b	bass
bar	baritone
b dr	bass drum
bn(s)	bassoon(s)
br bd	brass band
cbn	contrabassoon
CD	compact disc
cel	celeste
ch	choir, chorus
cl(s)	clarinet(s)
CIT	Cork Institute of Technology
CMC	Contemporary Music Centre, Dublin
cond	conductor
cor ang	cor anglais
CRC	Cultural Relations Committee
cymb	cymbals
db	double bass
DCO	Dublin Chamber Orchestra
ded	dedicated to
DMus	Doctor of Music
DOP	Dublin Orchestral Players
fl(s)	flute(s)
GPO	General Post Office (Dublin)
gui	guitar
hn(s)	horn(s)
hp	[pedal/concert] harp
hpd	harpsichord
IMMA	Irish Museum of Modern Art
Ir hp(s)	Irish harp(s)
LP	long play record
MAI	Music Association of Ireland
MC	music cassette

MS	manuscript
MusB	Bachelor of Music [TCD]
MusD	Doctor of Music [TCD]
narr	narrator
NCH	National Concert Hall, Dublin
NLI	National Library of Ireland
no.	number
NSOI	National Symphony Orchestra of Ireland
NUI	National University of Ireland
ob(s)	oboe(s)
op.	opus
orch	orchestra
org	organ
p timp	pedal timpani
perc	percussion
pf	piano
pr pf	prepared piano
rec	recorder
rev.	revised
RÉSO	Radio Éireann Symphony Orchestra
RÉ/RTÉ	Radio Éireann/Radio Telefís Éireann
RIAM	Royal Irish Academy of Music
RTÉSO	Radio Telefís Éireann Symphony Orchestra
s	soprano
s dr	side drum
str	string
str qt	string quartet
t	tenor
tam	tam tam
tamb	tambourine
TCD	Trinity College Dublin
tgl	triangle
timp	timpani
tpt(s)	trumpet(s)
trbn(s)	trombone(s)
v, vv	voice, voices
va(s)	viola(s)
vc(s)	cello(s)
vn(s)	violin(s)
wbl(s)	wood block(s)
xyl	xylophone

INTRODUCTION

Brian Boydell (1917–2000) was one of the foremost Irish composers and a central figure in developments in music in Ireland in the later twentieth century. He was widely recognised not only as a composer, but also as a performer, broadcaster, public lecturer, musicologist, member of the Arts Council, and as professor of music at Trinity College Dublin (TCD) from 1962 to 1982. A man of wide interests and accomplishments, he was already establishing a reputation as an artist before making the decision in the mid-1940s to devote himself wholly to music. Brian Boydell's centenary year in 2017 was marked by a series of events including a two-day conference hosted at the Royal Irish Academy of Music (RIAM) and TCD that celebrated his incomparable contribution to the musical, cultural and academic life of Ireland in the latter half of the twentieth century. The centenary provoked a renewed interest in Boydell's life and work, which is reflected in the essays in this volume, many of which have grown out of research presented at the conference.

This is the third book dedicated to Brian Boydell, building upon and complementing Cox, Klein and Taylor's edited volume *The Life and Music of Brian Boydell* (2004) published shortly after his death, and the recent edition of his memoir *Rebellious Ferment* (2018), edited by his son Barra. Also worthy of note is Gareth Cox's comprehensive article in *The Encyclopaedia of Music in Ireland* (2013). The present expansive collection of essays is testament to the immense scope of activities, commitments and achievements of Brian Boydell, and to the infectious enthusiasm with which he contributed so much to the nation. It includes insights on lesser-known works and underexplored cultural activities alongside fresh viewpoints on previously researched areas. As such, the essays underline the book's broad potential readership, which is also underscored by the diverse range of contributors to the volume. The breadth of connection that Boydell continues to engender in generations of scholars and fellow enthusiasts is remarkable, and this is reflected here by contributions from those working in the fields of musicology, performance, art history and archive studies, including both past pupils and current students of music.

In constituting a re-evaluation of Boydell's myriad contributions and their place within the wider contexts of musical, cultural and artistic developments in Ireland in the twentieth century, the contributions to this book have benefited from the two decades since his death in 2000, within which new or revised reflections and perspectives can emerge. That said, the volume makes no attempt to be a comprehensive survey; however, given that Boydell was a natural-born archivist, retaining every letter, newspaper cutting or other document relating to his work, not to mention engagement diaries, musical notebooks and scores, the significant archive housed in the library of TCD – donated by the Boydell family – provides a wealth of future research potential, not only on the life and work of Brian Boydell (including his activities as a conductor and performer which are not covered in the present volume), but also as a valuable source of Irish social and cultural history.

Brian Boydell's life and work can be difficult to summarise, given the wide range of his interests and achievements. More than once he has been described as a 'renaissance man', the course of whose life was never restricted solely to that of being a musician. Indeed, it may be said that his infectious enthusiasm lies behind his extensive accomplishments. Born in Dublin on St Patrick's Day 1917 into a prosperous family, Brian Boydell was educated in England, first at the Dragon School, Oxford, then at Rugby public school, before eventually gaining a first-class degree in natural sciences at Cambridge University. It was at Rugby where Boydell first displayed the inherent rebellious nature that would remain with him throughout his life. Notwithstanding his progress from 'angry young man' of Irish music and anti-establishment artist in the 1940s to his position later in life at the apex of the Irish musical establishment, Boydell remained something of a rebel, never quite abandoning this spirit displayed in his youth. It was also at Rugby that he first formally expressed his musical talents under the direction of Kenneth Stubbs. Further tuition in organ and piano at Heidelberg preceded his increased engagement with music at Cambridge where he became an active member of the University Music Society and listening club, took singing lessons, sang in the Clare College chapel choir, and had technical training in piano with a pupil of the concert pianist Solomon Cutner. While all of these engagements fed into his later contributions to a developing musical culture in Ireland, it was the strict technical regime attached to the Solomon style of piano teaching that had the most significant, and detrimental, impact on Boydell's relationship with the piano, both in terms of his decision to discontinue performing as a soloist and the formation of his strong sentiments about how best to engage the young piano student in the joy of playing rather than imposing technical exercises written by those who had nothing musically worthwhile to say.

After graduating from Cambridge, his father supported his attendance at the Royal College of Music in London where he studied composition with

Patrick Hadley and Herbert Howells, in addition to taking oboe, piano and voice lessons. Upon the outbreak of war in 1939, Boydell returned to Ireland where he began carving out a central place in the musical and cultural life of a newly emerging independent nation. Despite the enormity of his contributions to composition, performance, pedagogy, musicology and cultural activity, he never felt truly accepted as an Irishman in his own time. Boydell is now, however, acknowledged as one of Ireland's most significant composers of the twentieth century. Moreover, as a musicologist, he was one of the pioneers in the development of modern Irish historical musicology, publishing seminal research on music in eighteenth-century Dublin and contributing to *The New Grove Dictionary of Music and Musicians* (1980) and the chapters on 'Music before 1700' and 'Music 1700–1850' to *A New History of Ireland*[1], among other standard reference sources; as Harry White has commented, 'Deprived of the empirical foundations so sturdily provided by Brian Boydell, the cultural history of music in Ireland would lose much of its authority'.[2] Through over 1,000 radio and television broadcasts on music starting in the mid-1940s, he became a household name throughout the country. He was known as a performer, most notably as conductor of the Dublin Orchestral Players for over 20 years, as well as conducting the Radio Éireann Symphony Orchestra on many occasions, and as founder-director of the renaissance music vocal ensemble, the Dowland Consort; he also taught singing at the RIAM in the 1940s and early 1950s. He gave public lectures on music the length and breadth of the country, acted as adjudicator at the Feis Ceoil and other competitive music festivals not only throughout Ireland but in England, Hong Kong and Canada. During the early 1940s he studied painting with the abstract artist Mainie Jellett and became involved with the White Stag Group, which he described as 'a motley group of artists and intellectuals, who wished to escape to a neutral country'. It was within this context that he developed his interests as a painter, strongly influenced by Surrealism. He was an often-outspoken agitator for music as one of the founders of the Music Association of Ireland (MAI) and a long-time member of the Arts Council, as well as of other bodies concerned with the support and development of Irish cultural life. An honorary DMus of the NUI (1974) and Fellow of the RIAM (1990), he was elected to Aosdána, Ireland's affiliation of creative artists, in 1984. Above all, Brian Boydell is perhaps most often remembered as professor of music at TCD from 1962 to 1982, shaping the School of Music under his leadership into one of the most dynamic music departments in the country.

Most of these facets are represented in this collection of 15 essays, many of them intrinsically overlapping through references to cultural events, compositional developments, creative output, or Boydell's own words. The central theme running throughout the book is that of Irishness and the search for cultural identity and an individual creative expression, both in terms of

Boydell's personal journey as an outsider searching for his compositional voice, and his fervent belief that Ireland as a cultural nation needed to find its own identity in art music within the wider European context. The essays are grouped into two sections: Part 1: 'Boydell as Composer' comprises eight essays that constitute an evaluation, in one form or another, of Boydell's compositional output; Part 2: 'Boydell as Contributor to Irish Musical and Cultural Life' includes the remaining seven essays, featuring discussions and analyses of his vigorous contribution to musical and cultural activity in varying guises: as educator, musicologist, agitator, broadcaster and painter. The collection is bookended by two complementary appraisals, one by a past student, the other by a former colleague. In the opening essay, Joseph J. Ryan commences with a consideration of Brian Boydell as renaissance man by setting out the national context within which he strove to find his individual creative voice. Ireland, as an emerging independent state was, as Ryan puts it, neither 'conducive to the creation of original art music' nor was music literacy an educational priority. Branded an outsider, Boydell represented the 'shifting social milieu': Anglo-Irish, atheist, pacifist, polymath, activist, the list goes on. It is well-known that Boydell regarded his string quartets as central to his compositional identity, commenting that this was a genre in which 'one couldn't hide within the medium'. Ryan uses his discussion of Boydell's string quartets over a half-century to posit that he found his creative voice quite early in his compositional journey, and while his accent matured over the course of his career in his exploring a range of forms and instruments, he never felt the need to experiment beyond conservative western norms. Indeed, Ryan suggests that being 'one scientifically trained', Boydell's output could be characterised as somewhat predictable and not as rebellious as he himself had aspired to be. Perhaps this 'dangerous modern noise' was as far as he could stretch less musically literate contemporary Irish audiences in comparison with their European counterparts. In the complementary closing essay, Niall Doyle provides both a personal reflection on his own experiences of the 'great man' of music in Ireland, and a retrospective overview of Boydell's accomplishments, most notably as a dynamic force for change in music in Ireland. Doyle asserts that when Boydell spoke, one could not help but listen, and that he leveraged this authority in 'being a particularly powerful advocate for change and a highly effective leader and collaborator in making change happen'. Speaking with his metaphorical Arts Council hat on, Doyle also puts forward suggestions for how those in the arts in Ireland might follow Boydell's lead, noting the impact of the economic downturn and continual financial uncertainty for music.

However conservative Brian Boydell's work may be viewed today, Axel Klein suggests in his essay that Boydell, alongside Fleischmann and May, infused Irish art music with continental inflections, thus impacting the next generation of composers and effectively ending the introverted parochialist tendencies of previous compositional output. With an enthusiasm that Boydell would attest to, Klein takes on the mammoth task of penning an appreciation of his often-overlooked orchestral music over a 50-year period. In his discussion of several 'inscapes', he sets out not only to balance perspective on Boydell's contribution to the genre, but also to discuss Irishness within Boydell's orchestral output, its potential meaning and to what extent it appears across the works. Klein notes that Boydell's idea of Irishness in music was not that of the 'Stanford, Harty, Anglo-Irish approach', which he saw as a shortcut to any meaningful and honest contribution to the art, but rather that by expressing one's sense of place in one's community and tradition through 'an unconscious influence', the creative artist could make a valuable contribution to the international language of music. The point here is that Boydell saw himself as Irish because he lived, worked and contributed to his Irish community, and he pays homage to Ireland's cultural heritage not through the inauthentic quotation of Irish folk tunes, but in celebrating the mythology of the ancient island and drawing from its poetry, stories and landscape. Boydell also considered himself part of the European concept, and it may even be argued that he thought of himself as a composer within a global cultural domain, the subject of *In Memoriam Mahatma Gandhi* (1948) being an example. Shauna Louise Caffrey takes up the thread of mythology in her consideration of Boydell's lesser-known early orchestral work *Magh Sleacht*. Having conducted extensive searches for scored materials, Caffrey uncovered previously undocumented and unpublished materials including one of Boydell's sketchbooks, from which she comparatively examines the 1947 short-score draft (the original draft of the work) against the revised 1948 score to reveal Boydell's individual process of editing a work, which included the recasting of material and appending of a new ending. Again here, discussion moves to Boydell's expressive identity where he strives to articulate himself musically through internationally-recognised language that would 'automatically be coloured' by virtue of being Irish. Laura Anderson's contribution deals with Boydell's musical scores to the documentary films of Vincent Corcoran and Patrick Carey from the 1960s and 1970s that elide images of Ireland's ancient past with its new identity as represented by emerging industry and development. This speaks directly to Boydell's desire to represent a modern, European, outward-facing Irish culture within his music, that neither denied its heritage nor depended solely on it for musical material. What we see here is the more experimental side of his compositional output; however, as he himself admitted, he would never have placed this music in the concert hall, nor did he express any real interest in technological developments in music beyond their use for recording or playback purpose.

The subsequent four essays by Aylish E. Kerrigan, Philip Graydon, Clíona Doris and Mary Louise O'Donnell feature evaluations of Boydell's idiomatic writing for voice and instruments, with Kerrigan and Graydon focussing on his formative period and works featuring voice, and Doris and O'Donnell on his more mature works for harp. Kerrigan explores six of Boydell's 12 early songs for low voice composed between 1935 and 1942, the earliest when he was just 18 and at Rugby, and most of which were later withdrawn by the composer. In spite of this, Kerrigan argues that this collection of songs still holds value in the wider discussion of the development of Boydell's early compositional style, especially when viewed in order of composition. From a performer's perspective, and notwithstanding the technical difficulties in the songs, Kerrigan asserts that they are noteworthy due to 'their expressive qualities and for the composer's faithful interpretation of the text'. Philip Graydon picks up where Kerrigan leaves off, focussing on the single work *The Feather of Death*, op. 22, composed in 1943 as a cycle of three songs for baritone solo, flute, violin, viola and cello. This work's significance is vital to an understanding of Boydell's compositional development as it signals a definitive shift away from painting as a member of the White Stag Group towards fulltime musical composition. It also reflects a new stylistic expression in Boydell's music, what Graydon sees as 'contemporary European modernism' in its bringing together of Boydell's shared interests in music, art and the written word. In this way, Graydon reinforces the importance of Kerrigan's exploration of his early style. The impact of developments in gramophone technology is also emphasised here, and a recently unearthed contemporary private recording of the work with Boydell singing the baritone solo part (as he did at its premiere) not only provides us with invaluable insights into the composer's interpretation of his own work in performance, but it also supports future preparation of performances of the work while reflecting recording techniques and practices in the mid-1940s.

Clíona Doris contextualises her discussion of Boydell's *A Pack of Fancies for a Travelling Harper* (1970) for solo pedal harp by introducing his complete output for harp, both pedal and Irish. This complements Mary Louise O'Donnell's appraisal of the musical collaborations of Boydell and the harpist Gráinne Yeats, explicitly focusing on works in the Irish harp repertoire. Both of their discussions emphasise the importance of the performer in championing the output of the contemporary composer in order to cement works within the canon of art music in Ireland. Doris notes that *A Pack of Fancies* is one of only a small number of works within which Boydell looks to Irish traditional music, and as in the compositions discussed by Caffrey and Anderson, the spirit of ancient mysticism and the sounds of the past are evoked here. She shows how, through his in-depth exploration of a borrowed pedal harp,

Boydell produces a work that is wholly idiomatic in performance and stylistically achieved. In tracing the work's compositional origins, performance history and reception from 1971 to the present, Doris concludes that *A Pack of Fancies* is now well-established as a major concert work in Ireland. Another similarity with Caffrey's and Anderson's essays arises in Mary Louise O'Donnell's contribution, namely that of Boydell's collaborative relationships. Here, O'Donnell addresses Boydell's writing for Irish harp in the context of his working relationship with the harpist Gráinne Yeats. Without such collaboration and friendship stemming from Yeats's commissions for Irish harp, and the resulting compositional output, O'Donnell posits that the contemporary repertoire for the instrument would have remained significantly depleted. She analyses Boydell's compositional devices in *Four Sketches for Two Harps*, op. 52 and *Three Yeats Songs*, op. 56a, and, confirming Ryan's arguments above, she notes that the *Sketches*, whilst imaginative, neither contain any avant-garde techniques nor do they push instrumental boundaries, although Boydell does explore chromaticism in the second *Sketch*. That said, O'Donnell does assert that the *Sketches* set the standard for future writing for the Irish harp by Boydell's contemporaries. Yet again, we see his affinity with text and its setting for voice, in this instance the poetry of W. B. Yeats in the technically difficult *Three Yeats Songs* for singer-harpist. Unfortunately, as O'Donnell concludes, these songs show little development in Boydell's compositional language for the harp.

The remaining essays in this volume traverse Brian Boydell's assorted exploits in varying capacities, from musicologist and educator, to broadcaster and agitator. In discussing Boydell's involvement in musical developments at TCD chapel, Kerry Houston notes the significance in this context of his appointment as professor of music in 1962. In contrast to most of his predecessors who had either been cathedral organists or were otherwise active as church musicians, he was neither, and nor was he a practicing Christian. While his relationship with what he saw as quite a traditional musical establishment was never easy, Boydell drew on his experience at Cambridge, where he had held a choral scholarship, to revitalise music in the College chapel. He severed the existing musical links with the Dublin cathedrals, establishing the College chapel as an independent, university-based musical institution with its own director of chapel music, organ scholar and choral scholars. He also took great interest in the chapel organ, arguing for a completely new instrument which was to be the first neo-classical organ installed in Dublin.

There is no doubt, given the diverse range of contributions to this book, that Brian Boydell embodied what Ita Beausang in her essay calls 'the spirit of an age'. Beausang focuses on Boydell's work as a musicologist attempting to recover music in Dublin in the eighteenth century, notably through his two books *A Dublin Musical Calendar 1770–1760* (1988) and *Rotunda Music in Eighteenth-Century Dublin* (1992), both published after his retirement from TCD. On the one hand, it seems odd that such an important contemporary figure would want to focus on Ireland's cultural past; and yet, on the other hand, perhaps his looking to the past signals his search for answers to questions of Irishness and identity, both personal given the contentious dichotomies of Gaelic–Anglo-Irish and Protestant–Catholic so much a part of his own heritage and upbringing, and as a way of building a national cultural legacy beyond that of traditional folk music. Again, as Beausang outlines, we see the value of Boydell's earlier scientific training, turning it to music research carried out in a systematic and highly organised manner. It also illustrates the respect with which he treats the past and its tangible documentary artefacts. As can be seen in contributions by Houston, Teresa O'Donnell and Dignam, Boydell's cause is always rooted in the people of his nation, in this instance focussing on the stories of performers, amateur musicians, audiences and members of society: real individuals in their authentic social circumstances. Whilst he would have abhorred the term musicologist, as Harry White explains in his contribution to Cox, Klein, and Taylor mentioned above, the more contemporary term cultural historian might have appealed to him more.[3]

Reflecting comments by other authors throughout this collection, Teresa O'Donnell notes that Brian Boydell's involvement with the MAI was driven by his desire to remove Irish contemporary music from its parochial environment and firmly position it within a developing European context. In embodying cultural progress for a modern age, Boydell and others in the MAI built the foundations for future generations of composers and performers to thrive. In evaluating his contribution to the association, O'Donnell provides an overview of the MAI's establishment in 1948, its aims and objectives, and Boydell's involvement in its various educational and advocational activities and initiatives, successful or otherwise. These included organising a festival of concerts and lectures for the bicentenary of J. S. Bach in 1950, establishing a working group for composers which brought about the Dublin Festival of Twentieth-Century Music, one of the precursors to the current New Music Dublin festival, and contributing talks to the People's College, still in existence and now involving contemporary composers such as John Buckley. Yet again, the debate surrounding Irishness appears in this essay, as O'Donnell discusses the tensions that existed between members of the MAI and the Irish public service. She references Richard Pine's writing on broadcasting in Ireland, where Boydell, Anthony Farrington and Olive Smith were said to have been considered by officials in Radio Éireann (RÉ) as distrustful of both the Irish government and RÉ, calling the MAI an Anglo-Irish clique.

Boydell's expressive and commanding voice as a radio broadcaster forms the basis for Barbara Dignam's discussion of select early broadcasts he made for RÉ, explicitly concentrating on the rhetoric and central messages within the texts of his broadcast typescripts. The typescripts are presented by Dignam as valuable historical, cultural and musicological artefacts deserving of examination both for the insights they provide into artistic developments in the emerging Republic and the formation of its cultural identity at home and within Europe, and what they reveal about Boydell's convictions and philosophies around such developments. Through examining the rhetoric of advocacy in series such as 'Music for the Ordinary Listener', 'Music for the Amateur' and his sizeable contribution of 97 'Topical Notes', the essay uncovers links to the same elements that Boydell was advocating for within the MAI, notably the importance of music appreciation, amateur music-making, a national music education policy, the need to broaden listeners' awareness of the wealth of music available and, above all, the sharing of enthusiasm and joy one can experience from engaging with music. It is the expressive and appropriate language that Boydell employs when communicating directly with various audiences, his use of humour and analogy, and his talent for storytelling that illuminate the typescripts.

Peter Murray discusses Boydell as painter, an aspect of this renaissance man that perhaps few will be familiar with. In cultivating his identity as a painter, Boydell was drawn, as he was in music, to innovation, influenced for example by the Cubist style of Mainie Jellett and Evie Hone and the Surrealism explored by members of the White Stag Group mentioned in Philip Graydon's essay. Murray paints the Bohemian existence that Boydell enjoyed in Georgian houses around Baggot Street and Merrion Square during the 1940s and the various colourful characters that he was acquainted with, including Nigel Heseltine, son of British composer Philip Heseltine ('Peter Warlock'), whose poem *The Lamenting* Boydell set to music, as discussed by Aylish E. Kerrigan in her essay. It was through this acquaintance that Boydell received his first formal employment as a composer, writing and performing incidental music for settings of Heseltine's plays at the Olympia Theatre. Murray notes that most of Boydell's Surrealist paintings include plants and landscapes reminiscent of his education in the natural sciences.

In quite a unique contribution, Ellen O'Flaherty invites us inside the Brian Boydell Archive at TCD, discussing the processes involved in cataloguing the substantial collection gifted to the institution by the Boydell family in 2001, and which amounts to 30 banker's boxes of documents, correspondences, and various artefacts including cassette recordings. O'Flaherty provides a first-hand account of the challenges encountered and the ultimate rewards gained during the process, as well as the opportunities and prospects that this collection affords the researcher and enthusiast. Like other authors to this book, O'Flaherty stresses the dual importance of this collection as not only a 'mine of information' on Boydell himself, but also an exceptional historical, social and cultural resource documenting a momentous period in Irish cultural life in the second half of the twentieth century.

The lack of published editions of music by Brian Boydell as arguably the foremost Irish composer of the mid to later-twentieth-century is both deserving of comment and reflective of the conditions faced by Irish composers during his lifetime. As observed in *The Encyclopaedia of Music in Ireland*, '[e]xamples of music publishing houses in modern Ireland are scarce, a factor which has been to the detriment of musical composition and dissemination.'[4] During most of Brian Boydell's career as a composer, overseas publishers expressed little if any interest in music by contemporary Irish composers. Rare exceptions in Boydell's case included his accompanied part song written for a primary school, *Noël*, published by Curwen in 1960, and two short piano pieces written for younger pianists, *The Sleeping Leprechaun* (1945) and *Dance for an Ancient Ritual* (1959), published by Ricordi in 1959. Since 1985 the Contemporary Music Centre (CMC), founded by the Arts Council to support and encourage the composition and performance of new music by Irish composers, has made Brian Boydell's full range of compositions (alongside that of other Irish composers) available in the form of bound photocopies or digital scans of the original manuscripts. Isolated works have also been published in printed form by the CMC, including his piano solo *The Maiden and the Seven Devils*, op. 90 (commissioned as one of the test pieces by the 1994 GPA Dublin International Piano Competition) in *Piano Album I* (1993), and *Come Sleep*, from *Two Madrigals*, op. 54 (1964), in the anthology of pieces by Irish composers for mixed choir *Choirland* (2012). Two of the *Four Sketches for Two Irish Harps* (1962) were included in *Irish Harp Book* (Cork: Mercier Press, 1975) and more recently *Confrontations in a Cathedral*, op. 84 for harp, percussion and organ was published (together with Anne-Marie O'Farrell's *The Lauding Ear*) in 2017 by Creighton's Collection, Cardiff, and *An Album of Pieces for the Irish Harp*, op. 88, is scheduled for publication in 2021 by 80 Days Publishing, Tyninghame (UK). However, Brian Boydell's major orchestral and chamber works by which he is perhaps best known, including his string quartets, remain unavailable in commercial, printed editions.

A similar situation pertains to commercial recordings of Brian Boydell's music. The Discography elsewhere in this volume includes a broad cross-section of his works that have been recorded at some stage, but few of these are commercial recordings that have enjoyed wider distribution. While the situation has improved in more recent decades, the fact that the 1997 Marco Polo CD dedicated to Brian Boydell's orchestral music is often the only recording of his music available on music streaming services reflects the relative lack of general availability of his music, as too that of many Irish composers.

However else his place and achievements in Irish musical life of the twentieth century may eventually be judged, perhaps above all, Brian Boydell's life – and indeed anything he undertook – was marked by his enthusiastic and energetic commitment. We invite you to engage with the essays in this collection and to enjoy exploring the various facets of this most remarkable character.

BARBARA DIGNAM AND BARRA BOYDELL
Dublin
August, 2021

PART I: BOYDELL AS COMPOSER

ONE

MUST NOT MAKE HIS NATIONALITY AN EXCUSE FOR HIS BEHAVIOUR: BRIAN BOYDELL, CREATIVE IMPULSE AND ACCENT

Joseph J. Ryan

The centenary celebrations for the birth of Brian Boydell in 2017 served to remind us vividly of a most colourful personality whose many talents, energy and flair for communication combined to establish him as one of the most influential voices in shaping the course of music in Ireland in the twentieth century. The breadth of Boydell's interests and his progress from an early involvement in renaissance music to life as a renaissance man has arguably clouded an assessment of his contribution as a creative artist. And yet it is clear that the creative impulse was one that persisted throughout his career and one that is central to his character. But the question is whether after the passage of time that will remain the case.

This essay seeks to explore Boydell's creative impulse and accent and that sense of searching for a personal voice. What makes his case especially interesting is that the context in the newly independent Ireland was not conducive to the creation of original art music at a time and in a place where musical literacy and acquaintance with the broader international movement in relation to modern music was especially low. That Boydell persisted and, indeed, was successful in establishing himself in the vanguard of an admittedly small group of Irish voices says much for his characteristic determination and resilience. The course of Boydell's search for an individual creative style is considered here with particular attention to his works in the string quartet form.

Boydell was an unlikely composer; his ultimate rise to the status where he was to be regarded by some as the composer laureate of Ireland was even less predictable.[1] His background and initial education and training suggested other paths, and promising ones too. The son of respected Dublin maltster James Boydell and his wife Eileen, Boydell was born into a successful Anglo-Irish homestead. While Boydell's father was successful in business he was essentially conservative; it was his mother who had more catholic tastes and was the culturally progressive partner. Born in Howth in 1917, Boydell lived with his family in various houses in Dublin as the malting business on Cork Street in the south inner city prospered. In the 1920s James Boydell and his family lived in the palatial Ashurst in Killiney, a Victorian mansion to the south of the city and later the home to the South African ambassador to Ireland, Melanie Verwoerd, and prior to that, and not without some irony, the long-time residence of the Catholic archbishop of Dublin, John Charles McQuaid. That the archbishop was walking in the steps and working in the room where earlier the young Boydell had established his experimental laboratory was probably not uppermost in the prelate's mind but it is a pithy reminder of the shifting social milieu in the newly independent country. For Boydell, this privileged background was the catalyst for his subsequent success but, based on his own testimony in interviews given in later life, it rankled with him. It was not the privilege that rankled, but rather the sense that this informed the perceptions of his countrymen who defined him as of a type and that that type was not of them. He felt it made it difficult to win acceptance within his own land. Boydell could eventually respect the lineage he inherited from such as Stanford and Harty, but creatively he abjured that tradition. This also points to a fundamental dichotomy that may well have contributed to the search for a distinctive creative voice. Boydell never reneged on his nationality: he made his life in Ireland (not that he ever entertained the thought of living elsewhere), but he struggled with articulating that personality and was equally and consistently minded not to have his nationality determined by any popular and politically indentured wave that fashioned an expression he thought reductive and constraining. In his view, one could be close to the land outside a direct dependence on folksong. Boydell had the confidence to see Ireland as a member of a European community of peoples long before that was to become a formal political and economic prospect; this too informs his writing. His music proposes that his national identity was not going to be predetermined elsewhere nor was it to be defined through seeking maximum distinction from the European canon nor from the art expression of a neighbouring island. In a country that increasingly rejoiced in rebels, Boydell was an artistic rebel against the prevailing orthodoxy. That demanded some courage and that Boydell was embraced as an avant-garde eccentric in a way suggests something about how peripheral art music was in the newly-independent state. The very basis for that perception is questioned here.

We have it from his own testimony that it was while a boarder in Rugby School, which he professed to hate other than his engagement with music, that Boydell first became conscious of his distinctive status as an Irishman; this was cemented by the comment from his housemaster that provides the title for this essay. That too rankled, and the notion of Boydell as an outsider was to persist.

Given his background and social standing, Boydell couldn't but court this reputation. He was an imposing figure with a striking and sonorous voice that was a substantial asset in his significant role as an excellent communicator and champion for music. Informing this was an infectious curiosity and enthusiasm for life that proved a winning combination. In brief, Boydell established himself as a character on the Dublin scene, but a character of substance. Underlying this was a core of conviction, both technical and philosophical. His music attests the importance he attached to the original voice; and notwithstanding his own testimony that in early life he was politically naive and too culturally engaged to understand the dynamics of the time, he was a committed pacifist. What Boydell would have described as the individual atmosphere of Ireland could inform a musical spirit that did not rely on a particular form or preordained expression.

Boydell portrayed himself musically as an autodidact, the self-taught composer. He clearly took pains to listen to modern music but how centrally his style was coloured by such as Schoenberg, Bartók, Webern, Berg and Hindemith is a matter for debate. He records, for example, how influenced he was by the music of Prokofiev. In a retrospective interview, Boydell noted that he 'was very influenced by Prokofiev for some time and it was a shared enthusiasm with a great friend of mine. We used to listen to records avidly, spend all night listening to them and so one partly made up there.'[2] The want of access to live performance of modern music in the new Ireland was indeed compensated for through gramophone recordings. But Boydell also had exposure to performances during his time of study in London and through travel including study at the Evangelical Church Music Institute of Heidelberg University. And while he was somewhat dismissive of what he gained through study with Patrick Hadley and Herbert Howells in the Royal College of Music, London, there can be little doubt that such a valuable exposure informed his thinking. He worked in Ireland under the tutelage of John Larchet, professor of music in University College Dublin, but while admiring the latter's dedication and work ethic, he did not consider Larchet a preeminent teacher of composition. Boydell also expressed the view that too formal an education could be unintentionally constraining; he talked of composers being shackled by a system and that working to a received plan would inevitably interfere with the composer's personality.

While his output proposes an eclectic approach to composition, Boydell was clear that his string quartets were of central importance to him; he stated that 'they are the works I would save if everything else was lost'.[3] The quartet has always been the most intimate of forms, the most personal. Taking a lead from Beethoven, the form offers a window into the inner soul of the creator. It was the purity, the transparency, of the form that attracted Boydell; it was the fact that, as he said, one couldn't hide within the medium. He was to compose three complete quartets, one in each decade commencing in the 1940s. He also produced the *Adagio and Scherzo*, op. 89, as two quartet movements late in his career. It is interesting to consider the stylistic approach to the form and across a period spanning almost half a century.

Boydell had written his String Quartet no. 1 in 1949, the very year that saw the first performance in Ireland of Frederick May's quartet. Boydell was quick to acknowledge the quality of the older man's work and I have proposed elsewhere that Boydell cannot but have been influenced by the older writer's expression.[4] In the view of Gareth Cox, this initial quartet established Boydell's compositional language.[5] There was also a necessary pragmatism in his espousal of the form. In an age when the country was not concerned to promote musical literacy and was not building an audience for the art, winning a hearing for music that was different was a constant challenge. Boydell proved himself canny and resilient and could marry the creative impulse with the practicalities of realising a performance. As a form, the quartet was not only intimate, but also financially manageable. In his interview with Michael Taylor he noted that 'I like writing quartets more than anything. I think it is the finest of all mediums, but the other reason was that quartets here wanted them.'[6] The very opening cello line of Boydell's quartet appears to pay respectful homage to May's achievement (ex. 1).

Example 1: String Quartet no. 1, bars 1–8

There is, and perhaps appropriately for an initial essay in the form, a sense of searching in the opening *Larghetto*. But there is also a sense of confidence from the outset; Boydell scores the first movement thinly in places and he is not shy in leaving lines exposed, which speaks to that feeling of the search.

Within the work there are elements that we can recognise in later works: the insistent energetic rhythmic figures, for example. These are often paired with a sharp dissonance that invests the second movement with a dynamic sense of contrast (ex. 2).

Example 2: String Quartet no. 1, 2nd movt., bars 1–8

The fugue that follows allows the academician to emerge. Also characteristic is the fact that material is used sparingly here. The opening falling fifth is balanced with an ascending run that is later given in augmentation. It is juxtaposed against the earlier driving rhythm to round a movement that is focused and appealing. The alternating semitone–tone opening of the first movement is echoed in the final one, and the approach affords us insight into the composer's stylistic preference. Boydell says he was at this stage unaware of the music of Messiaen and especially the latter's use of modes of limited transposition with alternating half and whole steps. The *Allegro* opens with a driving energy and fuller scoring affording a contrast to the opening movement. The alternating fast and slow sections that centre on the three-note initial theme provide a fragmented conversation before the whole ends on an affirmative C major chord.

The octatonic scale that is employed here is not original and the technical examination of this and its antecedents are well documented by Gareth Cox in his essay 'Octatonicism in the string quartets of Brian Boydell'.[7] The adherence to this underlying construct allowed Boydell to be in a sense both modal and modern; the technique also confers a coherence that is further cemented through the use of classical elements and even forms, as is evident in his last work in this form.

The late *Adagio and Scherzo*, op. 89 of 1991, two movements for string quartet, demonstrate a consistent stylistic approach. The work was commissioned for the quatercentenary celebrations of the foundation of the University of Dublin (Trinity College) where Boydell had held the chair of music for two decades from 1962. In listening to the piece, one is reminded of Boydell's penchant for the avoidance of virtuosity in music. Again, the octatonic scale is employed but is informed by more traditional classical techniques. A four-note motif presented initially in the viola provides the thematic focus that is consistent with the creative perspective in the three completed quartets; it more particularly echoes the creative approach evident in the second quartet (ex. 3).

Example 3: *Adagio* and *Scherzo*, bars 1–9

From the opening, there is a confident coherence in this work. The *Adagio* is sparse from the outset; the lines are exposed and consciously hesitant but the work is also informed by a plangent lyricism. It is a bleak landscape that finds contrast in the appropriately playful *Scherzo* that follows. This betrays the familiar sectional approach alternating slower searching passages with faster affirmative statements. The use of the falling scale motive, evident from the very outset, acts as one of the unifying techniques, as does the detailed examination of the assured chords that are followed by a leap of a seventh in a sequential central passage before the transition to a tranquil trio section. The composer respects the classical form with a return to the *Scherzo* but on this occasion with reference to the more tranquil material of the trio before a characteristic final affirmative scalic conclusion.

This integrating compulsion is particularly well displayed in the third string quartet, no. 3, op. 65, completed by the composer on 2 December 1969 and dedicated to the RTÉ String Quartet, who gave its first performance in the National Gallery of Ireland, Dublin, in September 1970. For the listener open to engaging with the music of Boydell for the first time and with a view to establishing an opinion on the question posed by this essay, this third string quartet offers a good place to start. It is arguably the finest realisation of his approach to the form. And while the inner sections can be discerned clearly, the work is fashioned as a single integrated movement. The opening shimmer has that characteristic sense of searching for direction before a small germinal theme is presented and explored (ex. 4). There is an energy and momentum within this creation that is compelling. Like its companions in the form, it pays homage to the lineage through conscious use of standard contrapuntal techniques including the favoured fugal approach.

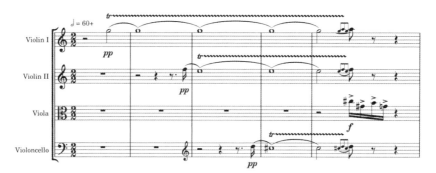

Example 4: String Quartet no. 3, bars 1–5

The String Quartet no. 3 is a single structure of some 18 minutes in duration and it reveals much that is characteristic about his creative approach. It is also the work that the composer refers to as 'an avowal of [his] musical beliefs'.[8] The initial pianissimo shimmer descends through the violins in succession and to the cello in a tenor register before the release is offered in the viola. The cluster that contextualises this forms a diminished triad. The manner of the energetic viola interjection, a falling fourth, rising third and concluding downward fourth, remains seminal to the work and is emphasised in unison by the upper three voices toward the conclusion of the quartet. This contiguity of build and release leads to a falling scalic motive in the first violin that informs the remainder of the work; the plaintive, unaccompanied falling tone at the close of the phrase (bar 31) provides an emotional reference point. It preludes a halting downward-third theme introduced in bar 34 by the second violin. This reflective turn is evident throughout the work. As for other themes cited, Boydell revels in extending, exploring and probing the core motive as the work unfolds.

At bar 158 there is an inversion of the opening filigree shimmer in a section that sees the cello gently iron out and present the energetic theme with *pizzicato*. The repetitive C♯s that follow are again characteristic of a musical trait that one encounters in Boydell. It is recitative-like and presages further exploration. This takes the form of the third, then fourth and fifth being announced and repeated in conversational style through the upper voices. At bar 180 this turns to a lyrical exchange where the theme describes a seventh before expanding further. This is juxtaposed with a reflective presentation of the initial theme. The *accelerando* that follows further investigates this material. The economy of approach and the constant shifting metre are also characteristic. The chordal statements from bar 294 lead to a step-wise rise four bars later that accompany the exploration of the rising fourth that ultimately leads to the fugal statement at bar 310 (ex. 5).

Example 5: String Quartet no. 3, bars 310–28

This is an energetic theme given *forte* that is the fuller working of the rising fourth exploration. The *ritardando* that follows heralds the return of the opening theme with the plaintive falling step at the close. The affirmative unison C♯s that mark the conclusion of the work are confident and anchor the work conclusively. The listener cannot but conclude that Boydell is crafting his statement through detailed exploration of focused material and is making much of this. The quartet evidences his experimentation with uneven rhythms and careful juxtaposition of slow and faster sections; it reveals a confident composer playing with form and limited material.

Within the confined world of Irish art music in the mid-twentieth century, Boydell cannot unreasonably be regarded as progressive and even subversive; it's a perception he would have enjoyed. But an alternative reading can equally be proposed. Here was a renaissance man for whom original composition was important but not the sole focus of his existence. He wished to contribute to an Irish expression but not at the price of having to be reductive in approach.

That he was methodical and even determined in his approach is suggested in his decision in 1944 to hire a room in the Shelbourne Hotel in central Dublin where together with like-minded friends he presented a recital of his recent chamber works.[9] This was in the days before the national broadcaster had assumed a responsibility to champion new Irish creativity. Boydell provided music for such recitals and as a vocalist and conductor, most notably of the Dublin Orchestral Players, he created opportunities to ensure that the voices of emerging Irish composers were provided with a platform. As one scientifically trained, perhaps it is not surprising to conclude that Boydell discovered the path to original expression through the use of elements that were consistent and even predictable. He married this to a faithfulness to the greater European art music forms and techniques. In this Boydell achieves a coherence of style that was to serve him for his long creative life. In working so, Boydell, it can be argued, and in no pejorative sense, is more conservative than is sometimes suggested. The search for that personal voice was one that was reconciled relatively early in Boydell's life. His chamber music, which is central to an appreciation of his creative impulse, attests a consistency of style. He did not struggle long to find a distinctive voice and while his music proposes that he valued discovering and honing his distinctive musical accent, there is no sense from the music that he felt compelled to go on changing this accent. His characteristically humorous description of the popular perception of his first essay in the quartet form as 'definitely a dangerous modern noise' is telling.[10] It is a commentary on the narrow and determinedly conservative Irish cultural scene of the mid-century, but deeper reflection proposes that Boydell's creative stance was neither as alarming nor revolutionary as was sometimes suggested. Thus while the soundscape was undoubtedly novel and perhaps even unwelcome to many Irish ears at the time, the music is coordinated and coherent to a degree that excludes it from being defined as anarchistic.

This proposition can be tested through a consideration of Boydell's second full work in the form. The String Quartet no. 2, op. 44, is a mature work of 1957 dedicated to the Benthien String Quartet of Hamburg and was first presented by them on St Valentine's Day 1959 in University College Cork. It can be regarded as the distillation of Boydell's approach to the form. The lyrical seed from which the slow opening movement is wrought is first delivered gently in viola and then cello (ex. 6). For a composer whose oeuvre is noticeable for the range of forms and media he was willing to explore, the essential intimacy of this expression is apparent from the first notes. The opening creates a lonely elemental feeling with its sparse open writing and short phrase lengths.

Example 6: String Quartet no. 2, bars 1–8

An increasingly insistent polyphonic exploration follows, but the listener is consistently returned to the opening motifs before the movement comes to a gentle close. The second of the two movements provides a dramatic contrast with its driving rhythms evident from the outset. Marked *Allegro*, it too is infused with a lyrical spirit but ever over that persistent rhythmic propulsion. The scoring is fuller here, the performers busier as the metre shifts continually. Characteristically there is some late respite with brief exploration of a minor third theme followed by a leap of a seventh that recalls the germinal essence of the opening movement before the work closes with the rhythmic reaffirmation and a bright diatonic close that again is a distinguishing feature of Boydell's style. It suggests a willingness to return home after a journey.

The circular quest that informs Yeats's *The Wanderings of Oisin* might find more prosaic echo in the creative journey of another. Boydell set out consciously to craft a distinctive accent and did so successfully. This is evident through all his string quartet writings. But he remains located technically and musically within the received traditions of western art music. The diatonic reasserts itself in his writing just as his native humour and optimistic outlook are in evidence throughout his works and even in this most intimate of forms. So too, the modal inflection of the lyrical writing in the second quartet can be defined as being infused with as much native spirit as any folksong. Boydell would not have defined it so, but perhaps he too was fated artistically and in the closing words of Oisin to 'dwell in the house of the Fenians, be they at flame or at feast'. Moreover, and perhaps with an irony that would have pleased one who delighted in being subversive, it can be argued that he was indeed to make his nationality an excuse for his behaviour.

TWO

MUSICAL INSCAPES: AN APPRECIATION OF BRIAN BOYDELL'S ORCHESTRAL MUSIC

Axel Klein

Brian Boydell was one of the most prolific Irish composers of orchestral music in the middle decades of the twentieth century. His catalogue of compositions includes twenty-seven orchestral works written between 1941 and 1988, three of them in concerto form with a solo instrument and including five works of incidental music, in addition to nine vocal works that also feature an orchestra.[1] Yet, the focus of critical attention to Boydell's music often lies on his chamber output, in particular his series of string quartets, with the orchestral music receiving comparatively little attention. When pressed to decide which works he would save if everything else was lost, Boydell chose the quartets[2] and not any orchestral work, although on an earlier occasion he also named *In memoriam Mahatma Gandhi* and the Violin Concerto.[3]

The present essay does not set out to question this assertion nor to 'redress' the perspective, but rather to balance it somewhat in order to give some more attention to Boydell's corpus of orchestral scores. This is done in the conviction that it is in his orchestral music that the composer's skill in creating colour, force, timbre and moods comes out in a more diversified and arguably more impressive way than in his chamber music – quite apart from the greater public echo that orchestral music necessarily receives in the concert hall and which has therefore had a greater influence on forming the public image of Boydell from an audience point of view.

A thread that will be running through this discussion is the question of Irishness, how it is reflected in Boydell's intentions and how it is audible in his music. The purpose of this approach is again rooted in the desire to balance the perspective. In recent years a number of academic publications have dealt with the issue of music and identity in Ireland – and this should not surprise us in a country that has seen such strong political, linguistic and cultural divides in the course of its history. Art (or 'classical') music has a particularly difficult standing in this ongoing debate. For instance, in his *Music in Irish Cultural History* (2009) Gerry Smyth manages to ignore art music almost completely.[4] In John O'Flynn's *The Irishness of Irish Music* (2009), roughly 12 out of 200 pages are devoted to 'classical music' — and in neither of these publications is Boydell mentioned.[5] Mark Fitzgerald and John O'Flynn's edited volume *Music and Identity in Ireland and Beyond* (2014) is a rare exception in its inclusivity towards art music, but Boydell's music is rarely mentioned in it.[6]

Joseph J. Ryan makes an interesting observation in 'Nationalism and Music in Ireland' (1991) in relation to the music of Brian Boydell:

> While it must be conceded that the majority of his compositions lie outside the scope of this study, and indeed were written at a time when national influence was on the wane, they are wholly consistent in that none makes any concession to parochialism.[7]

For many critics (and for many years), art music with any audible Irish musical identity risked being regarded as 'parochial' (as if Sibelius, Dvořák, Albéniz or Villa-Lobos had been parochial composers!), implying that a composer should not attempt such a direction if he wanted to be taken seriously. But Ryan does remark that, of Boydell's compositions, 'none makes any concession to parochialism'.[8] It will have to be seen in how far Boydell's music may actually be interpreted as contributing to musical nationalism — provided that the term 'nationalism' is read with a *positive* connotation (meaning cultural identity), and not a negative one (meaning parochialism).

The main reason for including this perspective here is that it was so important for the composer himself — despite the fact that he eschewed what he coined a 'plastic shamrock' idiom and the 'temptation to "write down" to a popular audience' (based on the overt use of tunes and rhythms of Irish traditional music).[9] In the well-known and frequently quoted interview that Charles Acton conducted with Boydell in the Irish-American journal *Éire-Ireland* in 1970, the discussion at one point turned to the national in music. Boydell's opinion was:

> By living in a community and by living in a country with certain types of scenery, certain types of traditions, a certain type of atmosphere, he [i.e. the creative artist] absorbs that atmosphere so that it affects his creative personality. The important thing is that if one is writing absolutely honestly, then the things that one has absorbed by being part of that community will come out in one's writing.[10]

But he was keen to point out that a contemporary Irish composer should not use the 'Stanford-Harty Anglo-Irish' approach as did so many composers of his generation:

> . . .surely it is better to use a reasonably international language, so that one can make a contribution from one's corner of the world to the international language of music, rather than taking a short cut.

This part of the interview ended with Acton's question:

> C. A.   In other words, you have got this unconscious influence from the country of which you are a part?
> B. P. B.   Well let's say that's what I hope.

In discussing the orchestral music of Brian Boydell, I will therefore seek to identify, within the necessary limits of an essay, where this influence occurs and how it manifests itself. Brian Boydell clearly wanted to be identified as an 'Irish' composer, albeit as an internationalist among them. Parochialism was far from him. What has often hindered his perception as an 'Irish' composer, however, was his English public-school education – which left behind a strong English accent in his speech – as well as studies in Cambridge and Heidelberg – which provided him with an educational background that was wider than that of most of his musical contemporaries in Ireland. Yet, it is high time that we reappraise the Irishness in Boydell's art, be it ever so subtle, and reaffirm his stance that a true Irish identity does not need folk song quotations to manifest itself.

Another general remark about Brian Boydell's music, in particular with respect to his harmonic language, will not be out of place here, since it applies to his orchestral music as much as for other genres – and, as Gareth Cox has repeatedly remarked, has not changed much in the course of his career, apart, perhaps, from an element of maturation.[11] Boydell has always been very outspoken, in his very own humorous way, about the dodecaphonic and serial avant-garde of the first half of the twentieth century, the proponents of which he simply dismissed as 'the serial boys'. In the 1970 interview with Charles Acton he said:

> I believe implicitly in tonality to this extent, that any group of notes which are played do imply a tonic, whether you like or not, and whatever the serial boys may say. . . All musical sounds contain thirds, fourths, fifths and the primary intervals. Therefore, I think it is unnatural to try and avoid such things. . . I often wonder what the serial boys sing in the bath.[12]

After initial influences ranging from Wagner to Moeran, Boydell's principal models were Jean Sibelius (1865–1957), Ernest Bloch (1880–1959) and Béla Bartók (1881–1945), as well as the harmonic theories of Paul Hindemith

(1895–1963). Cox also sees similarities with Olivier Messiaen (1908–92).[13] With little liking for the western avant-garde, Boydell wrote in an idiom of expanded tonality, often using – initially unconsciously – a scale of alternate tones and semitones that was later to become known as the 'octatonic scale'. This scale needs nine steps to reach the octave and tends to be ambiguous as to major or minor preferences.

Boydell's explicit condemnation of the serial avant-garde has earned him the epithet 'conservative', especially in the context of other works performed – like some of his – at the Dublin Festival of Twentieth-Century Music between 1969 and 1984. In retrospect, writing from a present-day perspective, Boydell's assessment 'I do not think that the *avant garde* is the music of the future'[14] may, arguably, have proven true. Hardly any younger composer today writes in a 1960s or 70s idiom (or in one directly evolved from there in the same spirit), and tonal approaches of various kinds now seem to have lost their terrors. In the once popular criticism of modestly modern Irish composers like Boydell it is also frequently forgotten that in most European countries a tonal harmonic language of sorts has remained at least as prevalent as the avant-garde; their representatives are in the process of being rediscovered and reappraised. Moreover, Boydell's importance in an Irish context of the 1940s and 50s is that – together with Aloys Fleischmann and Frederick May – he introduced a hitherto unheard Continental voice into Irish art music. With the generation that followed, this group effectively ended the artistic isolation in music that Ireland had been suffering from since independence.

* * *

In the present overview I shall look at a representative selection of Brian Boydell's orchestral works. Despite what I said above, this selection is not based on his 'most Irish' works but on representativeness for the time in which a piece was written, on the artistic and public success that he had with it, and on selecting works from the entire span of his creative life. Irish influences do not appear in all of his works.

As with many other composers, Boydell shared reservations about his 'early' works:

> ...*early* works...are all right when somebody has heard the later works first. I am not in the least ashamed of them, but I am afraid of their creating the wrong impression. That goes for everything I wrote up to the period of the *Five Joyce Songs* and the first string quartet. (That is up to the late 1940s).[15]

I shall follow this guidance and avoid very early works like *Pregaria a la Verge del Remei*, op. 14 (1941 – a fantasia on an old Catalan chant) and three works dating from 1942, the theatrical overture *The Strings are False*, op. 16, the tone poem *Laïsh*, op. 17, and the *Satirical Suite*, op. 18a.

'SYMPHONY FOR STRINGS', OP. 26 (1945)

The *Five Joyce Songs*, op. 28a – quoted by Boydell as a dividing line – date from 1946, as does the revised version of the *Symphony for Strings*, op. 26, originally of 1945. It is a rarely performed work of his that has never received critical attention. Since its first performance on 30 October 1945 by the Dublin Orchestral Players (DOP) under the composer's direction, the work has only been played again twice, in 1954 and 1960, by the Dublin Chamber Orchestra (DCO) under Herbert Pöche, the German viola player with the then Radio Éireann Symphony Orchestra (RÉSO), who had founded the DCO.[16] The sizes of the ensembles (DOP and DCO) suggest that the work has perhaps never had the intended effect of a string orchestra at full size.

The *Symphony* is one of the few works written by any of the Irish composers of Boydell's generation in the symphonic (rather than mere orchestral) genre, even though it is scored for strings only – if we disregard the symphonies of the somewhat older Ina Boyle (1889–1967) that were also written in this period but not performed. Generally, the 'triumvirate' of Fleischmann, May and Boydell were hesitant about the term and the concept of a symphony, although all three wrote orchestral music. Later, Boydell wrote *Symphonic Inscapes*, op. 64 (1968), and there is a *Sinfonia votiva* (1977) by Fleischmann; but these titles more or less confirm the problematic attitude of these composers to the symphonic genre. That Boydell in 1945–6 did not write a symphony for full orchestra is probably also due to the lack of instrumental forces at the time. The RÉ Orchestra was not yet large enough – an expansion followed in 1948[17] – and the same goes for Boydell's 'own' DOP that he conducted from 1943 to 1966.

Yet, the scoring of the *Symphony for Strings* is as varied as can be. Both first and second violins are divided into two groups, as are the cellos, so that the music starts out in eight parts (two first violins, two second violins, violas, two cellos, double bass). In the course of the work, the two voices within one group occasionally merge and divide again. The work is in three movements without subtitles. The first begins with nearly 40 bars marked *lento*, moves to an extended *Allegro molto ritmico* section and returns to the first tempo to conclude. The second is a slow movement, and the third is marked *Allegro*. The first and last movements, scored with one sharp, suggest E minor, but the scale he is mainly using is, in fact, the Dorian mode on E with its characteristic major sixth, C♯. The first movement in particular is tonally ambiguous, moving between the Dorian mode and the natural minor scale in E with its sixth step on a C♮.

Like the majority of Boydell's compositions, the motivic material of the Symphony derives from a small initial cell, in this case beginning in bar 2 with the sequence E – F♯ – G – F♯ – E, following a *fortissimo* opening chord consisting merely of the keynote and the fifth, consciously avoiding the third, which would have decided the tonality in favour of major or minor. On its repetition, the theme is harmonised in fourths, creating a 'medieval atmosphere' that is intensified in the expansion of the motivic cell in bars 10–15, where the theme in (unison) first violins is accompanied by second violins in fourths, while the theme is also expanded, including interval leaps common in medieval music such as the fall from A to C♯ in bars 11 and 13. The rather plangent opening creates an 'ancient' mood without copying all too directly any clear references to medieval music (ex. 1).

Example 1: Symphony for Strings, 1st movt., bars 10–15

The following *Allegro molto ritmico* section is written in 2/4 time and forms the main part of the first movement. Though still in the ambiguous E minor / Dorian harmony, it is considerably livelier. From bar 128, the music takes on a more fluid form characterised by an alternating movement between two pitches in the second violins and violas with an ensuing cello motif. Although this technique is a well-established device in string music generally, this passage strongly, albeit briefly, reminds one of the slow, second movement of E. J. Moeran's *Symphony in G minor* (1937), a work largely written in and inspired by the south west of Ireland. The ending of this passage leading to bar 143 most definitely recalls Moeran (ex. 2).

Example 2: *Symphony for Strings*, 1st movt., bars 136–44

With this in mind, much of the preceding motivic work and quartal harmony can also be attributed to Moeran's influence, which Boydell had expressly acknowledged for his early works. In the *Symphony* we can probably envisage how it manifested itself. On this section, the *Irish Times* commented that the motivic development, combined 'with a strong rhythmic surge[,] makes the work most attractive and interesting'.[18]

Although notated without a key accidental, the second movement, marked *Lento*, takes up the initial theme from the first movement transposed to B flat minor, on a solo viola. The whole movement is characterised by an interplay between solo instruments (in all groups except the basses) and *tutti* playing. The motivic work recalls even more strongly the slow movement of the Moeran Symphony, now applied to its theme rather than the accompanying pattern.

In the third movement Boydell leaves the Moeran influence behind. Returning to the E minor-dominated tonality of the first movement and notated mainly in 9/8 and 3/4 time, the movement is marked by rhythmic variety, strong accentuation, and the clever use of *pizzicati*. A number of convincing creative ideas drive the music to brief climaxes in short succession, such as in Example 3, marked *Poco più mosso*, where the application of repeated pitches on straight beats in the higher strings contrast with some dynamic playing in cellos and basses, making this passage particularly effective. This is harmonically enforced through interval tensions using pitches foreign to the scale such as E♭ and C♯.

Example 3: *Symphony for Strings*, 3rd movt., bars 256–61

The mood relaxes considerably with a strong *rallentando* in bar 303, followed by 32 bars of *maestoso* playing in 3/4 time that bring back the original theme from the first movement in rich harmonic colours, bringing the *Symphony* to a close after about 23 minutes.

In the *Symphony for Strings* we see Boydell in the process of self-definition. Two movements recall Moeran, but the third sees a marked development with independent ideas and more individual structural and harmonic approaches. In the absence of any programmatic ideas that might help with interpreting his intentions, one cannot seriously read any Irishness into the score. All there is are allusions to Moeran, who was himself inspired by Irish landscape, but any Irish inspiration in the *Symphony for Strings* is ultimately Moeran's, not Boydell's.

'IN MEMORIAM MAHATMA GANDHI', OP. 30 (1948)

Deeply moved by the death of the Indian politician and human rights activist Mahatma Gandhi on 30 January 1948, Boydell began immediately to work on a commemorative orchestral piece that was to become one of his most frequently performed works.[19] It received its first performance on 20 July 1948 with the RÉSO under the composer's direction. Since then it has received numerous further performances in Ireland, sometimes with less than a year in between, the most recent on 10 January 2020 with the RTÉ National Symphony Orchestra under George Jackson. It has also appeared on the – so far only – commercial CD exclusively of Boydell's orchestral music.[20]

Like the *Symphony for Strings*, *In memoriam Mahatma Gandhi* opens with a single chord played fortissimo, here a quartal chord based on D♭. The whole score, though without any key signature, suggests D flat major, but Boydell's penchant for small interval steps produces numerous exceptions, and the main melodic cell already contains two of them as the theme moves down from G via G♭ and F to D (ex. 4).

Example 4: *In memoriam Mahatma Gandhi*, op. 30, bars 1–6 (cor anglais solo)

The work is written in one movement of about 11 or 12 minutes in duration, structured into an *Adagio* opening followed by a funeral march that commences after about 4 minutes (from figure E in the score) and which forms the main part of the work. The at-first-sight unclear tonality of the *Adagio*, with its frequent pitches that belong neither to the notated key (C major / A minor) nor its concluding clear D flat major, is worth a closer look, specifically the pitches foreign to any of these scales, in order to perhaps identify an octatonic scale. The most frequently occurring foreign pitches are G, A, and D. G and A are indeed contained in an octatonic scale commencing on D♭, but D is an exception. But the scale does contain both G and G♭, the most characteristic interval step in the theme. In other words (and independent of the question whether this has been applied consciously or not), the octatonic scale on D♭ largely explains the mood of the *Adagio*, but Boydell would not be Boydell if he had completely adhered to a 'system' like that of octatonicism.[21]

The central part of the work, marked (in a curious mixture of Italian and French) *Tempo di Marcia Funèbre*, is characterised by the regular beat on a timpano, occasionally interspersed with a little dotted figure (ex. 5).

Example 5: *In memoriam Mahatma Gandhi*, op. 30, bars 46–51 (timpano solo)

What follows is an extremely well-made orchestral crescendo that builds up an impressive climax with the full resources of a symphony orchestra including brass and timpani (ex. 6). Just before the calm ending, the funeral march subsides into what Frederick May has described as a mood 'of unearthly peace'.[22]

In memoriam Mahatma Gandhi is a moving piece that derives its effectiveness from the solemn character of its music and the composer's credible sympathy with his subject. These qualities far outweigh the fact that we are not dealing with 'modern' music at the height of the late 1940s avant-garde. At the same time, the music is not mawkish or in any way unbearably plaintive. It is clearly the voice of a contemporary composer who brings a global view into Irish music not only with his subject matter but also in the seriousness and sincerity of his expression.

Example 6: *In memoriam Mahatma Gandhi*, op. 30, bars 79–84

VIOLIN CONCERTO, OP. 36 (1953–4)[23]

In October 1953 Brian Boydell completed his Violin Concerto, one of the few works of his that he revised after he had heard the first performance (on 1 October 1954). The revised version of November 1954 was first performed on

29 June 1955. In both cases the performers were Jaroslav Vanaček (violin) and the RÉSO under Milan Horvat. In the score Boydell acknowledged the support he received from Vanaček in writing the solo part, and the work was dedicated to him.

It was Boydell's first exercise in the concerto format. At the same time, it is one of his most substantial orchestral works, with three movements and lasting about 30 minutes. The movements are headed *Allegro ritmico*, *Lento* and *Rondo: Allegro scherzando e molto ritmico*. The headings alone give an impression of the rhythmical fireworks that the listener can expect.

The first movement is in sonata form. Rapid scale passages in semiquavers are characteristic for this movement in 2/4 time. From the beginning, the character of these passages becomes apparent, typical for Boydell in scales of alternate tones and semitones, starting here (bar 1 in the orchestra) from G – A – B♭ – C – C♯, followed by the solo violin (from bar 8) with B♭ – C – D♭ – E♭ – E, then C♯ – D♯ – E – F♯ – G. In combination, we have a perfect octatonic scale starting from G. In fact, the solo violin that had started on B♭ continues the scale with the sequence E – F♯ – G – A – B♭, in order to conclude another perfect octatonic scale – in both cases even written as an ascending scale. This is, in the main, the pitch material we are dealing with here.

From bar 11 (in 9/8 time), the solo violin expands these short cells to a rapid scale extending over several bars ending on a trill, followed by the first theme of the exposition (in the orchestra). Though staged in a dramatically perfect way, the theme appears initially as little more than incidental. The thematic character of the motif is manifest only after it has been taken over by the *tutti* violins and violas and a number of isolated citations in solo bassoon, cellos and (again) the solo violin as the starting point of a renewed rapid scale passage. Now, the solo violin expands the theme a little further (ex. 7).

Example 7: Violin Concerto, 1st movt., bars 44–8 (solo violin)

A little later (bars 59–63), this variant of the theme is also taken up by the strings in *tutti*. There follows an extended passage during which the solo and the *tutti* violins busy themselves with various continuations and variations of this theme that is so rich in melodic and rhythmic potential.

The second theme is of a completely different nature. The direction now reads *Meno mosso*, and the tempo slows down from about 116 to 76 beats per minute. The strings play repeated triplets on the same pitch, which together form a chord of fourths and seconds (or ninths). Out of this material, the solo violin develops its theme.

In what follows there is an attractive collaboration of violin and bass clarinet (which will be further expanded in the second movement). At the present point it is as yet limited to an echoing function by the bass clarinet, which first repeats the second theme and then all the last pitches played by the solo violin. In a very measured approach, the remaining strings play some attractive dissonant material.

Towards the end of one of its scales the solo violin concludes with a motif that will be heard several times from here on. The similarity of this motif with typical phrases from Irish traditional tunes is intriguing (ex. 8).

Example 8: Violin Concerto, 1st movt., bar 110 (solo violin)

The orchestra, at this point reduced to very few instruments, begins from bar 111 with a variant of the second theme and grows again to full force. Now the theme ends on the quintuplet as in Example 8, which enhances the effect of an old Irish lament, followed by another orchestral climax, which precedes the solo violin cadenza (which Boydell wrote out in full).

The following reprise is more like another thematic development with the previous themes and motifs varied, alienated, set against each other and variously orchestrated. Especially striking are bars 291ff. where the formerly rather delicate theme undergoes a strident variation by the brass section.

The second movement of the Violin Concerto commences with muted strings and horns, increasing the tension with brief *forte-piano* (*fp*) elements. The likewise muted solo violin begins a declamatory motif that occurs throughout the movement, intensifying by several transpositions. The tonal material here is closely related to the initial phrases of Boydell's first string quartet, op. 31, of 1949. The ending of this motif on a quintuplet ornamentation is a reminder of the first movement. Now marked *tranquillo* and *espressivo*, it resembles an Irish traditional lament. A strongly melismatic variant of it particularly underscores this argument (ex. 9).

Example 9: Violin Concerto, 2nd movt., bar 33 (solo violin)

Particularly magical is a phrase during which solo violin and bass clarinet begin an interplay, accompanied by shimmering violin tremolo and the harp plucked in high registers (ex. 10).

Example 10: Violin Concerto, 2nd movt., bars 92–7

After a brief climax shaped by some very skilful brass arrangements and followed by brief statements of the previous thematic material, the movement ends on plaintive *glissandi* of the solo violin and a calm harp solo.

The third and last movement combines the rhythmic refinement of the first with the melodic drama of the second movement. It contains rousing rhythmic passages through syncopation in the drum and horn parts. In an ensuing section the solo violin takes up a number of the rhythmic and melodic elements that shaped the first two movements while the orchestra restrains itself in terms of volume, which leads into a second extended cadenza. A number of fast-paced sections, driven by the solo violin, bring the movement and with it the concerto to a close.

The Irishness of Boydell's Violin Concerto expresses itself in a very subtle but identifiable form. Many listeners might not notice because, although they relate to Irish traditional music, these melodic elements are not harmonised in a conventional way and do not necessarily use the same interval leaps as a traditional fiddle piece would. Furthermore, Boydell neither quotes from a folksong nor does he apply any traditional dance rhythms. The subtle use of traditional Irish characteristics would have been those elements that Charles

Acton and Richard Pine had in mind when they wrote that his music 'is international and, at the same time, distinctively Irish, without striving after Irishness'.[24] It is also what Boydell himself had in mind when he said:

> I think perhaps I use the sort of characteristic Irish melismata unconsciously, and perhaps the prime example is the slow movement of my violin concerto, which I think is very Irish.[25]

* * *

Boydell's interest in Irish subject matter had been increasing since the late 1940s. An early example among his orchestral scores is *Magh Sleacht*, op. 29 (1947), subtitled with its English translation as *The Plain of Prostrations*. The piece is named after an historic plain in County Cavan that is associated with ancient legends and where some 80 historic monuments survive today in an area of just 4 square kilometres (see Shauna Louise Caffrey's contribution to this volume).

'THE WOOING OF ETAIN', OP. 37A AND OP. 37B (1954)

Similarly programmatic are the two orchestral suites under the title *The Wooing of Etain*, op. 37a and op. 37b (1954), the *Megalithic Ritual Dances*, op. 39 (1956), *The Deer's Cry*, op. 43 (1957) for baritone and orchestra, and *Ceol cas corach*, op. 46 (1958). In these works Boydell evokes a world of ideas based on the prehistoric and Celtic history of Ireland, with landscapes imbued with ancient legends and historic events. Some of these works are also inspired by poetry (or modern poetic recreations of old sagas), like *Magh Sleacht* and *The Deer's Cry*, the latter featuring an English interpretation by Thomas Kinsella of the old Irish poem 'Faeth Fiadha'.[26]

In all probability Boydell did not follow any other composer's ideas or influence when he conceived these scores. Stylistically, they are, of course, far removed from the Celticism of earlier generations of composers on the British Isles – think of Stanford, Harty, Bantock, Boughton, etc. Likewise, the music of Irish-based Celticist composers such as Thomas O'Brien Butler (1861–1915) and Robert O'Dwyer (1862–1949) was not performed during Boydell's lifetime, and this fate would also include the music of the consciously Irish-Celtic-influenced, Paris-based composer Swan Hennessy (1866–1929).[27] Their rediscovery is a development of the twenty-first century; Boydell cannot have heard their music.

A literary, if not strictly 'poetic', influence has been at work in *The Wooing of Etain*. The actual opus 37 is Boydell's incidental music to the play of the same name by Padraic Fallon (1905–74), which saw its performance as a radio play on Radio Éireann not before 28 October 1956. The orchestral suites were first performed on 31 October 1954 at the Gaiety Theatre, Dublin (Suite no. 2, op. 37b), by the RÉSO under Milan Horvat, and on 20 November 1954 at Carlow Town Hall (Suite no. 1, op. 37a) by the DOP under Boydell. Suite no. 1 is in 5 movements lasting approximately 15 minutes and Suite no. 2 is in 4 movements lasting some 13 minutes. The suites have never been performed together, probably because of their rather different orchestrations (Suite no. 1 uses a larger and more varied orchestra). But both have enjoyed several repeat performances in the course of the following years, most recently in November 2000.

'The Wooing of Étain', or 'Tochmarc Étaíne' in Irish, is a medieval legend, part of the so-called Mythological Cycle but also employing characters from the Ulster Cycle and the Cycle of the Kings. The rather complex story involves Étain, known as the most beautiful woman in Ireland, who becomes the wife of Midir after Aengus, following Midir's demand, has performed a number of difficult tasks for Étain's father. But Midir's former wife Fuamnach transforms Étain into a fly and she is blown by a storm to a distant place where the fly is accidentally swallowed by the wife of Étar who becomes pregnant, whereby Étain is born a second time.[28] Since the story is so complex and contains a number of fantastic twists and turns, it is perhaps no wonder that Boydell's music consists of so many parts that are all duly named in the headings of the various movements. Both suites, therefore, though working well as orchestral music in their own right, are highly programmatic.

Harmonically, both suites are rather easy on the ear. Suite no. 1, for instance, opens in a clear E minor, but Boydell still leaves himself a backdoor by doing without a key signature – and, in fact, the piece modulates considerably through various tonalities, with or without a key signature, but keeping a rather clear tonal language throughout. As Denis Donoghue, the *Irish Times*' music critic, remarked:

> As tuneful easy-to-listen-to music this might surprise those of the composer's admirers who are accustomed only to his more serious side, but good musicians have more than one string to their bow, and lack of versatility has never been one of Mr. Boydell's failings.[29]

Donoghue later described it as 'clever pastiche, written with tongue in cheek and no concern for profundity'.[30]

Due to its more diversified instrumentation, the second suite, op. 37b, is more effective than the first. It includes a number of beautiful themes and some very well wrought highlights that show Boydell's skills as an orchestrator. It is these skills, however, that make one wonder whether or not the 'unreal' and fantastic elements of the Celtic saga could not have inspired some more daring music.

'MEGALITHIC RITUAL DANCES', OP. 39 (1956)

The *Megalithic Ritual Dances*, op. 39 is Boydell's best known work of this series of Celticist compositions dating from the roughly 11-year period between 1947 and 1958. It has become something of a favourite of Irish audiences thanks to its many performances in the course of the past 60 years, eclipsed only by the composer's *In memoriam Mahatma Gandhi*. It was completed in January 1956 and first performed at the Gaiety Theatre, Dublin, on 12 February 1956 by the RÉSO under Milan Horvat. It has appeared twice on commercial recordings: on a 1956 Decca LP and a 1997 Marco Polo CD.[31]

The work is to be played as one movement of approximately 17 minutes although it consists of 6 different parts, namely *Introduction: Maestoso – First Dance – Second Dance – Introduction (reprise) – First Dance (reprise) – Final Dance*. As is usual with Boydell's orchestral scores he does not indicate any key signature, but a number of tonal structures are deployed including (in the *Introduction*) a 'nearly' octatonic scale starting from C♯,[32] and a Dorian melody as the theme of the *First Dance* (which one might also interpret, or extend, as D minor). Graydon also identified 'a pentatonic 'cello line, replete with the 'Irish' melisma', a procedure that recalls the solo violin part of the Violin Concerto.[33] As in previous works, he also frequently employs quartal harmony[34] to enhance the impression of 'antiquity'.[35]

Generally, the *Megalithic Ritual Dances* continue the route taken in *The Wooing of Etain* as a very accessible work with a clear programme, in this case referring to Neolithic Ireland and the (presumed) dances performed during burials and similar rituals at megalithic tombs. Whether or not such dances were actually performed at the time and what their music was like is neither historically established nor important in this context. Boydell takes the listener on a journey of the mind and persuades his audience to follow his fancy. What is clear, though, is the composer's abiding and continuing interest in Ireland's prehistoric past that found another outlet in this composition.

'Dance' is the most frequently occurring term here as that is what the work is about and that is what gives the score its rhythmic framework. Fleischmann called it an 'Irish *Rite of Spring*, evoking a fantastic world of primitive imagery', pointing out the similarity of Boydell's and Stravinsky's approach, even going to the extent of claiming that 'some of the more up-to-date adventurers in compositional techniques would find [this] difficult to emulate.'[36]

Example 11: *Megalithic Ritual Dances*, bars 13–19

Be that as it may, there are a number of convincing phrases and well-designed transitions between the various parts. For example the *Introduction* actually consists of two *maestoso* sections divided by a calmer interlude during which wind, brass and strings gradually subside towards bars 14–16, and when the double basses accompanied by bass drum and gong set in at bar 17 the whole mood is mysteriously transformed (ex. 11) to make way for an even more vehement orchestral force in the second section. This is just one of several instances in the score where Boydell shows his mastery in shaping drama and effect. Often, the melodic material of the lyrical passages is presented by a solo oboe, as in the *First Dance* with its pentatonically tinged motif.[37]

The most striking quality of the score, however, is its rhythmic variety. The three dances are in 2/2, 6/8, and 11/8 (the latter a rather complex one for an actual dance, an amalgam of 4/4 and 3/8). Frequent syncopation, markedly in the first section of the *Second Dance*, may safely be ascribed to the influence of Stravinsky and Bartók though it is not in the least derivative. Boydell spoke about this in an interview with Michael Taylor, and although he did not specifically mention the *Megalithic Ritual Dances* in this regard, the *Final Dance* might well suit the description:

> Also in the fifties, I think it came from an enthusiasm for Stravinsky and Bartók (particularly the Romanian and Bulgarian rhythms), [Bartók] is experimenting with uneven rhythms... I find this idea of a group of three happening in a string of groups of two enormously exciting, giving it a sort of spring-board effect, it is like that extra hop before you take a dive off a spring-board, and it hurls the rhythm forward. One of the things that I find most stimulating is the rhythmic excitement of music and that is why an awful lot of contemporary music bores me stiff, because it just does not move at all.[38]

Certainly, boredom is no criticism that one could hold up against this score. The critic in the *Irish Times* (unnamed but probably Denis Donoghue) was particularly taken with the rhythmic impetus of the work and particularly of the *Final Dance* when he heard the first performance:

> This section is extremely thrilling, and when it ends one is really breathless from excitement. More than most of Mr. Boydell's works, it has a sustained drive that never flags even through the quiet phase, and the timpani part is sometimes of an emotional *tour de force*.[39]

More recently, Ó Dochartaigh expressed his admiration for the piece from an audience perspective:

Listening to these *Megalithic Ritual Dances* is a thoroughly enjoyable experience; Boydell has the genius to draw the listener into that unknown, far away, epoch and he does this by an act of pure imagination.[40]

'ELEGY AND CAPRICCIO', OP. 42 (1956)

Boydell wrote just three *concertante* works for orchestra, the most substantial being the Violin Concerto, op. 36, followed by the *Elegy and Capriccio*, op. 42 for clarinet and string orchestra, and the eight-minute *Richard's Riot*, op. 51 (1961) for a solo percussionist with (full) orchestra. He seems to have had reservations about the star cult surrounding solo performers and the expectations of virtuosity, on the part both of the performer for whom the work is written and of the audience.[41]

In terms of virtuosity, the *Elegy and Capriccio* starts as a slow burner. In fact, when the clarinet first enters (in bar 5) it hardly sticks out from the rest of the ensemble. Its two movements of almost equal length combine to about 13 to 14 minutes.

According to the score, the second movement was written a year earlier than the first: the *Capriccio* is dated December 1955, and the *Elegy* December 1956. It was written for Michele Incenzo, then the principal clarinettist of the RÉSO, and the *Elegy* only was performed in a live broadcast with Incenzo and the DCO under Herbert Pöche (who had already conducted Boydell's early *Symphony for Strings*, op. 26) on 14 March 1956.[42] The first performance of the full work probably took place on 21 January 1958 with Incenzo and the RÉSO under Milan Horvat. Other clarinettists who have performed the work include Brian O'Rourke (at the 1980 Dublin Festival of Twentieth-Century Music with the New Irish Chamber Orchestra under Seóirse Bodley) and John Finucane. The latter first performed it in January 1986 with the RTÉ Concert Orchestra and later recorded it for CD with the RTÉ National Symphony Orchestra conducted by Robert Houlihan, resulting in a most pleasing audio record of a remarkable piece of music.[43]

In his brief booklet notes to the CD, Finucane expressed his opinion about the Irishness of the score by stating '. . .the *Elegy and Capriccio* has, I feel, the distinct Irish flavour of a bygone age.' With all due respect to the artist's interpretation, such a 'flavour' is in this case extremely difficult to identify in the score. It is not contained in any 'Celtic' programme, and the melismatic ornaments in melodic lines, though such exist in the score, are not necessarily Irish in character, certainly not as much as in the Violin Concerto.

The two movements, starting with a slow one marked *adagio*, somehow appear as a second and third movement of a full concerto, as if a lively first movement was missing. Still, the opening *Elegy* has quite a characteristic charm as a very solemn opener. Again, there is no key signature, although Boydell may well have indicated one as the piece stands initially in a clear E flat (natural) minor that seems ideally suited to the elegiac mood. Underlying the carpet of bowed strings is a brief plucked *ostinato* pattern of three descending pitches, B♭ – A♭ – E♭, played by two thirds of the celli – and it seems a very clever idea to divide the celli so that one third of them plays the same pitches *arco*. This has the eminently suitable effect of softening the *pizzicati* to some extent. The pitches of the *ostinato* pattern occur throughout the *Elegy*, being taken up by other string parts as well as now and then in the solo clarinet.

The clear E flat minor tonality gradually dissolves in the course of a *crescendo* from bar 10, with a number of pitches foreign to the scale that result in some dissonant interval clashes (ex. 12), heightening the tension before the peaceful mood returns by bar 18.

Example 12: *Elegy and Capriccio*, here: *Elegy*, bars 1–15

Another climax occurs around bars 33 to 36, driven forward by a more excited clarinet, and similarly from bar 55ff. before the *Elegy* slowly calms down again. It ends on a very interesting albeit brief chordal shift, involving a quintal chord based on E♭ with a preceding suspended C♭ in the violas releasing to B♭ (ex. 13).

Example 13: *Elegy and Capriccio*, here: *Elegy*, bars 66–72

The *Capriccio* poses, of course, more technical challenges for the soloist, resulting from the faster tempo, higher note values, melodic lines that are both punctuated and syncopated, and frequent changes in tonality. In fact, it is difficult to pin down any tonality for the movement that is held for any length of time. There is a brief return to the E flat minor tonality of the *Elegy*, but there is also a clear-cut C minor scale (bar 26 in the clarinet) – that would be

Example 14: *Elegy and Capriccio*, here: *Capriccio*, bars 103–9

related to the major variant of the dominant E♭ – and a number of unusual chords in the strings that seem to belong nowhere. The movement is marked by elaborate contrapuntal and canonical writing and, of course, by its rhythmic variety, as may be expected from a *Capriccio*, with some very well-made interplay between the soloist and the string orchestra (ex. 14).

Still, compared to the rhythmic fireworks of the *Megalithic Ritual Dances*, the 'caprices' of the *Capriccio* are noticeably more restrained. This is what disturbed the critic Charles Acton when he wrote after the first performance:

> The Capriccio itself has a well-sustained liveliness, but not enough caprice... I would have expected Mr. Boydell to insist on a little more air, a little more sprightliness, in all this vigorous, lively music.[44]

Not having been entirely happy in 1958, Acton seems to have changed his mind somewhat when he heard the work again in 1980 played by Brian O'Rourke:

> Brian Boydell's miniature clarinet concerto... deserves far more frequent airings. This was a pleasure to hear in itself... it is easy on the ear and refreshingly direct.[45]

Notwithstanding the directness of the score, there are at the same time such little harmonic experiments (illustrated in Examples 12 and 13) and a harmonic freedom in the *Capriccio* that make the present work seem much less compromising in comparison to the preceding orchestral scores. If the distance from traditional functional harmony inherited from the nineteenth century is one measure of modernity, then the *Elegy and Capriccio* is one of Boydell's most modern scores to date.

'SYMPHONIC INSCAPES', OP. 64 (1968)

Some years appear to have passed before Boydell wrote another substantial orchestral work. In the meantime, *Ceol cas corach*, op. 46 (1958) has been compared with the composer's String Quartet no. 2, op. 44 (1957) as being 'much alike in mood, in harmonic texture and thematic content and development',[46] and there was the rather light *Shielmartin Suite*, op. 47 (1959). But it must also be considered that in the years before the *Symphonic Inscapes* Boydell wrote major cantatas like *Mors et vita*, op. 50 (1961) and *A Terrible Beauty is Born*, op. 59 (1965) as well as some incidental music.

Boydell's *Symphonic Inscapes* may be regarded as his second attempt at tackling the symphonic genre, after the *Symphony for Strings*, op. 26 in 1945–6.

Apart from a general cautiousness in applying the term 'symphony', another reason for the avoidance of that 'pure' term is the origin of the work. As with *The Wooing of Etain* suites, the *Symphonic Inscapes* derive from incidental music, in this case the film scores Boydell wrote for three landscape movies by the director Patrick Carey (to whom the work is dedicated), namely *Yeats Country*, op. 57 (1965), *Mists of Time*, op. 61 (1967) and *Errigal*, op. 63 (1968) (see Laura Anderson's contribution to this collection). Consecutively, these make up the material of the three movements of the *Symphonic Inscapes*. Boydell explains that in these film scores, 'I created a number of musical figures which seemed to have possibilities of symphonic development denied in the time-bound context of film music.'[47] Although, therefore, Irish landscape provided the 'programme' for the film scores, Boydell insisted that 'this is not a descriptive landscape-symphony. Evocative pictures may have inspired the material, but the working-out of the ideas reflects personal emotional feeling rather than objective painting.'[48] Graydon even claims that the *Symphonic Inscapes* is a '*mostly* abstract work' and 'one of Boydell's more "uncompromising" works in musico-linguistic terms'.[49]

For the title, and specifically the term 'inscape', Boydell referred to the English poet Gerard Manley Hopkins (1844–89) for whom it expressed the quality that defines the uniqueness, the essential meaning, of any given or natural object, adding that he wished to express in sound the 'inscape' of the films' images. Coincidentally, the American composer Aaron Copland (1900–90) also wrote an orchestral piece of music around the same time with the same inspiration, called *Inscapes* (1967), one of the composer's few dodecaphonic works. It is not very likely that Boydell knew about it.

According to the score, the *Symphonic Inscapes* were completed on 24 September 1968. The first performance took place at the Gaiety Theatre, Dublin on 26 January 1969 with the RTÉSO conducted by Albert Rosen. It has enjoyed a number of further performances and was issued on an LP in 1974 by the same performing artists.[50]

Another of Boydell's remarks in his original 1968 programme note is of interest, being directed at a potential analyser of the score:

> I am anxious not to encourage an analytical approach to this work, and would prefer to let it speak more directly through the senses. Some specific guide-lines may however be of some help especially in the first movement... though I don't intend to spoil the pleasure of the clever people to whom I leave the game of counting up the notes to see how far it can be termed a 'serial' work.

This should not be read as a concealed invitation to actually test the serial qualities of the work. Rather, it is a statement that expresses a certain amount of 'frustration-turned-scorn' about musicians and critics who, especially during the 1960s, did indeed enjoy the 'game of counting up the notes' and casting their judgement about a work's quality based on the presence or absence of 12-note 'series'. Boydell did not use a 12-note row or any technique derived from there. As Gareth Cox has remarked so succinctly, Boydell had 'established a modernist legitimacy for his music throughout his career by quietly ignoring serialism altogether, integral or otherwise'.[51]

That said, Boydell's music does derive from motivic cells which he called 'cornerstones' and which are defined by 'a series of notes piling up one on top of the other' – that is how far his concessions to the 'clever people… counting up the notes' go. The key cell is a theme of three notes that occurs in many

Example 15: *Symphonic Inscapes*, 1st movt., bars 68–73 (woodwind and brass)

tonalities and consists of the interval of a rising major seventh followed by a descending fourth. This first occurs in the horns in bar 8 (starting from D), followed by clarinets in bar 11 (starting from G), and this 'piles up', for instance, in bars 70ff. in woodwind and brass (ex. 15). It becomes an extended motif in the strings from bar 70, which develops into the main material for the more excited parts of the movement, driven forward by brief, quick interplays between the strings and the woodwind. It is these intervals rather than the pitches that permeate the whole first movement.

From bar 192, a short *lento* passage provides some breathing space, and Graydon has rightly identified an oboe melody – preceded by a brief harp motif and accompanied by some very soft sustained brass sound – as an example of 'that unconscious ethnic Irish influence that so naturally and tellingly pervades his output'[52] (ex. 16).

Example 16: *Symphonic Inscapes*, 1st movt., bars 195–8 (solo oboe)

The tonality of the first movement is extremely difficult to determine (and I won't do Boydell the favour and count up all the notes). A look at the ending of the movement may illustrate this. Though it ends peacefully on a dominant C (with a hint of the fifth), the preceding pitch collection in the strings is extremely chromatic, containing, *inter alia*, both C♯ and D♭, and F♯ and G♭.

The second movement, marked *Lento*, both introduces new (the *fortissimo* repeated brass pitches, bars 2–3) and recalls previous material (the initial 'cornerstone' motif, here in the cor anglais, bars 5–8), which the opening page of the movement in the score nicely illustrates (ex. 17). This is the basic material of the whole, fairly short movement. The repeated pitches are later taken up by the strings and develop into another very Irish-sounding motif in the character of a lament (bars 37–42 and 76–81). The characteristic 'cornerstone' motif with various extensions works very well with the repeated pitches, heightening the dramatic expression of the movement considerably. The final sustained sound is a chord of five notes that appears to combine a G major seventh chord (in strings and flute) with a C in the bassoon (G – B – C – D – F♯).

Except for a calm *tranquillo* section, the third movement does not introduce new thematic material. It starts immediately (i.e. without any long pause) after the *lento* movement, but the considerably faster overall tempo transforms the repeated pitches idea of the slow movement into a forward-

Example 17: *Symphonic Inscapes*, 2nd movt., bars 1–8

driving rhythmical firework (in Boydell's words, 'an earthy bacchanale of rhythmical energy'). Many bar changes give the impression of a syncopated rhythm although this is not notated in a traditional way (bars 110 to 125 feature 11 bar changes in 16 bars, including 5/8, 2/4, 3/4, 3/8). The *tranquillo* passage is a masterwork in instrumentation, with a base provided by harp and celesta and motivic work in celli and horns. The 'bacchanale' brings the work to an end after some 22 minutes.

Charles Acton seemed thrilled when he sat down to write his review of the first performance of the work in January 1969, describing it as 'beyond doubt, the most accomplished orchestral work Dr. Boydell has yet written' and the whole performance 'a major event'. While I don't agree with the superlative 'the most accomplished' (because there are more works of the same level of quality), the *Symphonic Inscapes* is a major achievement that urgently needs a new commercial recording that would spread its fame internationally.

'JUBILEE MUSIC', OP. 73 (1976)

Another leap in time brings us to Boydell's *Jubilee Music*, in fact his next orchestral composition after the *Symphonic Inscapes* of eight years before. This time a main reason may be sought in the increasing amount of time Boydell invested into his professorship at Trinity College Dublin (TCD) and his historical research into eighteenth-century music in Ireland. Another factor may have been the increasing competition for commissions. Since around 1950, the number of capable and original composers in Ireland had probably more than doubled. The jubilee in question was the 50th anniversary of broadcasting in Ireland that was celebrated with this special commission from a composer with a deep involvement in Irish broadcasting, both as a composer and an educator on radio and television.

Jubilee Music, op. 73, is a one-movement piece of about twelve minutes in duration. It was first performed on 3 October 1976 in the Gaiety Theatre, Dublin, by the RTÉSO under Albert Rosen. It had a repeat performance on 9 September 1977 in the St Francis Xavier Hall under Colman Pearce's direction, but has since slept soundly in the archives of RTÉ. The piece is in many ways a typical Boydell – which bears its own risks. There are parts in which he repeats himself, others in which he emphasises more overtly what is important to him, and yet other parts where he tries something he has never done before and had always expressly eschewed: that of using an Irish traditional tune, and he does so twice.

Very recognisably (or predictably?), Boydell sets the beginning on rolling drums and *maestoso* brass arrangements, as well as using repeated pitches that drive the rhythm forward, as we have seen before particularly in the last movement of the *Symphonic Inscapes*. There are themes that – as overtly as never before – use melodic curves and melisma familiar from Irish traditional music (here an extended solo flute line beginning in bar 18, continued by a solo oboe for bars 24–6; ex. 18). In his programme note, he calls this episode a 'short "celtic twilight" link'. This leads to a brief section where the strings imitate the searching for radio frequencies in the early days of broadcasting, illustrated by successive trills through the parts of the string section (lasting until bar 54).

Example 18: *Jubilee Music*, bars 24–32

Another very clear Irish-inspired tune appears in the strings in bars 168–75, followed by another one in the solo oboe (bars 179–89), which is then taken up in the strings (bar 191ff.). But really odd for all who know Boydell's attitudes to the use of Irish traditional music in original compositions is his quotation from bar 226 of the jig 'Patsy Mack' in the solo violin (or is it a fiddle?) and later on of the song 'O'Donnell Abú' (Boydell erroneously calls this 'Donald Abu') – the former as a reminder 'of many broadcasts of Irish dance music' (programme note), the latter being RTÉ's station signal since the mid-1930s. Of course, there is a reason why he uses these tunes, but would he have done so if he had received a commission for the station's 25th or 30th anniversary? Probably not.

Charles Acton's review of the first performance was not quite as enthusiastic as on previous occasions. But he caught the essence of the music (and the celebratory occasion) when he wrote:

> Professor Boydell has perhaps the one completely identifiable musical language of all our composers and also a tendency to short-winded themes which lead to an episodic quality. However, he used these qualities to put forward an occasional piece containing a number of ideas symbolising the life of the station.[53]

And when he witnessed the repeat performance a year later he added dryly: 'Hearing it again I found it occasional music that is not maturing very well.'[54]

'MASAI MARA', OP. 87 (1988)

In all fairness it cannot be denied that Brian Boydell's most creative and original period when he had a unique standing in Ireland was the three decades from the 1940s to the 1960s – shared only, perhaps, by Aloys Fleischmann and to some extent by Gerard Victory, A. J. Potter and later the young Seóirse Bodley. He began this period as 'the naughty boy of frightfully modern music'[55] and ended it with mature works composed at the height of his creativity, including the *Symphonic Inscapes*, op. 64 and, perhaps, the String Quartet no. 3, op. 65 (1969). In his orchestral music, the *Jubilee Music*, op. 73, and the following *Partita concertante*, op. 75 (1978) are pastiches of his former self, the latter quite openly an adaptation of previous chamber works (the *Five Mosaics*, op. 69 and the *Impetuous Capriccio*, op. 75a).

For many, therefore, *Masai Mara*, op. 87 came as a surprise – would he have something new to say, at the age of 71? Yes, he would indeed. It was not a stylistic turnaround, and he had not become an avant-gardist overnight; but Michael Dervan, the new music critic at the *Irish Times* (a paper that now, not of Dervan's fault, devotes much less space to art music than in previous decades), noted 'an exploratory character to the music, unusual in the work of an Irish composer who is now in his seventies'.[56]

As with every real musician, Brian Boydell had always been a very perceptive man with a gift for and an intense interest in observing his natural as well as his social environment. He liked travelling, and in his diaries often made notes about flora and fauna of the regions he visited. One such journey led him to Kenya when he visited the famous national park Masai Mara, a large protected ecosystem populated by lions, leopards, rare birds and migratory species like zebras and gazelles. In his programme note, Boydell writes about his fascination of 'being a guest of the animals in *their* land' and his subsequent 'strong urge to communicate in music' what this experience meant to him. In particular, it meant to him a sense of awareness of how endangered this natural world was, due to 'human greed and misguided ideas of "progress"'.[57]

In other words, with *Masai Mara* Boydell returns to programmatic music, but for the first time this has no connection to Ireland, and it is the rather 'exotic' nature of his own experience that is a key to understanding what makes *Masai Mara* so different.

The piece is written in one movement of about twelve minutes in duration and may be divided into two very quiet outer parts and a more agitated central section. The beginning and closing sections serve to illustrate the beauty and fragility of (almost) untouched nature, with the central section demonstrating the destructive influence of human beings on such a landscape. There is a positive message in that Boydell returns to the peaceful mood of the beginning as it offers the hope that destruction may in the end be overcome by the power of nature, but there clearly remains a risk.

The 'otherness' of this score, compared to his earlier music, does not express itself in any new approach to harmony or notation. We are dealing with a tonal score centred on E, and there are many hints of octatonality, very clearly, for instance, in the lines of the first violin in bars 83–6 with an octatonic motif based on a scale of E – F♯ – G etc. (ex. 19; only the eighth step, D♯ or E♭, is missing).

Example 19: *Masai Mara*, bars 83–6 (strings)

The striking 'new acoustic' of *Masai Mara* has its origin in Boydell's novel use of a tenor recorder, which occupies the role of an exotic bird against the background of an often static orchestra that creates 'atmosphere' rather than contrapuntal harmony. In his score, Boydell describes his demand on the

Example 20: *Masai Mara*, bars 66–70

instrument: 'A Renaissance model is preferable to Baroque type. The intonation should <u>not</u> be precise.' He also devises some special notation asking the player to bend the notes slightly flat or sharp of the indicated note.

For instance, a line above a note that goes up and down represents the bending of the given note in this manner. Example 20 illustrates how this is applied in the score. In Michael Dervan's words, sections like this revealed 'an almost other-worldly appeal', and the credit for this goes to the masterful orchestration that gives the tenor recorder its space by positioning it against the static low strings and harp in quartal harmony.[58]

* * *

'I think I'd like to be known for somebody who was sincere and honest in what he tried to be.'[59] In his desire to be honest, sincere and true to himself, Boydell was uncompromising. He undoubtedly found a way for himself to formulate a cosmopolitan and, yes, contemporary voice in Irish art music that is very comprehensible to non-Irish audiences as well. In Gerard Manley Hopkins's sense, each of his compositions represents his own musical 'inscape' of the idea he has wanted to convey. Moreover, his cultural and political attitudes inform much of his (orchestral) music, resulting in musical expressions of these 'inscapes' that are highly credible because they are personal. This includes his love of Ireland, its prehistoric monuments and impressive landscapes, but he also goes beyond his own regional experience in works honouring an Indian pacifist or an African nature park.

While the importance of Brian Boydell as a composer working in Ireland during formative periods in its cultural history has been developed here to some extent, the question remains how influential he may have been, not in his role as an educator in university and the public sphere, which is a different matter, but as a composer. In this regard, I think his greatest importance lies in the cosmopolitanism that he brought to a conservative country often hostile to social and cultural progress. This he had in common with Aloys Fleischmann and Frederick May, but Boydell was the most consequential and persistent among them. Ireland's own cosmopolitan development since membership of the European Union in 1973 has been phenomenal, and in music, Boydell was a precursor of this trend.

In purely musical terms, nobody really followed in his artistic footsteps. Diatonic tonality in Irish music has either developed into neoromantic pastiche or dissolved into unrecognisability. Cosmopolitanism is now a given, it no longer affords special mention. But there is a heritage, perhaps, of a Celticism in art music that has survived the social changes because of its adaptability to individual modes of expression and its timelessness. There are composers who, as a personal characteristic or in certain periods of time, have explored Ireland's Celtic or prehistoric past in modern music – some of the orchestral scores of the young John Buckley (b. 1951) in the 1970s, the 'Mad Sweeney' series of works in all kinds of genres by Frank Corcoran (b. 1944), selected scores by Michael Holohan (b. 1956) and Fergus Johnston (b. 1959) – composers who grew up as concert-goers hearing Boydell's orchestral music, and some of whom were students of Boydell at TCD. Perhaps, as unconscious as Boydell's own Irish influence was, some of Boydell's influence more or less consciously worked its way into present-day composition.

THREE

'AVERT THY SMITINGS': A STUDY OF *MAGH SLEACHT* (1947)

Shauna Louise Caffrey

In April 1946, Brian Boydell began sketching fragments of a three-movement masque by the title of *Magh Sleacht*. The work, first performed in 1947 by the Radio Éireann Symphony Orchestra (RÉSO), was both dedicated to and conducted by Jean Martinon. Despite numerous broadcast performances on Radio Éireann (RÉ) and seemingly positive reception, the work has since fallen into such obscurity that a cursory search – either online or within a library catalogue – is more likely to turn up references to bardic poetry and Irish mythology than to Boydell or his music. Why has this work, a thematic predecessor to *Megalithic Ritual Dances*, op. 39 (1956), endured in a state of limbo: largely absent from lists of Boydell's works, unpublished and unperformed – or so it seems – since 1948? The following essay seeks to shed some light on this elusive work and to chart its development from sketchbook to completed score. The work's place within Boydell's wider catalogue will be discussed, as will its inspiration, performance history and reception. A vast majority of this study has been conducted using unpublished sources, and while as many lines of enquiry have been followed as possible, there are a number of questions regarding the work that remain unanswered. The following pages seek to give as complete an understanding of the work as the documents currently available can provide, but acknowledge that more information could be gained from further studies – possible avenues for which will be discussed in the conclusion.

'MAGH SLEACHT' UNEARTHED

The rediscovery of *Magh Sleacht* and subsequent research for this paper was the result of the study of one of Boydell's sketchbooks, a small volume held by Trinity College Dublin's Manuscripts & Archives Research Library, numbered 11128/6 (2014). Containing sketches dated from 1946 to 1956, the sketchbook contains preliminary work for *In Memoriam Mahatma Gandhi*, String Quartets nos. 1 and 2, *The Buried Moon* and a number of other works, and is characterised by Boydell's meticulous dating and labelling of his entries.[1] Entries for the year 1946 are largely concerned with a work entitled *Meag Sleacht* – which was later to be retitled *Magh Sleacht* – with the earliest known reference to the work occurring on the first page alongside a sketch from April 1946.[2] The only printed records found in the initial search for *Magh Sleacht* were those in *The Life and Music of Brian Boydell* and a small number of newspaper reviews. The information presented in these, in Hazel Farrell's 'Compositions by Brian Boydell', and the contents of Boydell's pocket engagement diaries for the year 1947, confirmed that the work had been first performed by the RÉSO in September 1947, which later documentation was to support.[3]

The RTÉ Archives, the RÉ collections, RTÉ Music Librarian and National Symphony Orchestra records were consulted in search of a score, performance information and any possible recordings without success. Having exhausted all external sources, the search for documentation was returned to the Manuscripts & Archives Research Library. Here, with thanks to assistant librarian Ellen O'Flaherty, a number of new documents were brought to light. The first uncovered were those in folder 11128/6/MAGH SLEACHT/2 (Box 31), which comprises three handwritten viola part-books for the work and four violin II parts (also handwritten), all of which had undergone revision by Boydell in 1948. These were followed by the final draft of the score 11128/6/MAGH SLEACHT/3 and folder 11128/6/MAGH SLEACHT/1, which contained the remaining orchestral part-books and early draft material of the work.

'MAGH SLEACHT' DISSECTED: A COMMENTARY

The discovery of score, parts and draft material for *Magh Sleacht* presented a particular opportunity to examine the transition of a work from draft to completed score, and to trace the alterations made to the work following its first performance. As the cataloguing of Boydell's documents is an ongoing process, there are as yet no specific references for the various draft pages present in folder 11128/6/MAGH SLEACHT/1.

An inspection of folder 11128/6/MAGH SLEACHT/1 revealed five violin I, one violin II, one viola, four cello and two double bass parts; parts for horns I to IV, trumpets I to III, two tenor trombones, one bass trombone and one tuba, flutes I and II, piccolo, oboes I and II, cor anglais, clarinets I and II and bass clarinet, bassoons I and II, and a miscellany of pages, some of which proved to be draft material for *Magh Sleacht*, and some of which have yet to be identified. The draft material is written on a variety of loose pages of different measurements. The material for movements one and two is written in pencil and is, in both cases, incomplete. The most complete and easiest of the movements to distinguish is movement three, in part due to the fact that the ink in which it is written has not yet undergone the process of deterioration that has affected the other drafts. Presumably there existed earlier draft material of this movement – and later drafts of movements one and two – but they could not be located in the Trinity College Dublin (TCD) collections. The recovered draft of movement three appears to have been the final short-score draft of that movement before the work was copied into the complete score, as a number of errors correspond between it and the final score. The final score (11128/6/MAGH SLEACHT/3) takes the form of a blue hardback manuscript book containing programme notes, front matter, and the complete score of *Magh Sleacht*. Measuring approximately 260 mm by 352.5 mm, the non-standard sizing and lack of a manufacturer's watermark suggests that the volume may have been assembled and bound by Boydell himself, or at his request. Originally comprising 106 pages of score, the 1948 revision decreased the number to 104. Plates 1 and 2, respectively, show page 89 from the completed score (11128/6/MAGH SLEACHT/3) and page 7 of the draft found in folder 11128/6/MAGH SLEACHT/1, and illustrate some of the alterations made to the score following its first performance in 1947. Page 7 presents a short score version of bars 145–70 of the earliest complete edition of the score, with page 89 presenting the newly inserted bars 152–6 of February 1948.

Page 7 measures 251 mm by 362.5 mm long, with a left-hand margin of 29 mm, a right of 31 mm, and top and bottom of 24 mm and 24.5 mm respectively. The page features 22 staves, measuring 192 mm by 6.5 mm deep. Page 7, unlike the draft scores of the first and second movements, is written entirely in black ink with the exception of a number of pencil notations. Although one may presume that these marks were made during the revision of the work in 1948, an examination of the following pages shows a dating in the same pencil grading on page 11 of the third movement as 20 July 1947.

Page 89 of the final score presents, at first glance, something of a puzzle. Taking the place of the original pages 89, 90, 91 and 92, the page is glued in place between the stubs of the margins of two removed sheets, the marks of which can be seen in the left-hand margin. Comprising five bars of material scored for full orchestra, the page is filled out in black ink, with notations made in red and blue pencil, and red and green ink. Consultation of a copy of *Hymne Variation et Rondo* from Northwestern University's Jean Martinon papers identified the pencil marks as corresponding to Martinon's handwriting and typical conducting marks.[4] However, those made in red and green ink correspond to the hand of Boydell himself, and are drawn over pencil outlines. A faint outline of the letter 'M' and a box can be seen below the eighteenth stave in bar 154. The green ink markings, judging by the thickness of the lettering, were made in some kind of marker pen, while those in red, based on the spreading and thinning of the ink in the middle of the pen-strokes, were made using a fountain pen. The page, which measures 260 mm by 352.5 mm, contains 24 staves of length 215 mm, with margins of 23 mm on the left, 22 mm on the right, and top and bottom of 15.5 mm and 18 mm. Overleaf is a blank page, with music continuing on the following sheet (original numeration 93 scribbled out and replaced with 90).

The alteration illustrated by these examples is just one of a number made to the final movement in Boydell's revision of the work. As can be seen by comparing the two, bar 153 of the 1947 short-score draft corresponds roughly with bar 152 of the 1948 revision, as does the first note of bar 154 (1947) with that of bar 153 (1948). Similarly, bar 167 (1947) corresponds with that of 154 (1948) with the preceding sextuplet figure appearing across woodwind and strings in the final score. As such, this alteration functions for the most part to remove the material from the latter part of bar 154 to the opening notes of bar 166 of the 1947 score from the work. This necessitated the renumbering of bars and pages, with page 93 becoming page 90, bar 175 becoming 162, and so on. Similar alterations occur at various points across the score, leading to numerous page and bar re-numberings, particularly in movement three. The first instance of this occurs on page 77 in the finished score, wherein two bars were pasted over the original material, with what would have been bars 92, 93, and 94 (1947) becoming bars 92 and 93.[5] Page 93 sees a number of bars that appear in the 1947 draft crossed out; however, it is unsure if this alteration was made in the editing process of 1947 or during the 1948 revision.[6] Even the conclusion of the work was not safe from glue and scissors, as 1948 saw Boydell attach an entirely new ending, adding a number of pages in the process. The examination of page 101 shows a new bar pasted in, followed by the addition of three new pages replacing bars 226 to 232 of the 1947 draft. The manner in which these were entered – with the back of the sheaf pasted to 1947's page 105 – has effectively obscured the earlier ending, although page 106 of the 1947 edition can still be seen.

The work itself comprises three movements: a *Prelude*, *Adagio* and final *Allegro frenetico*. Details in the front matter of MS 11128/6/MAGH SLEACHT/3 indicate that the duration of the work in its entirety is approximately 20 minutes. The effect of the revision process discussed above upon the performance of the piece can be seen in Boydell's amendments to his notes on the time of the performance – with the second movement dropping from 7 minutes 45 seconds to 7 minutes 30 seconds, and movement three from 6 minutes 30 seconds to 6 minutes.[7]

While not explicitly programmatic, as will be discussed in the following pages, the work's scoring is evocative of a series of moods and images outlined in the front matter of MS 11128/6/MAGH SLEACHT/3. The *Prelude* sees scenes of pastoral idyll interspersed with persistent 'call[s] to the religious festival' that the work as a whole explores. The 'primitive equivalent of the church bell' presents itself as a rising fourth motif. Although present at first in brass above *sul ponticello* strings and timpani rolls, over the course of the first movement the motif comes to be passed throughout the orchestra, its continual intrusions and the increased presence of chromatic passages creating a sense of urgency as the movement draws to a close.[8] Boydell's description of the *Adagio* movement suggests a processional quality, evinced in the pulsing, repeated *pizzicato* notes in double bass and bass drum. The instrumentation of this movement perhaps reflects Boydell's own preferences as a musician, highlighting solo oboe and flute. Although overwhelmingly sombre, the *affretando* passages that punctuate this movement see denser textures and dotted rhythms prevail over the lighter solo passages, the repeated notes and chromatic movement throughout the orchestra a sonic signifier for the 'fear and apprehension' the composer's notes allude to.[9] Similar sonic characterisations are present in the final movement, in which the frenzied elation of the festival itself is apparent in the densely textured, rapid chromatic passages and frantic repeated notes.

INCEPTION

Magh Sleacht's composition occurred during a period of great creative success for Boydell. Having returned to Ireland from England following the outbreak of war in 1939,[10] by 1946 he was laying the foundations for what was to become a long and illustrious career in music in Ireland. Already the conductor of the Dublin Orchestral Players (DOP) and professor of singing at the Royal Irish Academy of Music, the mid-1940s saw Boydell embark on an additional career: that of broadcaster for RÉ.[11] Between these three, Boydell's profile as a musical authority was quick to be established in the eyes and ears of the public, with the directorship of the DOP providing a number of opportunities to have his works publicly performed. It was, however, his connection with RÉ that proved the most integral to *Magh Sleacht*, as will be discussed below.

As alluded to previously, the title *Magh Sleacht* is one that is steeped in the Irish folkloric tradition, being a direct reference to the ancient megalithic ritual site of the same name. Now known as Moyslaught in Co. Cavan, it is believed to be the site at which the Milesians (the mythical ancestors of the Celtic Irish) worshipped the god Cenn Cruaich, the 'lord of the mound' to whom first-born children were sacrificed. The La Tène style Killycluggin Stone and Corleck Head preserved at the Cavan County Museum are believed to represent aspects of the grim deity:

> **Moyslaught**
> [Mag Sleacht. Mag(h) Slecht. Plain of Adoration]
> The site where the Milesians worshipped Cenn Cruaich. It is said they sacrificed children on this site.[12]

Boydell's familiarity with this subject matter appears to have sprung from the poetic sphere, as he states that 'the work is based on an ancient Irish poem about 1000 years old.'[13] It is possible that this reference is to the poem *Mág Shamhradain, Brian, Lord of Magh Sléacht* by sixteenth-century bardic poet Tadhg Dall O'Huiginn (a translation of which had been published by Lambert McKenna in 1940).[14] It is, however, a somewhat more modern poem that appears in the score to *Magh Sleacht* – specifically a work by Caoimhín O'Conghaile. Entitled *Mágh Sleacht*, the poem is typed – presumably in its entirety – and pasted into the final draft of the work.[15] The poem details a ritual to appease the god Crom Cruaich, and the invocations of his followers as they proceed to the ritual ground. Both Crom Cruaich and the ritual site, Magh Sleacht (see reference above for alternate spellings), also referred to in Boydell's subtitle to the work as 'the plane of prostrations', play prominent roles in Irish mytho-history:

> **Cenn Cruaich**
> [Blood Crescent. Crom Cruach. Cromm Cru(i)ach. Lord of the Mound]
> A deity to whom firstborn children were sacrificed. He was later known as Cromm Cruaich and his image, made of gold and silver, was worshipped by the Milesians. It was overcome by St. Patrick and sank into the earth.[16]

Letter 11128/2/2/163 clarifies the relationship between the poem and musical work. Seemingly written at the request of Boydell, O'Conghaile (signing off the letter with the Anglicised name Kevin) states that his poem is intended to 'bring about the spirit of Magh Sleacht, of your work, and of the old poem at once'. While the letter itself is not dated, it is likely that the date of the poem (30 August 1947) as it appears in the score is also that of the letter, or that the letter was sent shortly thereafter. While the presence of the poem in the final draft of the score and its shared title with Boydell's work could be seen as being indicative of a programmatic relationship, the notes provided in the front matter clarify Boydell's position on the subject. Stating that the work is 'allegorical' rather than programmatic, he tells us that 'it has a programme, but the programme is not definitely connected with particular passages in the music.'[17] O'Conghaile's letter affirms that the poem is not intended as an 'afterthought programme', but rather a complementary piece that – rather than expressing the ancient through the language of contemporary European music – expressed it through the medium of contemporary poetry.[18] In a letter dated 21 May 1947, the Australian-born British conductor and composer Dr Hubert Clifford lauded Boydell's apparent foregoing of programme:

> Your symphony sounds exciting – you have an evocative subject, even though you seem to be steering clear of the programme music implication of the Stone Circles. I think this [is] wise of you.[19]

While Clifford had yet to examine the work in either sounding or score form – he was to request a copy of the score and recordings of the work in later letters[20] – Boydell's apparent neglect to mention O'Conghaile's poem would support the notion that the poem (and its letter) were created at a later date as suggested. The emphasis placed upon the allegorical nature of the work by Boydell speaks of an independent yet concurrent relationship between the musical and extra-musical in *Magh Sleacht*: the music does not diverge completely from its source material, but seeks to evoke rather than illustrate the precise details of the poem. The atmospheric quality created as a result of this – particularly in the third movement – was to become the subject of some discussion in reviews of the work following its initial performance.

In later years Boydell would revisit the subject matter of ancient pagan ritual in *Megalithic Ritual Dances*, and spoke of a lasting fascination with prehistoric Ireland in a 1989 interview with Michael Taylor:

> I also wrote a work which Martinon conducted [to] which I gave an Irish title *Magh Sleacht* bringing out my intense interest in the ceremonies which went on in Megalithic Ireland around the stone circles, an interest I shared with Arnold Bax.[21]

This preoccupation with what could ostensibly be called Celticism may seem at odds with Boydell's professed aversion to nationalism; however, the musical language by which he chose to express it is suitably bereft of traditional Irish idiom to adhere to his preferred method of musical communication:

> If you live in this country and are of this country, those influences soak into your bones and therefore we felt our job was to express ourselves in an internationally

understood language, in fact the language of contemporary European Music. What lay behind that language would automatically be coloured by the fact that you were Irish and lived here, without having to try and be Irish.[22]

PERFORMANCE HISTORY AND RECEPTION

The complete performance history of *Magh Sleacht* is, for want of a better word, short. Having been performed three times over a period of eight months between September 1947 and April 1948, the subsequent disappearance of the work from Boydell's performed repertoire is something of a mystery, as what reviews have been found appear to be largely favourable. The first performance of the work took place on 5 September 1947 in the Phoenix Hall,[23] following daily rehearsals from 1 September.[24] Performed by the RÉSO conducted by Jean Martinon, the broadcast went out at 7.10 p.m. as part of a concert programme that included Rosenthal's *Les Petits Métiers* and Tchaikovsky's 'Pathétique' Symphony.[25] Reviewed the following day in the *Irish Press*, the work was:

> said to be a descriptive of rites connected with human sacrifice in Pagan Ireland – fear and frenzy being the emotions chiefly depicted. There was no suggestion of Irish idiom or mode of thought in the composition, which is obviously the work of a competent musician with a good knowledge of orchestration. The pastoral adagio made a pleasant interlude; the frenzied atmosphere of the close was cleverly suggested, but became almost too painful.[26]

It appears that not all shared the views of the *Irish Press* contributor, however, as Boydell later recalled the response of fellow composer Seóirse Bodley: 'He got up and walked out when it was performed because it was too modern for his ears.'[27] It should however be noted that, if Boydell was referring to the work's first performance in 1947, Bodley was only aged 14 at the time.

Aside from the young Bodley's recalled disdain for the work, surviving responses from Boydell's peers are few and far between. The only known chain of correspondence regarding *Magh Sleacht* is that between Boydell and Dr Clifford, which provides a valuable glimpse into the relationship between the two. Having requested and received both the score and recordings of *Magh Sleacht* in October 1947, Clifford's letters to Boydell are written in a largely encouraging and constructive tone. The recordings sent to Clifford were those of the September 1947 performance, to which his initial response was as follows: 'First impressions were very favourable. The work has perhaps more promise than the Song Cycle, but rather less attainment in the more difficult medium of the orchestra.'[28] Stating in the same letter that he felt it 'an impertinence to volunteer [his reactions] unless they are definitely requested',[29] Clifford's later epistles included a more detailed criticism of Boydell's execution of the piece, describing it as:

> a work which had great power in places and revealing a genuine musical talent... What I felt that the work lacked as a whole was the ability to sustain your thinking consecutively. Your inspiration was genuine but spasmodic. The resultant impression was that the work lacked continuity.[30]

Whether or not Clifford's feedback was a motivating factor behind the revision of the piece in February 1948 is unsure; however, the press response to the later performances on 2 and 23 April 1948 echoed their earlier praise: 'There was a fine orchestral colour and an impressive breadth of style in the Prelude to *Magh Sleacht* by Brian Boydell.'[31]

Both performances saw a return to the Phoenix Hall, and to the RÉSO with Martinon at the helm. The second was held at the same time as its premiere some months before. Although the performance was set to air at 7.10 p.m., a 'Call for Enquiry' by Michael McMullin published in *Radio Review* a number of days later reveals that the broadcast was affected by 'a breakdown of approximately 3/4 hour... covering the entire period during which we were to hear an orchestral work'.[32] This particular article is the only newspaper clipping pertaining to *Magh Sleacht* that could be found in Boydell's scrapbooks. The final known performance of the work was that of 23 April 1948, during which only the *Prelude* was performed.[33]

As no further reviews were found in Boydell's correspondence or scrapbooks, the only view that can currently be formed as to how the work was received must be based upon the sources given above. As the 1989 interview with Michael Taylor illustrates, Boydell spoke of the piece suggesting that its lack of revival after 1948 was not as a result of an attempt to expunge the work from common memory. The erasure of Boydell's signature and place of residence (Cabinteely) from the final pages and from the flyleaf of the final draft suggests that the piece was perhaps submitted to a competition, although at present little evidence to confirm this has been forthcoming.[34] If this is the case, the result may have been a contributing factor to the disappearance of the work from the spotlight, but it is equally possible that the work was merely displaced from the repertoire by some of Boydell's more mature works. Nonetheless, *Magh Sleacht* has been resigned to the fringes of public knowledge, rarely discussed outside of chronologies of Boydell's works.

CONCLUSION: ONWARDS TO THE 'PLAIN OF PROSTRATIONS'

This study began as that of a sketchbook, and grew to become the hunt for an eventual examination of a work that had not – and to our knowledge still has not – been heard or performed in over 70 years. The report given here of *Magh Sleacht* is by no means exhaustive, and instead functions more as an introduction to the work rather than a complete analysis of its inner workings. Further studies of the work will doubtless continue to uncover material, and there are several avenues of pursuit that could be taken to further our understanding of it. There is the matter of the recordings sent from Boydell to Clifford to be explored – for while TCD is in possession of a number of tapes belonging to Boydell, these are later cassettes, and contain no reference to *Magh Sleacht* – and also the still somewhat mysterious 1,000-year-old poem. Although Boydell's correspondence with Hubert Clifford is the only one that could be found in the collections held by TCD that references *Magh Sleacht*, one may presume that at some point, letters were exchanged with Martinon on the subject, and perhaps further correspondence with Caoimhín O'Conghaile. The score itself provides numerous opportunities for further transcriptions or arrangements to be made, with the possibility of reconstructing the 1947 score through the short-score drafts or abundant part books. Having celebrated the centenary of Boydell's birth and legacy in 2017, *Magh Sleacht*, rediscovered, allows us a glimpse into his early compositional process and the lasting fascination that he held for the ancient history of Ireland. Just as his interest in the subject persisted, so too did *Magh Sleacht*, finally coming to light nearly 70 years since its composition began. With any hope, further studies will continue to illuminate this elusive and intriguing work.

APPENDIX

A list of the works contained in the sketchbook, Brian Boydell Archive, TCD MS 11128/6 (2014). The sketchbook is characterised by the meticulous labelling of sketches by Boydell, although when precisely this labelling occurred is subject to speculation. It is likely that, as the sketches were used in later drafts, they were labelled, and occasionally crossed out. Any material that has not been identified in this way by Boydell has been marked as 'Unspecified'. Any dates, where marked by Boydell, have been included in the Date column. Works named in the sketchbook that were not developed into completed works of the same title or ensemble are marked with an asterisk.

Page	Contents	Date
1	*Magh Sleacht*	April 1946
2	*Magh Sleacht*	
3	*Magh Sleacht* (references to p. 8)	
4	Unspecified	April 1946
5	Unspecified (possibly *Magh Sleacht*, references to p. 12)	
6	Unspecified (possibly *Magh Sleacht*, references to p. 12)	
7	*Magh Sleacht* (references to p. 23). Unspecified	
8	*Magh Sleacht*	
9	*Magh Sleacht*	
10	Unspecified (possibly *Magh Sleacht*)	
11	Unspecified	
12	Unspecified (references pp 5, 6, 7, and 34)	
13	Quartet (presumably Quartet No. 1)	May 1946
14	Unspecified	
15	Unspecified (possibly *Magh Sleacht*)	
16	*Magh Sleacht* (references p. 15)	
17	*Magh Sleacht* (references p. 7)	
18	Unspecified (possibly *Magh Sleacht*, references to pp 16 and 17)	
19	Unspecified	
20	Quartet, *Magh Sleacht* (references to p. 23)	
21	Unspecified	
22	*Magh Sleacht*. Unspecified.	
23	*Magh Sleacht*	
24	*Magh Sleacht*. Unspecified. (covers two pages)	24 September 1946
25	Unspecified (March, Lament)	
26	Unspecified (relates to p. 8)	
27	*Magh Sleacht*	
28	*Caprice for Wind Instruments**	18 January 1947
29	Unspecified (possibly a continuation of p. 28)	
30	*Magh Sleacht*	
31	*The Feather of Death* (references to p. 33)	
32	Unspecified (possibly continuation of p. 31)	
33	Unspecified (references to p. 12)	
34	Unspecified (references to p. 12)	
35	Unspecified (March time)	
36	*Magh Sleacht*	
37	Unspecified (reference to pp 12 and 14)	
38	Unspecified (reference to pp 12 and 15; possibly *Magh Sleacht*)	
39	Unspecified	
40	Unspecified	
41	Unspecified	

42	Unspecified	
43	Unspecified (reference to p. 15)	
44	Unspecified (reference to p. 37)	
45	*Quartet*. Unspecified	10 September 1947
46	*Quartet* (reference to pp 87 and 93)	11 September 1947
47	Intermezzo	27 September 1947
48	*Quartet*	
49	Unspecified	
50	Unspecified	
51	*The Buried Moon*	
52	*The Buried Moon*	
53	*The Buried Moon*	
54	Unspecified	
55	*Quartet*	
56	*Quartet* (reference to p. 33)	30 September 1947
57	*Quartet*	2 October 1947
58	*Quartet*	
59	*Quartet*	
60	*Quartet*	
61	*Quartet* (reference to pp 62 and 71)	
62	*Quartet*	
63	Unspecified (possibly *Quartet*)	
64	*Quartet*	
65	*The Buried Moon*	
66	*Quartet*	
67	*Quartet*	29 October 1947
68	*Quartet*	
69	*The Buried Moon*	12 November 1947
70	Unspecified	
71	*Quartet* (reference to p. 76)	
72	*Quartet* (reference to p. 74)	4 January 1948
73	Unspecified	9 December 1947
74	Unspecified (possibly *Quartet*)	
75	Unspecified	4 January 1948
76	*Quartet*	16 January 1948
77	Unspecified (reference to p. 45)	16 January 1948
78	Unspecified (reference to p. 81)	
79	*In Memoriam Mahatma Gandhi*	31 January 1948
80	Unspecified	
81	Unspecified (reference to p. 81)	
82	*In Memoriam Mahatma Gandhi*	
83	*In Memoriam Mahatma Gandhi*	
84	Unspecified	
85	Unspecified	
86	Unspecified	18 August 1948

87	*Quartet* (possibly *The Buried Moon*)	14 February 1949
88	Unspecified	
89	Unspecified	17 March 1949
90	*Divertimento for Clarinet, Oboe and Orchestra**	
91	Unspecified	
92	Unspecified (reference to pp 50 and 75)	
93	*The Buried Moon*. Unspecified	
94	*Quartet. The Buried Moon*	
95	*The Buried Moon*	
96	*The Buried Moon*	
97	Unspecified	25 March 1950
98	*The Owl and The Pussy-Cat*. Unspecified	
99	Unspecified	22 January 1951
100	Unspecified	
101	Unspecified (arrow to p. 102)	28 January 1951, 26 February 1951
102	Unspecified (Largo, reference to p. 105)	27 May 1951
103	Unspecified	27 May 1951
104	Unspecified	March 1952
105	Unspecified	2 June 1952
106	Unspecified (for a fugue)	June 1952
107	Unspecified	June 1952
108	Unspecified	August 1952
109	Unspecified	March 1953
110	Unspecified	15 June 1953
111	Unspecified (Episode III)	20 June 1953
112	Unspecified	
113	Unspecified	
114	Unspecified	
115	Unspecified	
116	Unspecified	
117	Unspecified	3 November 1954, July 1955, August 1955
118	Unspecified	
119	Unspecified	
120	Unspecified	
121	Unspecified	
122	Unspecified	
123	Unspecified	9 October 1955
124	Unspecified (accompaniment for a Funeral March)	3 November 1955, March 26 [??]
125	Unspecified (Adagio)	7 November 1955, 8 November 1955
126	Unspecified	26 February 1956
127	Unspecified	26 February 1956

FOUR

SOUNDING IRISH LANDSCAPE AND LIFE: BRIAN BOYDELL'S SCORES FOR DOCUMENTARY FILMS

Laura Anderson

Between 1960 and 1970, Brian Boydell worked on several film scores that would showcase Irish culture and landscape. He provided a score for Vincent Corcoran's production *Ireland* (1967, dir. George Sluizer), which promoted Ireland's history, economy and landscape, in addition to scores for three films directed by Patrick Carey and sponsored by the Department of External Affairs that showcased the Irish landscape: *Yeats Country* (1965), *Mists of Time* (1967) and *Errigal* (1968). Carey's films were sought after for international distribution following their release and were awarded multiple prizes. Radio Telefís Éireann (RTÉ) launched regular broadcasts at the end of 1961 and, as public service broadcaster, was keen to support productions that reflected positively on Ireland's culture and heritage. It is thus unsurprising that the organisation broadcast Sluizer's *Ireland* and Carey's *Mists of Time*. Another state body, the Irish Tourist Association, began to produce tourist landscape films for export during the 1930s and 1940s.[1] Support continued with Minister for External Affairs Seán MacBride's establishment of the Cultural Relations Committee (CRC) in 1950, an organisation that would foster Irish culture through film and function as a liaison between the Department of External Affairs and filmmakers.[2] For its part, the Department had supported films aimed at the tourist market and industrial promotion throughout the 1960s,[3] and the projects examined in this essay can be contextualised loosely in the former category, adopting a documentary visual style with voice-over alongside Boydell's scores.

Boydell was well known in 1960s Ireland as a composer of music for the concert hall, as a professor at Trinity College Dublin, and as a broadcaster on national radio and television on musical matters. Given his wide-ranging interests and projects, it is perhaps understandable that little attention has been paid to his film music in existing scholarship and it is hoped that this essay will be a first step towards understanding his engagement with this genre. Drawing on archival materials, the essay outlines Boydell's role in the film score production process and the role of his scores. Considering Sluizer's film *Ireland* and then discussing the Carey projects, I will highlight some commonalities of approach on Boydell's part and will suggest that these scores inspired him to adopt a more experimental compositional voice than in his scores for the concert hall.

ARCHIVAL INSIGHTS INTO BOYDELL'S COMPOSITIONAL APPROACH

Boydell had a deep interest in visual art – he was a member of the White Stag Group and a keen painter until 1944. He remained an active photographer throughout his life and this was a key factor in his attraction to Carey's work: visually they were on the same wavelength.[4] It seems he was captivated by the opportunity to compose for film:

> I'd done a certain amount of film music before, but I became absolutely fascinated, I love a challenge. And the great thing about challenge for film music is that you know in the end, dare we say this, nobody listens to the music. It's a sort of background there and therefore you can afford to experiment. And this is one of the things I adore doing.[5]

Boydell's comments about how his engagement with film afforded the opportunity for experimentation suggest that we might hear a different side to the composer's work with closer focus on his approach to audio-visual media.

The typical approach to scoring a film can be broadly described as: conceptualising and spotting the film; composition; recording; mixing and editing. Bearing this in mind illuminates some distinctive elements of Boydell's working methods. Examining the scores, it seems Sluizer and Carey provided Boydell with rough cuts of the films and that the composer was aware of the flexible way in which his music might be treated. Yet he also maintained strong views on the equal status of image and music, believing that they complemented each other rather than the music playing a mere supporting role.[6] His diaries reveal that he engaged with the other members of the crew, not just the director. For instance, when working on *Errigal*, he met with Peter Hunt (sound) and Ann Chegwidden (picture editor) in addition to Carey.[7]

Boydell prepared musical cues as would be normal for any film scoring project and adopted the usual terminology of reel number followed by cue number, '1M1' indicating the first cue on the first reel of film and beginning his timing sequences anew with the beginning of each cue. He adopted similar working methods for Sluizer and Carey's films, using a system of colour coding his scores to differentiate directions about musical notation from those relating to synchronisation points and timings.[8] Plate 3 shows an extract from cue 1M2 of *Yeats Country*, which illustrates that Boydell wrote his music mainly in black ink – he appears to have worked out ideas in pencil first. This was typical of his usual practice of composing in pencil and then, when the score was completed, making a fair copy in ink. He used blue ink to indicate shot numbers in boxes above the bars (cue 1M2 begins at shot 56) and he also included timings in seconds under each system noted in blue ink here (the duration is noted in seconds starting from the beginning of each cue). Also precisely noted is where the commentary should begin and end.

Ireland's music is written in black ink with edits and corrections of music, bar numbers and timing in pencil, and descriptions of scenes and timings in red marker pen. There are notes for camera movements and angles, tilts up, tracking shots etc., with important synchronisation points also clearly noted. *Mists of Time* follows the same approach with music written in black ink and timings noted in seconds in red/blue ink. However, this score employs far fewer shot numbers (in blue/red ink);[9] instead, timings and text descriptions aid synchronisation. As illustrated by Plate 4, *Errigal* adopts a very similar approach but includes additional annotations for tape, which seem to be a mixture of pre-recorded sound effects and some of the composer's own experiments with modifications to instruments, indicating its presence by wavy lines in blue ink. Boydell uses dynamics for tape (it begins *pp*) and decrescendo marks are used to show where it should fade out. Shot numbers and timings are recorded under the staves: shot numbers here are indicated by green ink with some scene descriptions, while time recorded in seconds from the beginning of each cue is noted in red ink.

These scores are not fair copies produced once all the decisions had been made about cues, since the last page of cue 1M2 of *Yeats Country* includes a revised stave pasted in on top of an earlier working out. Taking a closer look at the end of this cue reveals a written note: 'Without break 2 minutes 24 seconds, with first break 1 minute 28 seconds.' I interpret this as demonstrating the composer's awareness about the flexibility with which his music must be treated in this medium, aware that extracts of his cues might be isolated or truncated. Boydell was equally precise about the synchronisation points for his music in *Errigal*, following the same approach adopted for *Yeats Country* but also adding in descriptive text and drawing in images from the film. Looking at cue 1M3 (pl. 5), which details music to accompany a sequence of mist around the mountain, we can see that he wrote in descriptions under the system and included a drawing of the mountain peak to indicate which part of the cue should be heard at that point.

This close attention to synchronisation points and development of a personal method to ensure that his music would synchronise with the images as he intended, reflects the fact that Boydell acted as his own music editor, perhaps unsurprising on such a personal and small-scale project.

In another departure from a composer's usual working method on a film, Boydell appears to have 'composed in' flexibility into his music – preparing additional bars marked 'bis (if necessary for extra timing)' (see for example cue 1M5 *Mists of Time*).[10] There is also evidence that Boydell attempted to ensure musical continuity across edits by using double bar lines in blue ink (rather than the black ink used for the 'musical' double bar lines) to indicate where one shot ended and another began. Then he could indicate a note should be sustained across shots by means of a broken tie line (- - - - -) (see for example cue 2M1 of *Yeats Country*). Alternatively, he would indicate overlaps using arrows and text annotations (see for example overlapping of 2M4 and 2M5 of *Errigal*). In Plate 6, extracted from the end of cue 1M1 of *Errigal*, he notes to fade out music as required and superimpose cue 1M2.

In the case of *Ireland*, there is also flexibility written in; for instance, at the end of complex 7, Boydell notes that the last five bars can be adjusted to the end of the film as required and to 'fade on tape as required' at the cue's conclusion. However, the composer is very precise about synchronisation, with more detail about the types of shots at particular points and consideration of how metronome markings match the speed of the images. The first cue in *Ireland*, track along cliffs, includes the note 'minim = 52. 13 beats = 15 seconds.' This marking might be due to the nature of a different collaboration and a film that demanded more connotative, illustrative cueing to support the images. Furthermore, the archive demonstrates that the project underwent extensive revision over a period of time (the cover page records 'Autumn 1965. Completely revised December 1966', and the end titles are dated 4 January 1967),[11] and perhaps this enabled Boydell to be more precise about exact cue lengths.[12]

Boydell was involved in the recording of his scores,[13] and included notes about microphone placement throughout the manuscripts, for example, noting in *Errigal* 1M3(2) at shot 53 'Errigal': 'harp microphone down', and in 2M2, he writes at the start of the piano part: 'Suggest close mike on pfte to pick up resonance and pianist play softly.' Gillian Smith, who played harpsichord and celeste for *Errigal*, recalled that 'Boydell was completely in charge. There wasn't another conductor, he worked directly with us and told us what he wanted.'[14] He annotated the scores with suggestions for who might play certain instruments, the degree of care and reflection indicative of his serious attitude to film scoring. He did not treat this process with any less diligence than his concert scores. The scores also reveal a composer who was willing to work around musical logic for the sake of audio-visual effectiveness. Cue 2M2D from *Errigal* (pl. 7) is such a case of composing around the restrictions of musical grammar and taking the recording process into account. The figure indicates that the composer intended to capture the sound of the gong without its initial attack. Using his system of red ink to indicate the timings, he could place a visual bar line after his musical bar line and could show that the recording should conclude before the bar was completed.

'IRELAND' (DIR. GEORGE SLUIZER, 1967)

Ireland was broadcast in March 1967, most likely to mark St Patrick's Day,[15] and it represents a positive view of the increasing modernisation of Ireland alongside the country's ancient heritage. The film opens with a dramatic seascape and there are several scenes of natural beauty interspersed through the film, including wild horses and Dún Aengus, alongside scenes of Irish heritage and history, such as the Book of Kells, the Ardagh Chalice and a high cross. Most frequently, the viewer is presented with scenes of industry and development: new machines for turf cutting, spinning and weaving, Shannon airport and Waterford Crystal. Scripted by R. B. D. French, Philip O'Flynn was the narrator. Boydell's score for the film was played by the Radio Telefís Éireann Symphony Orchestra (RTÉSO) conducted by Philip Martell. The archive contains both a reduced score and the full score for a large orchestra (see Table 1 for a breakdown of the instrumentation of individual cues). The film is heavily scored with most scenes requiring music, and continuity is provided across the film by a principal theme.

Example 1: Theme transcribed from Complex 1, *Ireland*. (Courtesy of the Brian Boydell Archive, TCD MS 11128)

The woodwind takes prominence in the score with the oboe most often leading the theme (ex. 1). The music tends to be closely synchronised with the action throughout, with a scene focusing on the statues of significant figures and a voice-over describing Ireland's struggle for independence eliciting fanfares from brass and a richer orchestral palette. By contrast, in a scene of covering freshly produced peat with plastic (complex 11), Boydell employs dancing harps, instructing the harpist to play by drawing the palm of the hand vertically upwards over lower strings so that they squeak; approaching the top, the harpist should spread their fingers, turn the hand with fingers upwards and sweep over the upper strings. The harp is accompanied by rapid hemi-demisemiquavers on celeste and trills on woodwinds and strings, side drum with wire brush and both small cymbal and soft sticks ad lib independent of rhythm (celeste joins them), emphasising the wind rustling the plastic and lending magic to the operation. There is evidence that Boydell blurred the boundary between his music and the sound effects in this film: for example, at the end of complex 2, there is the following annotation: 'Suggest – hold last chord and fade recording as desired with natural sounds of curraghs on the beach.' This play with both extended techniques and with the boundaries of music and sound effects can also be heard in the scores for Carey's films, which arguably elicit even greater experimentation.

Description	Cue number	Instrumentation
Track along cliffs	Complex 1	fls, ob, cor ang, B flat cls, 2 bns, 4 hns in F, tuba, hp, vn 1, vn 2, va, vc, db, timp, large cymb, tam, b dr
Bulldozer and turf cutting	Complex 2	fls, ob, cor ang, cls, 2 bns, 4 hns, 2 tpts in B flat, trbns, tuba, vn 1, vn 2, va, vc, db, timp, s dr, cymb, b dr, xyl
Wild horses – Dún Aengus – Book of Kells	Complex 3	fls, ob, 2 cls, cor ang, 2 bns, 4 hns, 2 tpts, trbns, tuba, hp, vn 1, vn 2, va, vc, db, timp, tam, s dr, large cymb, small cymb
Hats in Derby Square leading directly to 5a	Complex 4	fl, ob, cl, bn, 2 tpts, vn 1, vn 2, va, vc, db, 2 wbls, tamb, xyl
Boys at parapet – Columns – Chimney stacks	Complex 5a	fls, ob, 2 cls, 2 bns, 4 hns, 2 tpts, trbns, tuba, vn 1, vn 2, va, vc, db, timp, s dr, tamb, xyl
High view O'Connell Street – Street scenes – Wedding	Complex 5b	fl, 2 obs, 2 cls, 2 bns, 2 hns, 2 tpts, hp, vn 1, vn 2, va, vc, db, s dr, tamb, cel

TCD Library – Statues – Museum	Complex 6	fl, 4 hns, 2 tpts, vn 1, vn 2, va, vc, db, timp, s dr, cymb
Museum – Memorial cross – Roofs of Dublin (End of Reel II)	Complex 7	ob, cor ang, cl, bn, 4 hns, 2 trbns, tuba, vn 1, vn 2, va, vc, db, timp, tam
(Beginning of Reel III) Continues from Complex 7. Shannon Airport – Spinning – Weaving	Complex 8	2 fls, 2 obs, 2 cls, 2 bns, 4 hns, 2 tpts, tuba, cel, hp, vn 1, vn 2, va, vc, db, s dr, wbl, timp, large cymb
Wheatfield – Bullocks	Complex 9	2 fls, 2 obs, 2 cls, bn, tpt, 3 hns, tuba, hp, vn 1, vn 2, va, vc, db
Launching of ship – Power station	Complex 10	2 fls, 2 obs, 2 cls, cor ang, 2 2 bns, 4 hns, 2 tpts, 2 trbns, tuba, hp, vn 1, vn 2, va, vc, db, timp, xyl, cel, tam, large cymb, b dr
Plastic effects	Complex 11	2 fls, 2 obs, 2 cls, hp, vn 1, vn 2, s dr with wire brush, small cymb soft sticks, cel
Finale	Complex 12	fl, 2 obs, 2 cls, bn, 4 hns, 2 tpts, 2 trbns, tuba, hp, vn 1, vn 2, va, vc, db, timp, s dr, large cymb, tam, b dr

Table 1: Instrumentation of cues in *Ireland*. (Courtesy of the Brian Boydell Archive, TCD MS 11128)

PATRICK CAREY'S DOCUMENTARY FILMS

Prior to working in Ireland, Carey had considerable experience of documentary filmmaking working for the Canadian Film Board and British Transport films, and on Columbia Pictures series of nature films, *The World of Life*. He moved back to Ireland in the early 1960s and established Aengus Films in 1964. Visually, his films made in Ireland are similar to his work in Canada – they are pictorial landscape films. Harvey O'Brien writes that without the voice-over 'it would be difficult to distinguish between scenes from *Yeats Country*. . . and those filmed elsewhere' and that 'this globalist eye is a mark of Carey's work.'[16] Aengus Films won its first contract in 1964, *Yeats Country*, a commission to celebrate the centenary of the poet's birth that is described by Kevin Rockett, Luke Gibbons and John Hill as probably 'the most widely seen Irish documentary ever produced'.[17] The Irish Film Archive holds correspondence that demonstrates the demand for both *Yeats Country* and *Errigal* in Ireland and abroad. An extract from a letter sent in March 1969 by the Irish Film Institute requesting more prints illustrates this demand:

You will be pleased to hear that bookings on this film average approximately forty per annum. When you realise that the average number of bookings on the films in the Library is 3.2 bookings per annum, you will appreciate the extraordinary demands which are made on the two prints of *Yeats Country*, which we have available for lending.

It is therefore with some hope that I ask if it would be possible for us to receive on deposit a few additional prints of this film and also a number of prints of *Errigal*, about which we have as many enquiries as for *Yeats Country*, which we have as yet not received from your Department.[18]

The Irish Film Archive also holds details of the types of groups that borrowed the prints for showings. Table 2 is a transcription of the distribution of copy A of *Yeats Country* between 1 June and 31 December 1966: the range of audiences was broad and included young and old, urban and rural.

Date	Type of Audience	Approximate Attendance
22/06/66	Business Firm	60
27–28/06/66	Girls' College	200
16/07/66	Boys' College	200
03/07/66	Television Studio	50
12/08/66	Business Firm	40
13/09/66	Countrywoman's Association	70
23/09/66	Seminary	130
07/10/66	Girls' Convent	200
28/10/66	Boys' College	200
04/11/66	Private Show	30
17/11/66	Business Firm	50
22/11/66	Boys' College	230
24/11/66	College	300
08/12/66	Film Society	350
16/12/66	Private Show	30
28/12/66	University	130

Table 2: Details of Showings of Department of External Affairs film *Yeats Country* for period 1 June to 31 December 1966. (Courtesy of the Irish Film Archive)

Yeats Country and *Errigal* were both classified as 'cultural propaganda' in the *Irish Times* and the former was very well received by the author of 'An Irishman's Diary', setting the tone for much of the press commentary:

If the Department of External Affairs had never done anything else in the field of cultural propaganda, they would have earned every laurel wreath at my bestowal for their latest venture in the medium.[19]

In a later column, dated 28 May 1968, the author notes the official nature of the private showing of *Errigal*:

'I regard Padraig Carey as one of the great Irishmen of our time', said the Tánaiste, Mr Frank Aiken, at a reception after the private showing of Mr. Carey's latest film, *Errigal*, in the Metropole Cinema. Mr Aiken amplified his statement by saying that Patrick Carey's films had brought the best of Ireland to the world, and to many of our own people as well. Replying to the Tánaiste, Mr Carey said: 'This film has been undoubtedly the best piece of sponsorship in Ireland so far – sponsorship of a very high international order.' While the primary credit for support goes to the Department of External Affairs, they share it with the Department of the Gaeltacht, Bord Fáilte and Radio Telefís Éireann, all of whom contributed to financing the film, and all of whom were represented at the preview, as well as members of the Diplomatic Corps and the other Government Departments.[20]

This review makes little mention of the score, except to note it as 'very effective'. Yet, Boydell's scores made a considerable contribution to the success of Carey's projects.

'YEATS COUNTRY' (1965)

Yeats Country was not the first project made by the CRC concerning the life and work of the poet. *W. B. Yeats – A Tribute* was released in 1950, produced by the National Film Institute of Ireland, scripted by John D. Sheridan and photographed by Georg Fleischmann. This earlier film also focuses on the landscape that inspired the poet, although it does not show any people in the landscape (which was typical of most contemporary tourist films).[21] Peter Hunt was employed for sound recording (and would later be hired for Carey's projects), yet, musically, the project sounds very different to Boydell's score. Éamonn Ó Gallchobhair, who was the most active stage composer of mid-twentieth century Ireland,[22] was chosen to score this film and he married an Irish folk melody style to the orchestral sound of Classic Hollywood.[23] Boydell went to see the film and recorded his impressions in his diary:

The film was really good – marvellous photography. The verse was excellently spoken by Mícheál Mac-Liammóir and Siobhan McKenna. Eamonn O'Gallagher [Ó Gallchobhair]'s music was restrained and very suitable, though never really inspired. There are many who will criticise this film because it is not quite what they would have done with the subject; but it remains something for this country to be proud of.[24]

Boydell had his chance to score a project on the same subject with a very similar ambition over a decade later.

Aloys Fleischmann wrote that Boydell was the 'obvious choice' when a composer was required to provide a soundtrack for *Yeats Country*. He had extensive experience working in the media and had already provided incidental music for Padraic Fallon's radio play *The Wooing of Etain*.[25] The opening shots of *Yeats Country* illustrate the official nature of the project and the key themes: to present sites associated with the poet in the west of Ireland, complemented by quotations from his work in Tom St John Barry's voice-over. The film has no narrative arc as such beyond loosely following the milestones of Yeats's life and, without the voice-over, the images are an ode to the landscape. Carey's keen concern with nature may have been a factor that contributed to his good relationship with Boydell, who also considered himself an environmentalist. In fact Boydell connected the inspiration of the Irish landscape with the poetry of Yeats, which must have made this project particularly attractive to him. He described the intertwined nature of the poetry and landscape as follows:

> The poetry of WB Yeats has, however, remained very special for me for as long as sixty years. It evokes the timeless magic of the Irish landscape which has inspired so much of my music.[26]

Table 3 outlines the instrumentation for the seven cues in *Yeats Country*. Boydell employed concert flute, alto flute, cor anglais, harp, timpani (sometimes played with wire brushes or timpani sticks or the handles of timpani sticks), small and large cymbals, tam tam and gong.

Scene Description	Cue	Instrumentation
Title music	1M1	fl, a fl (as sounding), cor ang (as sounding), hp, timp
Lake Isle of Innisfree – Sligo countryside	1M2	fl, a fl, cor ang, hp, large cymb, small cymb, timp

Glencar storm	2M1	fl, a fl, cor ang, hp, p timp, large cymb, small cymb, tam
Mountains	2M2	fl, a fl, cor ang, hp, timp, large cymb, small cymb, gong
Lake at sunset	2M3	a fl, cor ang, hp, timp
Knocknarea leaving	2M4	fl, a fl, cor ang, hp, timp, 2 p timp, large cymb, small cymb, tam
Drumcliffe – end titles	2M5	fl, a fl, cor ang, hp, timp

Table 3: Instrumentation of cues in *Yeats Country*. (Courtesy of the Brian Boydell Archive, TCD MS 4951)

He provided extensive technical directions for the harp, including playing it with hammer and bones in cue 1M2, mist. His directions for the harp in cue 2M1 Glencar Storm are as follows:

> Never damp strings unless indicated. Draw the palm of the hand upwards (longitudinally) over the lower strings (wire-bound) and then turn the hand over with fingers spread, towards the highest strings (producing a whistling sound which becomes a vague glissando effect).

Barra Boydell recalled that the composer would usually experiment with an instrument or consult performers about the effects obtainable, as he composed.[27] In the case of his next score for Carey this would lead to his own experimentation with prepared piano.

'MISTS OF TIME'

Carey directed and produced *Mists of Time* for broadcast by RTÉ in October 1967. Focusing on Irish megalithic tombs and stone circles, the film had a commentary spoken by Tom St John Barry who explains the setting of Hallowe'en, Samhain (the eve of All Souls), a pagan festival that centres on the belief that, as one year ends, time stops and starts again at dawn of the following day. Boydell's interest in these great stones had already been evidenced in his *Megalithic Ritual Dances* and this interest is paralleled in *Mists of Time*. This film is less heavily scored than *Yeats Country* and *Errigal*. Boydell composed eight cues for an ensemble comprising cor anglais, contra-bassoon, four horns in F, two violas, two cellos, percussion I and II (Table 4).

Scene Description	Cue	Instrumentation
Title music	1M1	cor ang, 4 hns, 2 vas, 2 vcs, cymb, xyl, pr pf, tam tam
Newgrange day sequence 'Nefertiti's face'	1M2A	cor ang, cbn, 4 hns, pr pf, 2 vas, 2 vcs
Newgrange day sequence contd. 'Eye'	1M2B	cor ang, cbn, 4 hns, 2 vas, 2 vcs, cymb, xyl, pr pf, gong
Shadows – Bricklieve – Darkness	1M3	cor angs, 4 hns, 2 vas, 2 vcs, cymb, pr pf, gong
Interior Newgrange at night	1M4	cor ang, cbn, 4 hns, 2 vas, 2 vcs, timp, cymb, xyl, pr pf, gong
Night sequence – sea	1M5 (there is a note on the fourth page that there is a 'possible break' which would divide the cue (1M5B begins with shot of Goddess eye stone))	cor ang, cbn, 4 hns, 2 vas, 2 vcs, timpi, tam, cymb, xyl, pr pf, gong
Stones rising out of water – Masks	1M6	cor ang, cbn, 4 hns, 2 vas, 2 vcs, b dr, cymb, pr pf, gong
Dawn – End of film	1M7	cor ang, cbn, 4 hns, 2 vas, 2 vcs, cymb, xyl, pr pf, gong

Table 4: Instrumentation of cues in *Mists of Time*. (Courtesy of the Brian Boydell Archive, TCD MS 4950)[28]

Prepared piano, an instrument associated with American experimental music and composers such as John Cage, was atypical of Boydell's compositional style for the concert hall and equally unusual in the context of 1960s film scoring. Figure 1 outlines the key the composer provided for the pianist.

Notation for Pianoforte: ("grand")
The strings are divided by the metal frame into 4 sections
U = upper section (never used)
UM = upper middle
LM = lower middle
L = bottom section
These sections of strings are activated as follows:
Fs = with the pads of the fingers (arrow up symbol) upwards (arrow down symbol) downwards
H = with a hard nylon brush (which will be supplied) (symbol of minim

with x in head) = hit the strings, (arrow up symbol) gliss upwards (arrow down symbol) downwards
S = with a soft circular polishing brush (which will be supplied)
Ts = with timpani or bass drum stick
(Wavy symbol) = continuous light glissando up and down (always on L)
The sustaining pedal is held down until ----------*

Figure 1: Cover page of Percussion II part, *Mists of Time*. (Courtesy of the Brian Boydell Archive, TCD MS 4950)

'ERRIGAL'

By contrast to the nonfiction narrative of *Yeats Country*, when making *Errigal*, Carey imposed his own narrative on images of the Donegal landscape, making the Errigal and Muckish mountains the main characters. He described:

> The weather, as far as I remember, actually did come from Muckish which was not a pretty mountain, it was a bit humpbacked, whereas Errigal had the classical shape of an artist's mountain if you like, so I made one the hero and the other one the villain. And they have a fight, which is quite absurd of course, but nevertheless they fight by throwing weather at each other and the hero of course wins, namely Errigal.[29]

Scene Description	Cue	Instrumentation[30]
Titles	1M1	fl, cbn, 4 hns, hp, vn, va, vc, pf, large cymb, small cymb, timp, gong, tape II
Medium shot of Muckish	1M2	fl, cbn, 4 hns, hp, vn, va, vc, hpd, cel, timp, large cymb, tgl
Mist sequence	1M3	fl, cbn, 4 hns, hp, vn, va, vc, pf, cel, timp, large cymb, small cymb, gong, tape II
Dark Muckish	1M4	fl, cbn, 4 hns, hp, vn, va, vc, hpd, timp, large cymb, small cymb, gong, tapes I and II
Errigal clearing	2M1	fl, 4 hns, vn, va, vc, cymb tape II
Muckish wind blowing dark clouds across	2M2	fl, cbn, 4 hns, vn, va, vc, pf, timp, small cymb, gong, tape II
Beginning of thunder	2M2A	cbn, 4 hns, vn, va, vc, timp, gong, tape II
Thunder	2M2B and 2M2C	tape effect
Errigal's reply	2M2D	cbn, 4 hs, vn, va, vc, pf, timp, gong, tape II (over-recorded effect)

After the thunder	2M3	fl, 4 hns, hp, vn, va, vc, pf, cel, timp, large cymb, small cymb, gong
Dawn sequence	2M4	fl, cbn, 4 hns, hp, vn, va, vc, hpd, timp, cymb
Panning down trees to Errigal	2M5	fl, cbn, 4 hns, hp, vn, va, vc, pf, cel, timp, large cymb

Table 5: Instrumentation of cues in *Errigal*. (Courtesy of the Brian Boydell Archive, TCD MS 4952)

Boydell was even more audacious in his experimental approach to *Errigal*. As illustrated by Table 5, he utilised the same core group of instruments as *Yeats Country* and the prepared piano of *Mists of Time*, but his instrumentation was expanded with contrabassoon, horns, violin, viola, cello, harpsichord and celeste, piano, a wider range of percussion and the notable addition of tape. Boydell's use of tape blurs the lines between music and sound effects in the film; he added in natural sounds such as curlews and experimented with tape effects to suggest the threat of Muckish. Indeed, cues 2M2B and 2M2C comprise only tape effects to convey the cats' paws effect of wind rustling on the surface of the lake water. The composer himself recalled the experimental nature of his music:

> I did some of the things in the music I wrote for Paddy Carey's films, which I'd never dream of putting on a concert platform. For instance, particularly I remember in *Errigal* using an effect with a paintbrush on the inside of a piano and putting it onto tape myself and fiddling around with the tape. Well that's not the sort of music I believe in putting on a concert platform, some people do but I don't.[31]

This quotation suggests that the medium of film permitted the composer to be freer than he felt he could be in the concert hall. The novelty of his effects was noted in music reviews, as Fleischmann comments:

> ... *Errigal* (1968) – in which novel but entirely appropriate effects have been brought about by devices such as the action of brushes on piano strings and the strings of the harp. All his film music is marked by an economy of sound, and an unerring sense of what Gerard Manley Hopkins would call the 'inscape' of the object on the screen.[32]

For many years, Carey wished to make a film without any words and he almost succeeded with *Errigal*. In fact, after the opening statements that introduce the principal protagonists and last just under two minutes, there is no more voice-over for the remaining 12 minutes of the project. His reasons for minimising voice-over were aesthetic: 'I was moving from *Yeats Country* towards my aim of getting commentary out because I thought that words tended to be more of a distraction and very often destroyed the atmosphere of what you were driving at.'[33]

Perhaps inadvertently, through the omission of the voice-over, the director upended the usual hierarchy of film's prioritisation of the human voice. This reversal is particularly acute in the case of documentary film, where the voice-over has a long-established role in conveying an air of authority and shaping the whole soundscape. As described by Michel Chion, '[I]n every audio mix, the presence of the human voice instantly sets up a hierarchy of perception... the presence of a human voice structures the sonic space that contains it.'[34]

Thus, during moments of voice-over, the narrator is prioritised automatically, and the music becomes a secondary aspect of the soundscape. John Corner's description of the intensifying impact of emphasising music in the documentary *Listen to Britain* (1941) is equally applicable in the case of Carey's films where, without the voice-over, music takes on the role of communicating the drama to the audience without the literalism of commentary, providing an aesthetic continuity to individual shots.[35]

CONCLUSION

The function of Boydell's scores and their contribution to these projects can be usefully evaluated with an eye on the genre of documentary film and its inherent tension between reality and fiction. Numerous theorists argue that music has no place in documentary film, undermining authenticity and realism. Yet I am inclined to agree with Holly Rogers who writes:

> Documentary may be underpinned by a realist aesthetic, but it often remains persuasive, subjective, emotional and narrative. As soon as an aesthetic decision is made, the line between the real and the fictional begins to flex.[36]

Given the pervasive use of music in fiction film, we can talk about a cinematic realism with music at its emotional core. Boydell's scores imbue Carey's films with a warmth and emotional connection to the landscape, devoid of any human players. In the case of *Yeats Country* his music provides another poetic strand and a subtle allusion to Irish music using an Irish harp, yet renders it strange through his experimental approach to its playing. As the author of 'An Irishman's Diary' on 9 April 1965 puts it:

Brian Boydell's music is never obtrusive and is exactly right for the mood of the film and all temptation to go overboard emotionally with script and commentary (always a danger with Yeats and Sligo as the subject) have been resisted.[37]

The composer's use of extended techniques, tape and blurring of music and sound effects in *Mists of Time* and *Errigal* draws the viewer into the landscape and his music takes on a more directly narratological role partly due to the move away from voice-over. This reflects the nature of his collaboration with Carey, which could be described as a meeting of like minds rather than music provided to an independently-conceived project.[38] Boydell reflected on the project so positively that he turned cues from the films into the basis for *Symphonic Inscapes*, op. 64 (1968), and dedicated it to Carey.

Engagement with Boydell's film music provides an insight into a more experimental side to the composer and close study of the manuscript scores reveals that he developed a personal method for working on these projects. His music contributed far more to the success of these films than was recognised publicly: the scores to Carey's films *Yeats Country* and *Errigal* were relatable for an international audience, presenting a positive audio-visual experience of the Irish landscape while the scores to *Mists of Time* and *Ireland* for Irish television offered a positive and creative reflection for home audiences. More broadly, study of these projects suggests a rich avenue for further research into music in short documentary film, revisiting the distinctions between practices for the concert hall and the cinema in Ireland.

FIVE

BRIAN BOYDELL'S EARLY SONGS FOR LOW VOICE

Aylish E. Kerrigan

Brian Boydell took his initial steps as a composer primarily through the solo song for voice and piano. In some cases (as noted below), orchestral accompaniment is also indicated, although no such arrangements survive. His only other compositions dating from before 1941 (excluding discarded juvenilia) are *Nine Variations on the Snowy-Breasted Pearl*, op. 2, for piano (1935), Oboe Quintet, op. 11 (1940), *An Easter Carol*, op. 12, for unaccompanied voices (1940), and *Hearing of Harvests*, op. 13, for baritone solo, choir and orchestra (1940). In a 1993 interview for Radio Telefís Éireann (RTÉ), he commented that:

> Naturally some of my earliest excursions in composition [were] in the form of songs. First of all, I myself was a singer, and the other thing too about a song is it is fairly easy to be performed. Performance in itself is a tremendous incentive to write music. I would write songs and sing them myself and other people would sing them as well.[1]

Singing would play an important role throughout much of Brian Boydell's musical career. He was a choral scholar at Clare College, Cambridge, studied singing in London in 1938–9 with Louise Trenton, and after returning to Dublin in 1939 he established himself as a singing teacher,[2] subsequently teaching singing at the Royal Irish Academy of Music (RIAM) from 1944 to 1952. He was active as a baritone soloist in Dublin through the 1940s and 50s, and between 1958 and 1969 he directed and sang in the Dowland Consort, which he himself founded.

This essay focuses on the early songs of Brian Boydell composed for low voice between 1935 and 1942. There are twelve songs in this category (see Appendix below), seven of which were later withdrawn by the composer without explanation. Six of the songs have been selected as examples of Boydell's early vocal compositions.[3] They all vary in style and contain a certain amount of harmonic and rhythmic experimentation. Only two of these songs are known to have been performed previously. These are *Wild Geese* and *Rushlights*, which were sung by the composer in the Cambridge Music Club in 1937.

'WILD GEESE'

Brian Boydell's earliest surviving song *Wild Geese* was composed in 1935 at the age of 18. A setting of a text by P. H. B. Lyon (headmaster of Rugby school), it was dedicated to his music teacher at Rugby, Kenneth Stubbs. According to Axel Klein, Stubbs had become a surrogate father figure for Boydell 'perhaps compensating for his own rather strict father figure who displayed such little interest in music'.[4] The manuscript is dated Heidelberg June 1935, although in his interview with Michael Taylor he states that he wrote it while still at Rugby.[5]

In 1935, after he left Rugby school, Boydell spent six months in Heidelberg at the Evangelisches Kirchenmusikalisches Institut (Evangelical Church Music Institute) where he studied organ and took private piano lessons. His stay in Heidelberg included a visit to a burnt-out Jewish village, which probably inspired his later pacifism and his lifelong concern with human rights. During this time he attended three performances in Mannheim of the entire *Der Ring des Nibelungen*. His love of Wagner was further nourished by attending *Tristan und Isolde* (after which he described himself as being unable to sleep, 'just walking around the place dreaming about this marvellous music'),[6] *Die Meistersinger* and *Parsifal*. He also attended *Die Frau Ohne Schatten* in Munich, during which performance he met Richard Strauss.

Boydell viewed *Wild Geese* as his first successful vocal composition and, as he stated in an interview with Charles Acton, he continued 'to be proud of the song throughout his life'.[7] The text by P. H. B. Lyons is a pleasant pastoral poem painting a picture of wild geese flying in formation overhead. Their beauty is compared to a 'song in the night' that pierces with 'an arrow of light'. The song is written in a simple style with a regular two-chord piano accompaniment and a consistent vocal line. It is very approachable and allows the voice to triumph, building to its final declaration in the last bars. There are no inherent pitching or rhythmic problems to be tackled. It best suits an even,

Example 1: *Wild Geese*, bars 20–4

legato vocal production and might easily be programmed at the beginning of a diverse vocal recital.

The first section from bars 1–24 compels the singer forward, emphasising the text 'a golden arrow under the sun' in bars 20–4 (ex. 1). This is followed by a middle section from bars 25–42, highlighting the words 'and pierced us' in bars 39–40 and partially resolving in bars 42–3 (ex. 2).

Example 2: *Wild Geese*, bars 39–43

The final climax of the song builds through bars 44–50 until the high F is reached in the final bars 51–4 (ex. 3).

Example 3: *Wild Geese*, bars 44–54

Composed at an early stage of his compositional development, the song is well-constructed although not harmonically adventurous.

'RUSHLIGHTS'

In 1935 Boydell also composed *Rushlights*, a setting of an anonymous text found in *TCD Miscellany*, a TCD magazine. He dedicated the song to W. R. Fearon, professor of biochemistry at TCD and an influential figure in Boydell's early life,[8] but later withdrew it. It is far more ambitious than *Wild Geese*, perhaps inspired by the myriad of images in this very romantic poem. The text describes a beautiful landscape: a still lake where the poet is observing 'wan lights' as the backdrop to plovers flying. The pervasive scent of irises prevails as the poet whispers 'I will take the dew cold stems of the rushes, and seven rushlights make'. The comparison is then made between the lake and the 'heart's dim places', which will be illuminated by the 'undying lights'.

The song begins *pp* with a five-bar arpeggiated piano introduction, mirroring the wind blowing through the rushes, and appropriate for the imagery of the text 'Orris green with rushes', 'the still, still lake', the 'wan lights', and 'wings upon the waters where plovers fly'. The folk-like vocal line lies in a comfort-

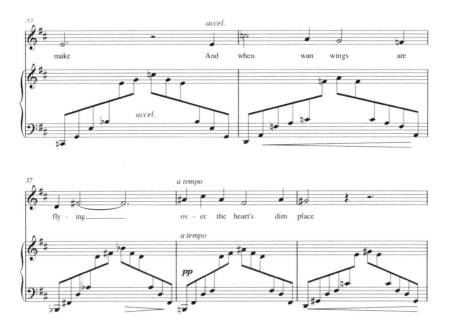

Example 4: *Rushlights*, bars 35–9

able octave range. Here we find a few surprising harmonic changes, as mentioned in Example 4, bar 38, but pitching is easily solved with careful consideration to the piano accompaniment in bar 37 where the B♭ in the treble clef is clearly heard, helping the singer pitch the A♯ in bar 38. Rhythmically the song is straightforward with a lulling 6/4 arpeggio accompaniment.

In the second verse the harmony intensifies with a romantic comparison of rushlights 'flying over the heart's dim place' (ex. 4). The setting concludes in the dominant major key as 'My seven lights undying Shall burn before her face' and the piano accompaniment gradually fades away.

'WATCHING THE NEEDLEBOATS'

In 1936, shortly after his stay in Heidelberg, Boydell composed *Watching the Needleboats* to a text by James Joyce and dedicated to his Cambridge friend Maurice Petit. He revised the song in 1937. Curiously, it was never performed but also not withdrawn. The economy of words maximises the impact in this poem. It is, as one would expect from Joyce, layered with meaning and sensual references. We note that the occupants of the needleboats are young as the poet hears 'their young hearts crying above the glancing oar', achieving with the word 'glancing' both fire-like flashing and impermanence. Then the poet hears 'prairie grasses sighing, no more, return no more', a contrasting, repetitive image. The second verse demonstrates brilliant use of language, 'vainly your love-blown bannerets mourn' evoking the weary and helpless nature of love which, like 'the wild wind that passes' will 'no more return'.

Vocally this short song is somewhat demanding with difficult pitching against the piano accompaniment, as in bar 11 when a B♮ in the vocal line is held against a tremolo octave C in the piano. The singer is required to move between legato and semi-recitative passages that conclude each verse in bars 17 and 32 respectively. As this song was not withdrawn, it might be used in a vocal recital, but the placement on the programme would be difficult as similar songs, *The Witch* or *Lamenting*, have been withdrawn.

The tempo direction 'Slowly, with the swing of gentle rowing' is expressed in the rhythm of the vocal line, which moves gently in semitones, whole tones and minor thirds. The piano part is quite complex with a heavy chordal structure and seems to be searching for a new style. With two repeated whole tone chords, the first four bars of the piano accompaniment (ex. 5) give a cluster effect. This continues in different forms communicating harmonic tension throughout the song.

Example 5: *Watching the Needleboats*, bars 1–5

There is a brief respite in bar 17 in the vocal line requiring the singer to use a recitative effect, which is echoed in bar 32, the final notes of the song. The last bars resolve with a descending pattern in minor thirds. Two sections of the song are quite awkward: bars 18–22 contain a stumbling rhythmic figure, followed by a dense harmonic piano accompaniment to the simple vocal line in bars 20–2 (ex. 6).

Example 6: *Watching the Needleboats*, bars 18–22

The most important line of the poem in bars 27–9, 'No more will the wild wind that passes return' is underscored with an unwieldy harmonic choice, unnecessarily complicating the vocal delivery (ex. 7).

'THE WITCH'

In 1938, while he was studying composition with Patrick Hadley and Herbert Howells at the Royal College of Music in London and working intensely on vocal technique with Louise Trenton, Boydell composed *The Witch*, to a text by W. B. Yeats. There is no record of a performance, it was not dedicated to

Example 7: *Watching the Needleboats*, bars 27–9

anyone and he later withdrew the song. The text of *The Witch*, by Yeats, is beautifully crafted. The first half of the poem is direct in its meaning and equates 'toil and grow rich' with lying with 'a foul witch'. The foreboding second half is dark, with the poet who aims for wealth being 'drained dry' and 'sought with despair'.

The dramatic, short 50-second song is, in my opinion, a veritable gem. The accompaniment is creative and varied, expressing the text perfectly. Short figures of two consecutive semiquavers are used to good effect throughout until expanded in the final bars 17 and 18 to a flaccid figure pointing the word 'despair'. The ensemble of the vocal line and piano accompaniment (ex. 8) is extremely original, effectively articulating the text perfectly.

Example 8: *The Witch*, bars 8–10

The ingenious piano part is based on repeated rhythmic semiquaver and quaver figures. The song concludes with a descending rhythmic pattern in the piano accompaniment, which creates a limping effect (ex. 9). This song would surely be welcomed in a group of early Brian Boydell songs in a vocal programme had it not been withdrawn.

Example 9: *The Witch*, bar 17

'AURELIA'

Aurelia, composed in 1939, was dedicated to P. B. Kinmonth. It was never performed and later withdrawn. It is a setting of a text by the wartime poet Robert Nichols. Boydell set the text in a harmless parlour song style. A vulnerable love poem, the emotions expressed are full of tenderness and longing. Only in the last line do we understand that this love is fraught with separation: 'Then my eyes with tears run over / And my very heart is broken'.

The vocal line is straightforward posing no technical problems for the singer. Why the song was withdrawn is again a mystery. This is an appealing love song, with a relatively simple accompaniment, using triplets throughout. The extended vocal line with its flowing piano accompaniment features duple against triple quavers, creating an interesting tension, and ending with the expressive phrase, 'And my very heart is broken' (ex. 10) followed by a six-bar postlude.

Example 10: *Aurelia*, bars 19–21

'THE LAMENTING'

The last song to be considered, *The Lamenting*, was composed in 1942 for baritone and string orchestra with a piano reduction. However, no record of the orchestral score can be found, suggesting that this scoring was intended rather than realised. *The Lamenting* was later withdrawn. The poem by the pacifist Nigel Heseltine is a stark argument against violence and war. The poet laments the 'drowning sorrow strong / Unspeakable tears of women'. This idea is expanded with the words 'Pierced tears numbing swollen eyes dripping' and 'Air in the windpipe making the moan'. In the last lines, the poet attempts to shut out the crying but the 'doors are eyes weeping'.

This very moving song poses no great difficulties in pitching or rhythm. The poem is well set, pointing the text in simple, explicit fashion. The piano accompaniment is sparser in style than *Watching the Needleboats* but it is otherwise similar, allowing the vocal line to declare its pleading message clearly. With a wide vocal range there is extensive use of repeated descending patterns in both voice and accompaniment (ex. 11).

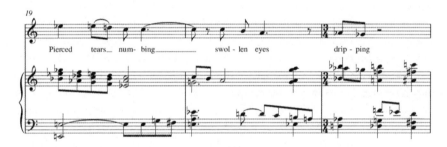

Example 11: *The Lamenting*, bars 19–21

This is a far more effective song than *Watching the Needleboats*. One is reminded of Anton Berg with good reason. In his memoir, Boydell refers specifically to Heseltine and this song:

> Nigel Heseltine... was the son of Philip Heseltine, the real name of the composer Peter Warlock. It was rumoured that he was a deserter from the British army enjoying refuge in neutral Ireland. But none of us minded in the least what might have been the murky past of any of our friends. It was what they could contribute to our community now that mattered. Whatever the truth of his past, the number of his unbelievable exploits in many distant lands, which he related for our fascinated entertainment, could hardly have been fitted into the limited life span

he had experienced. He was a good poet, and published in Dublin a volume entitled *A Four-Walled Dream*. I set one of these poems ('The Lamenting') to music in 1942. It was a very complex setting for baritone and string orchestra in the style of Alban Berg's early songs. I considered it as an experimental exercise.[9]

The withdrawal of this song is again curious and inexplicable.

CONCLUSION

We are left with the conundrum: why did Boydell choose to leave *Wild Geese* and *Watching the Needleboats* in his oeuvre of work and why did he withdraw four of the six other songs that I have considered? One may reasonably question the point of the efforts to analyse and understand the four early songs in this essay that have been withdrawn by Brian Boydell. It can be argued that Boydell put great value on well-constructed works. Although *Wild Geese* is not an adventurous experiment and does not herald Boydell's future compositional style, it is well constructed. Perhaps Boydell also did not withdraw *Watching the Needleboats* for the same reason, and he may have felt that the two songs best demonstrated the early stage of his development as a composer. What assumptions are possible? *Rushlights* may have been withdrawn due to some of the incongruous harmonic choices that he made in the song. Withdrawal of *The Witch*, with its effective, creative setting is difficult to understand. *Aurelia* may have been considered too simple, but it is also quite effective and again begs the question of withdrawal.[10] *The Lamenting* is a very compelling setting of Nigel Heseltine's poem. Was it withdrawn because Boydell viewed it as an experiment? Only the piano reduction survives. Did the string orchestra setting pose other problems?

Boydell was a true renaissance man adept in science, recognised as a painter, a baritone, an oboist and a pianist. However, it is revealing that in an interview with Charles Acton in 1970 he mentions the word 'ashamed' four times, and states that he is 'worried by being at an age which I may very likely be an old fogey'[11] (he was 53 at the time), in addition to referring to himself as 'we small people'.[12] Was he insecure about his place as a composer? Almost 20 years later in his interview with Michael Taylor in 1989, we find a much more confident Boydell, as he asserts regarding the *Five Joyce Songs* written in 1946 for baritone and piano: 'I simplified my technique on purpose for the Joyce Songs. The Joyce lyrics were enormously simple and straightforward.'[13] Later he states that 'the most valuable thing in all creativity is... honesty of purpose'[14] and that his String Trio of 1943 was 'the first work in which I found some kind of an individual voice'.[15]

Considered from the performer's perspective, these songs are notable for their expressive qualities and for the composer's faithful interpretation of the text. Although there are technical difficulties in the songs, as a singer Boydell understands the requirements for breathing, pitching and the limits of vocal range. Since four of the six songs considered in this essay were subsequently relegated by the composer to the 'withdrawn' list, we are left with the question: is it useful and/or important to reflect on these songs in order to understand the process of development and progression in the composer's early compositional style? Should they indeed somehow be restored and available to singers?

APPENDIX

The early songs of Brian Boydell
*Songs marked with an asterisk were later withdrawn by the composer

Wild Geese, op. 1 (1935)
    low v, pf; text: P. H. B. Lyon, ded Kenneth Stubbs, director of music at Rugby School

*Rushlights, op. 3 (1935)
    low v, pf; text: Anon. (from *TCD Miscellany*), ded W. R. Fearon

*Cathleen, the Daughter of Houlihan, op. 4 (1936)
    low v, pf; text: W. B. Yeats, ded Charles Acton

*She Weeps Over Rahoon, op. 5 (1936)
    low v, pf (str orch); text: James Joyce

Watching the Needleboats (1936, rev. 1937)
    low v, pf; text: James Joyce, ded Maurice Petit

Cradle Song, op. 10, no. 3 (1937, rev. 1943)[16]
    s, pf (str qt); text: John Berryman, ded John Berryman

*The Witch, op. 6 (1938)
    low v, pf; text: W. B. Yeats

A Child's Grace, op. 10, no. 1 (1938, rev. 1943)
    s, pf (str qt); text: Robert Herrick, ded P. B. Kinmonth

*Aurelia, op. 7 (1939)
    low v, pf; text: Robert Nichols, ded P. B. Kinmonth

The Bargain, op. 10, no. 2 (1940, rev. 1943)
    s, pf (str qt); text: Sir Philip Sydney, ded Marie Werner

*Alone, op. 15 (1941)
    low v, pf; text: James Joyce, ded G. V. K[eys].

*The Lamenting, op. 19 (1942)
    bar, pf (str qt); text: Nigel Heseltine

SIX

'WHITE STAG' EMBODIED: *THE FEATHER OF DEATH*, OP. 22 (1943)

Philip Graydon

In a letter dated 8 April 1945 to the English art gallery owner and patron Lucy Wertheim, the artist Kenneth Hall enthused: 'I know that here in Dublin we started with so much enthusiasm and I firmly believe that a great deal of the popularity that modern painting enjoys here now in a restricted circle is due to our efforts.'[1]

The collective of which Hall wrote was the White Stag Group: a loosely aligned cadre of (mainly) English émigré artists, whose aesthetic was influenced by continental modernism, not least Surrealism. Founded in 1935 by its sole, true 'members', Basil Rákóczi and Hall, the White Stag Group committed itself to the expansion of subjectivity in art and the then burgeoning field of psychotherapy (of which Rákóczi became a practitioner in equal parts). They adopted a symbol depicting a white stag on a black background: a symbol of the family of Rákóczi's close friend and confidant, Herbrand Ingouville-Williams, who encouraged the former's interests in psychology.[2]

As the Second World War approached in late August 1939, Rákóczi and Hall fled to Ireland. Thereafter they moved to Dublin in early 1940 and took rooms at 34 Lower Baggot Street where they revived their immediately prior, London-based activities – namely, the Society for Creative Psychology and the White Stag Group. Their first exhibition, which was held in April 1940, included the work of Mainie Jellett, one of the leading figures in the Irish artistic avant-garde of the day and, in time, teacher to the aspiring artist and composer, Brian Boydell.

By 1943 Boydell's standing vis-à-vis the White Stag Group was such that he joined a committee convened by Margot Moffett (whose husband was the architect Noel Moffett) to discuss the potential of mounting an exhibition examining the influences of the White Stag Group since their arrival in Ireland. That committee also included Thurloe Conolly (1918–2016), an assistant structural engineer turned full-time painter, who would eventually become a professional architect (and brother-in-law to Brian Boydell). Though encouraged toward such a career change by friends as eminent as the artists Evie Hone and Ralph Cusack, Conolly had an ambition to similarly explore further his impulse toward poetry; as he later remarked: 'I would have liked to write poetry – and maybe thought that I did, but now I know I did not, except for an occasional rare flash of words that seemed to come from nowhere.'[3]

Conolly's own direct association with the White Stag Group stemmed from 1942 when, on 17 April, he participated in a poetry reading that had been organised by Ingouville-Williams and included other figures such as William Clare and Bruce Williamson. In the same year, Conolly, Ralph Cusack and Anne Yeats painted sets for *The House of Cards*, a play by Frank Carney that was staged in the Gate Theatre, Dublin. A satirical comedy set in contemporary Bohemian Dublin, its music was composed by Boydell. *The House of Cards* may not have met with any great critical or public acclaim but it is notable insofar as it marks Conolly's first collaboration-of-sorts with Boydell as composer. The second and more auspicious occasion followed in 1943 when they collaborated on Boydell's work *The Feather of Death* – a cycle of three songs for baritone solo, flute, violin, viola and cello.

Perhaps unsurprisingly (given the paucity of opportunities in the early 1940s for public performances of contemporary music and the composer's own deep involvement in the visual arts via the White Stag Group), *The Feather of Death* was premiered at a concert of Boydell's chamber music held in the Shelbourne Hotel in January 1944 during the collective's Exhibition of Subjective Art. The latter, which was held at 6 Lower Baggot Street from 4–22 January, was the one originally mooted by Margot Moffett's committee during the previous summer and it featured works by 13 different artists selected by Hall and Rákóczi, among them paintings by Boydell and Conolly. Boydell's two pictures, *Atlas Approached* (pl. 8) and *The Return of the Wood* (pl. 9), were characteristically Surrealist-inspired creations; the art historian S. B. Kennedy suggests that their use of grotesquely-contorted branches, worm-like beings and other organic ephemera point to a not-so-mythical dystopia brought on by the war.[4]

On a less elevated plane, the White Stag Group was arguably responsible for injecting some glamour and intrigue into wartime Dublin via its artistic and literary fringe.[5] As one of the leading members of that fringe, Boydell certainly looked and played the part with panache. With his friend Lionel Kerwood he rented a house, 'Imaal', in Rathfarnham in April 1941, which quickly became 'a club for artists, scroungers and other friends', as he later described it.[6] Despite this depiction, most evenings at the house involved earnest inquiry into art and music.

Indeed, Boydell and his circle of acquaintances also held chamber music concerts at 16 Heytesbury Lane. Gatherings included Boydell, Charles Acton,

Paul Egestorff, William Fearon, Nigel Heseltine and Edward Oldham. Around 1943 Kerwood vacated Imaal and Conolly moved in. By now evenings at the house were taken up with what they called 'Surrealist Expression', embodied in drawings and texts that were often collaborative in nature. Light-hearted at base, this activity led to the establishment of the short-lived 'Rathfarnham Academy of Surrealist Art', whose participants produced texts, photo-montages and drawings. Boydell's sister Yvonne, who was also part of this particular group, went on to become Conolly's first wife upon the occasion of their marriage in 1946.

It was during this febrile period that *The Feather of Death* began to take shape. In 1942 Boydell had set Nigel Heseltine's poem *The Lamenting* to music,[7] but the following year he turned his sights to collaboration with Conolly. Conolly later described the occasion thus:

> I enjoyed writing words for a short song cycle while Brian worked at the score from the piano. Much of my writing at that time was influenced by Eugene Jolas, André Breton, James Joyce, Gertrude Stein and others who wrote for the quarterly review, transition, where *Finnegan's Wake* first appeared.[8]

Conolly began to value what he termed music's 'abstract nature', which he now saw as being of a piece with painting.[9] Despite this avowed belief his paintings of the day were more symbolist and subjective in nature. In February 1944, in a statement written for the Irish monthly magazine *The Bell* to supplement an article by the distinguished English art critic Herbert Read entitled 'On Subjective Art', Conolly professed: 'I should like my painting to react, not away from humanity but away from universal oppression, towards humanity... through the harnessing of dream images.'[10] Such potent theorising was the stock-in-trade of the White Stag movement as a whole, not least Rákóczi himself, who used the term 'psychological analysis' in describing what would become for him a lifetime's preoccupation with psychotherapy à la Freud, Adler and Jung.[11]

Conolly's own description of 'harnessing dream images' is an apt way of describing his literary style in the texts Boydell set in *The Feather of Death*. Fraught and freighted with symbolist imagery, the text of the opening song stands as an apposite introduction to the cycle; actually, the overall effect is one that could be described as profoundly psychotherapeutic:

The White Beach
My body drifts like ash on the singing wind,
searching.
Ravens thread the air with black embroidery

Like tunnels of glass are the waves on the beach
But the sea is an ivory breast with foaming nipples.
Terror stands stiffly in the wind
Your eyes are frosted with dread;
But your mind is a coiled ring, though your nostrils curl like wax shells.
My bones are as brittle as glass, and we are still as clay idols.
The air curdles, so cold is the world.

Musically, Boydell's op. 22 song cycle undoubtedly marks the emergence of his original voice as a composer. It marks an unambiguous turn from the English pastoralism of his earliest works toward a personalised European modernism well suited to Conolly's introspective exploration of the intimate connection between nature and grief. But while the style and mode of expression react effectively to that stimulus, the impetus behind Boydell's inspiration may well have sprung from a source that transcended the immediate.

As an undergraduate student at Clare College, Cambridge, in the late 1930s, Boydell developed an abiding interest in the music of the British composer Peter Warlock (the pseudonym of Philip Heseltine), not least his setting of poems by W. B. Yeats including *The Curlew*, scored for tenor solo, flute, cor anglais and string quartet, which its composer revised and published in 1922. As Boydell's son Barra has pointed out, the work must surely have been an influence on the Irish composer's not dissimilar scoring for *The Feather of Death*.[12] Moreover, in his memoir, Boydell speaks of this enthusiasm for *The Curlew*:

> With my musical friends we listened to records in each other's rooms, and developed wild enthusiasms for several composers regarded then as the avant-garde, including especially Alban Berg. Peter Warlock's setting of poems by W. B. Yeats, known as *The Curlew*, became a veritable cult. Another cult work was Berg's *Lyric Suite* for string orchestra. On strictly limited and carefully planned occasions we would listen to the newly available recording with all lights extinguished. A period of meditation would follow during which no one would breathe a word that might disturb the magic spell.[13]

One of those 'musical friends' was the American poet, John Berryman, whom Boydell met in February 1937 and with whom he cultivated a close friendship. In a letter sent to Berryman's biographer John Haffenden in 1972, Boydell described how Berryman became associated for a time with what the composer described as 'our frightfully aesthetic/intellectual group' that met in his digs on Midsummer Common.[14] Haffenden describes how, upon hearing Warlock's *The Curlew*, Berryman was convinced that the music should be experienced in the dark from then on. In a letter to his mother dated 23 February 1937, Berryman wrote: '*The Curlew* is beautiful but utterly despairing, the most desolate art I know.'[15]

In fact Berryman referenced directly Boydell's enthusiasm for *The Curlew* in the opening stanzas of his poem 'Friendless', commenting on how the young Dubliner introduced him to Warlock's music, and inferring how Boydell's sonorous tenor voice stood in direct contrast to the melancholic nature of the implicit voice contained in Warlock's settings.[16]

To be sure, Berryman's summation of Warlock's *Curlew* – 'voice of a lost soul moving' – could certainly be applied to Boydell's *Feather of Death*; the first song, 'The White Beach', opens with a descending, canonic figure that goes on to inform its entirety, before the voice enters in a decidedly disembodied fashion (ex. 1).

Example 1: *The Feather of Death*, 'The White Beach', bars 1–8

The incursion of marine imagery on the words occasions what then sounds like a return on Boydell's part to the pastoral style of his youth, before annunciation of the word 'Terror' jolts the music back to a more Bergian expressionistic palette (ex. 2). Thereafter, the music of the opening returns; the stark ending of the final line creates an effect recalling Warlock's *Curlew* in its unadorned bleakness (ex. 3).

Example 2: *The Feather of Death*, 'The White Beach', bars 12–27

Example 3: *The Feather of Death*, 'The White Beach', bars 42–5

Moreover, that association is made all the more pronounced if one considers an amateur recording made of 'The White Beach' around the time of its first performance in 1944. Featuring the original performers with Boydell himself (as on the occasion of its premiere) singing the baritone part,[17] it was digitally transferred from the source 78 rpm acetate disc and exists as a fascinating historical record, documenting not only the composer's interest in and advocacy of early recording techniques, but also the interpretative stance he took toward his own music.[18] Boydell possessed a wire recorder during this period and it seems plausible that it was this device that was used to record 'The White Beach' before its necessary initial transfer to acetate disc for private playback on a contemporary, conventional gramophone. Invented in 1898 by Valdemar Poulsen, wire recording or magnetic wire recording was the first early magnetic recording technology, an analogue type of audio storage in which a magnetic recording is made on thin steel wire. The wire is pulled rapidly across a recording head, which magnetises each point along the wire in direct relation to the intensity and polarity of the electrical audio signal being simultaneously supplied to the recording. By subsequently drawing the wire across the same or a similar head while the head is not being supplied with an electrical signal, the changing magnetic field presented by the passing wire induces a similarly changing electric current in the head, recreating the original signal at a reduced level. Such technology reached its heyday between the 1930s and early to mid 1940s, before the introduction of magnetic tape recording.

With regard to how Boydell may have directed the interpretation of his works, the recording of 'The White Beach' attests to the fact that the tempi he doubtless controlled (which he approximated at the foot of the title page of the score) were considerably slower than the more recent professional recording of the work.[19] While the latter-day performance captured on CD has the length of Boydell's first song clocking in at 2'06, the digital transfer of the 1944 performance of the work – registering an overall length of 3'35 – is much closer to that which he gave as being indicative upon completion of the score.[20] Apart from the likeness in mood and in some points of musical detail to Warlock's *Curlew*, the elongated tempo (more 'compliant', in metronomic terms, with Boydell's marking of 'dotted crotchet equals 76' atop the first page of his song) arguably articulates its structure with greater clarity than the later recording, while allowing the music to 'breathe' in a more idiomatic fashion.

The second song, 'The White Moon', is similarly integrated in a musical sense by an undulating motif in the flute, as a calm (albeit, bleak) 'sea picture' is sketched by the words. Once more, Boydell's slow-moving, contorted harmony recalls *The Curlew* (its opening, in particular), but the vocal melody is more angular (in the main) than that in the Warlock piece (ex. 4).

Example 4: *The Feather of Death*, 'The White Moon', bars 1–8

More striking overall, though, is the superstructural motif, which returns first in the cello and then in the flute, underlining an early example in Boydell's music of nascent octatonicism via its use of alternating tones and semitones (ex. 5).

Example 5: *The Feather of Death*, 'The White Moon', bars 15–19

Likewise, 'The Last Farewell' is infused by a theme characterised by a decorated rising fourth-falling second pattern, although the unity here is subverted as the mood of the text toggles from resignation to anguish. The song starts with Conolly's words at their most Surrealist in terms of imagery, while the flute weaves florid, tendril-like arabesques (ex. 6).

Example 6: *The Feather of Death*, 'The Last Farewell', bars 1–14

The pace starts to quicken consequently, driven relentlessly by the frenzy of the flute line, before ending abruptly (ex. 7).

Example 7: *The Feather of Death*, 'The Last Farewell', bars 39–47

Beyond the obvious, 'The Last Farewell' was a fitting choice with which to end their song cycle; moreover, Boydell's imaginative rendering in music of the 'winter wood [sweating] with fear' as the subject of the poem 'chop[s] the dripping trees in a fever of despair' and, equally, of the 'the cold wet roots [gripping his] throat' while '[holding him] fast between two dreams', brings to mind the composer's abovementioned contemporaneous paintings, *The Return of the Wood* and *Atlas Approached*. While Boydell went on to paint other works before deciding to forgo visual art in favour of music toward the end of the following year, perhaps the experience of realising that he could now satisfactorily – and successfully – distil his creative impulse into composition in a manner true to his inspiration made that decision all the more inevitable.

SEVEN

A PACK OF FANCIES FOR A TRAVELLING HARPER (1970): CONTEXT, PERFORMANCE AND RECEPTION

Clíona Doris

The harp is well represented in the composition catalogue of Brian Boydell and features significantly in the composer's concert programmes in his lifetime, most notably in musical celebrations for his 70th and 80th birthdays presented at the National Concert Hall, Dublin (NCH). He collaborated with many of Ireland's leading harpists, including Gráinne Yeats, Mercedes Bolger [Garvey], Sheila Larchet Cuthbert, Una O'Donovan, Caitríona Yeats, Denise Kelly and Teresa Lawlor, to produce solo works for Irish harp and pedal harp, voice and Irish harp, chamber ensembles and orchestra.

The main focus of this essay is the performance history and reception of his work for solo pedal harp, *A Pack of Fancies for a Travelling Harper* (1970), written for Una O'Donovan for a performance at the Dublin Festival of Twentieth-Century Music on 13 January 1971. In five movements, it is written in tribute to the Irish harper and composer Turlough Carolan (1670–1738) in the tercentenary year of his birth. In addition, the context and style of the work is considered in terms of Boydell's compositional output for the instrument.

WORKS FOR HARP

Brian Boydell wrote works for two forms of the instrument played in Ireland: the Irish harp with a lever mechanism, and the double-action pedal harp (Table 1). He wrote specifically for each type of harp, born out of a detailed study of each instrument, exploiting their distinctive characteristics in terms of pitch and harmonic organisation. For instance the *Three Yeats Songs* (1965) for voice and Irish harp is not suitable for the pedal harp due to the use of specific lever settings for individual strings, resulting in the instrument being tuned to several scales throughout its register.

Work	Instrumentation	Year of Composition
Quintet for Flute, Harp and String Trio, op. 49	fl, hp, str trio	1960, rev. 1966 and 1980
Four Sketches for Two Irish Harps, op. 52	2 Ir hps	1962
Three Yeats Songs, op. 56a	s, Ir hp	1965, rev. 1992
Musician's Song [*Love is an Immoderate Thing*], op. 56b	s, Ir hp	1965
A Pack of Fancies for a Travelling Harper, op. 66	hp	1970
Five Mosaics, op. 69	vn, hp (pf)	1972, rev. 1978 as *Six Mosaics*
Partita Concertante, op. 75	vn, hp, orch	1978
The Small Bell, op. 76	fl, hp, str qt, ch	1980
Confrontations in a Cathedral, op. 84	org, hp, perc	1986
An Album of Pieces for Irish Harp, op. 88	Ir hp	1989

Table 1: Brian Boydell, List of Works for Harp

Boydell's first main work utilising the pedal harp is the Quintet for Flute, Harp and String Trio of 1960, written for the Prieur Ensemble: André Prieur (flute), Jaroslav Vanaček (violin), Máire Larchet (viola), Maurice Meulien (cello) and Sheila Larchet Cuthbert (harp). In a review published in the *Irish Times* on 29 June 1960 entitled 'First-Class Chamber Music One of Festival Highlights', Charles Acton states: 'this work pleased me a great deal straight away. . . This may well be Dr Boydell's most complete and satisfying work to date.'[1] However, after such a positive reception, it seems that the work was not performed again until 1966, now with material from *Four Sketches for Two Irish Harps* (1962) incorporated into the revised first movement.[2] Once again the work had an impact on Charles Acton:

> I have a very clear idea indeed that it is a very fine work now – strong, powerful, taut; with a lot to say, very well said. We really must not be allowed to be without a performance for another six years. In any other country official arrangements would have been made to support the recording, publishing and foreign dissemination of such a good work.[3]

This work underwent significant revisions between its premiere in 1960 and its final version in 1980. A study of two recordings in the Contemporary Music Centre (CMC) from 1960 and 1981 illustrate Boydell's developing understanding of the instrument and its capabilities. The harp has a much more prominent role in the revised first movement, with extensive use of the *glissandi* effect and short solo passages that are absent in the original version. The second movement is not as extensively revised and the final movement, with its effective colouristic use of the harp throughout, remains unchanged.[4] Caitríona Yeats (harp), with Elizabeth Gaffney (flute) and members of the Testore String Quartet, performed the final version of the work at the National Gallery of Ireland on 6 May 1981 in a 'retrospective' concert of Boydell's chamber music works presented by Radio Telefís Éireann (RTÉ).[5]

In the intervening years, Boydell composed several works for Irish harp: songs with Irish harp accompaniment for Gráinne Yeats, and *Four Sketches for Two Irish Harps*, a series of four Irish harp duos for Mercedes Bolger and Gráinne Yeats. The next major work, *A Pack of Fancies*, returned to the pedal harp with an evocation of the sound world of the ancient music of the harpers and a homage to the music of Bach. It also displays an experimental character, with integrated extended techniques in the central movements, including the inventive exploitation of the fingernail buzz, described by Boydell as 'the harpist's nightmare'.[6]

His later works for harp, while they do not return to such an investigative soundscape, display a deep understanding of the instrument's mechanism and its harmonic and timbral potential. This is apparent in *Mosaics* (1972, revised 1978) for violin and piano or harp, which he later adapted to become the *Partita Concertante* (1978), for violin, harp and orchestra. His knowledge of the pedal harp can be clearly evidenced in comparing the harp and piano versions of *Mosaics*, where he recasts the same material to ensure that it is idiomatically adjusted for pedal harp, through enharmonic changes and alterations to complement the instrument's particular resonance and reverberation character. The main differences from the piano part are some registral octave changes, additional doubling to provide a stronger articulation and enharmonic changes to facilitate fewer pedal changes. In the *Scherzo* some of the melodic piano writing is not found in the harp part but is instead played on the violin. This may be explained by a need to reduce the requirement for multiple pedal changes, but perhaps also through consideration of the difference of the balance and sustain between the two instruments. The damping indications on the harp score are parallel with the pedalling indications in the piano version.

While it seems that *Mosaics* was conceived for piano or harp from the start,[7] it was not until 1980 that four movements were given a first performance on harp, in a concert presented by Concorde with Alan Smale (violin) and Denise Kelly (harp) at the Hugh Lane Municipal Gallery of Modern Art.[8] The same performers performed all five movements for harp in 1987 at a Music Association of Ireland concert in the NCH, presented in a tribute for the composer's 70th birthday.[9] Denise Kelly performed the work later in 1990 and 1992 with Sheila O'Grady (violin) in her 'Harp Plus' series in the Hugh

Lane Municipal Gallery of Modern Art and the NCH respectively.[10] Denise Kelly was also the harpist who premiered the orchestral version of this work, *Partita Concertante* (1978) for violin, harp and orchestra in 1983.[11]

Boydell composed three works involving harp in the 1980s: *The Small Bell* (1980) for choir, flute, harp and strings; *Confrontations in a Cathedral* (1986) for organ, harp and percussion; and *An Album of Pieces for the Irish Harp* (1989). Caitríona Yeats performed in the 1981 premiere of *The Small Bell* in an RTÉ concert of Boydell's chamber works with the RTÉ Singers[12] and Denise Kelly played the harp part in a 70th birthday concert in 1987.[13] *Confrontations in a Cathedral* was a specific commission from the Dublin International Organ Festival and written for the unique reverberance of St Patrick's Cathedral Dublin, by exploiting the spatial separation of the instruments within this acoustic. It is an affecting work and was recreated in the same acoustic in a performance to mark the centenary of the composer's birth by DIT Conservatory of Music and Drama (now TU Dublin Conservatoire) in 2017.[14] *An Album of Pieces for the Irish Harp*, his final work for harp, is a collection of short pieces written for solo Irish harp and commissioned by Teresa Lawlor. It again exploits the specific tuning settings of this type of harp.

'A PACK OF FANCIES FOR A TRAVELLING HARPER' (1970)

A Pack of Fancies for a Travelling Harper is a central work in Boydell's output for the harp. He had collaborated closely with the Irish harpist and singer Gráinne Yeats throughout the 1960s (see Mary Louise O'Donnell's essay elsewhere in this volume), becoming well acquainted with idiomatic figuration for the instrument and extensively exploiting the polytonal tunings across different registers achievable on the Irish harp. Material from the *Four Sketches for Two Irish Harps* had also been reworked into the first movement of his Quintet for Flute, [pedal] Harp and String Trio. Therefore, by the time he came to compose *A Pack of Fancies*, he was already conversant with the instrument, but this work sees him further deepening his understanding and widening his experimentation, especially in terms of colour, timbre and carefully judged use of extended techniques.

The work was written for Una O'Donovan, a former student of Sheila Larchet Cuthbert, and by then an accomplished harpist living in London and the co-principal harp with the orchestra of the Royal Opera House, Covent Garden.[15] Boydell sent the manuscript to her on 18 September 1970 and his letter to accompany the score provides insight into how seriously he undertook the commission and his study of the instrument:

I have just finished the harp pieces for you, and her[e] they are. I do hope that you like them, and that they don't pose too many insoluble problems. I have borrowed a harp, and have been living with it all the summer, trying things out – so I think all the things I have written work all right and are possible. If there are any problems, don't hesitate to let me know. I would also be most grateful if you think of any more effective way of doing things. There is still a reasonable amount of time, and we can change things by mutual agreement.[16]

Additionally under separate cover, he sent a 'special stick' for the fourth movement, 'A Dream of Ballyfarnon'.[17] Amusingly, the stick arrived before the score and Una jokes in a responding letter that '[t]he stick arrived the day before the music so I was puzzled to know whether it was a mistake, a practical joke or maybe the sum total of the piece!'[18] Boydell in his preface to the score writes that the harp 'remains one of the most awkward instruments to write for in any medium beyond a simple diatonic idiom.'[19] A similar sentiment is expressed for the Irish harp in a letter to Teresa Lawlor, when sending the score for *An Album of Pieces for the Irish Harp*: 'Here you are. What an impossible instrument you play.'[20]

Brian Boydell's writing for harp is more conventional in all his other harp works, employing only occasional use of *glissandi* and harmonics as effects. It is his use of carefully selected extended techniques that makes *A Pack of Fancies* particularly distinctive. In a 1970 interview with Charles Acton he speaks about this exploration:

> B. P. B. Just as I'm now actually writing a work for solo harp for the next contemporary music festival in Dublin [January, 1971] and I have borrowed a harp to find out what you can do with it.
> C. A.   A full concert harp?
> B. P. B. Yes, having done so with the Irish harp before that. So I am not averse to experiment... I am not going to advertise 'Look here, Boydell has produced this marvellous new gimmick.' That sort of thing does not interest me. Any gimmick I could produce would have to be thoroughly explored and thoroughly absorbed before I'd use it.[21]

In borrowing a harp to aid in his research, he explored the instrument's 'curious and often fascinating effects', which he carefully selected, having 'discarded all but a few which seemed naturally suited to the nature of the instrument, believing that the style of the music should grow out from the natural possibilities of the instrument'.[22] The effects chosen demonstrate a deep investigation of the instrument, with some quite individual timbral findings that are well integrated into the musical fabric of the work. The use of the fingernail buzz in 'Impetuous Impromptu' (ex. 1) is particularly unusual with its precise rhythmic execution.

Example 1: *A Pack of Fancies for a Travelling Harper*, III 'Impetuous Impromptu', bars 34–7

Una O'Donovan draws attention to this new technique in a letter, where she also provides an initial positive impression of the work, as requiring 'some practising'.[23] It is this effect and the rapid continuous ascending and descending nail *glissandi* of the second movement 'Caoin' that takes time to master effectively in performance (ex. 2).

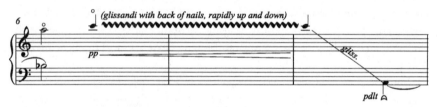

Example 2: *A Pack of Fancies for a Travelling Harper*, II 'Caoin', bars 6–8

Una O'Donovan also refers to the nail *glissandi* technique in the same letter, where she suggests using both hands in downward *glissandi* to produce a 'rapid rustling effect'.[24] However, Boydell responds with a detailed explanation of the sound he wishes to achieve, and while appreciating the practical knowledge of the performer, indicates that he has precise timbre in mind:

> I certainly accept any suggestion which you think will give a better or more practical effect. The main thing here is that it should be a continuous sound – we should not be conscious of each hand beginning a short downward gliss, so that we would get an effect of a number of separate downward glissandi.
>
> Do remember that you know so much better than I do what is more appropriate for the instrument, so don't hesitate to make such changes as long as they don't materially alter the kind of effect which you obviously know that I am aiming for.[25]

Nevertheless, it is the use of the adapted xylophone stick in the fourth movement, 'A Dream of Ballyfarnon' (ex. 3) that is the most distinctive effect employed, with the resulting iridescent *glissandi* played throughout the movement.

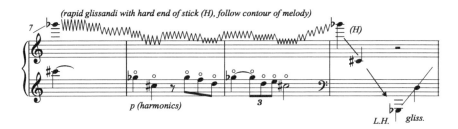

Example 3: *A Pack of Fancies for a Travelling Harper*, IV 'A Dream of Ballyfarnon', bars 7–10

Boydell provides comprehensive descriptions in his performance instructions for both the construction of the stick and the technique for its use. Correspondence between Brian Boydell and the harpist Derek Bell in the early 1970s provides some additional performance advice on the use of the stick and an insight into the composer's detailed intentions. Derek Bell writes:

> I must confess that today, not having a xylophone stick at my disposal, I used a pencil and a cimbalom hammer (both traditional style and Rácz style) so as get [sic] somewhat near the effects required. It was great fun![26]

Brian Boydell responds:

> I imagine a pencil would be too thin, and tend to slip between the strings – the Xylo stick touches two or more strings at one time, and doesn't 'bump' the strings.[27]

The fact that he also sent a specially designed stick to Una O'Donovan for the premiere provides further evidence of his crafting a specific sound through experimentation and practical harp research, thus ensuring the translation of the desired effect in performance.

The style of the work has two main eighteenth-century influences, that of the music of Bach and Carolan. The work opens and closes with two movements that evoke the musical landscape of Bach in a Prelude and Toccata. Throughout the work, two-part counterpoint is prevalent and there is a concise rhythmic and motivic design. The most experimental writing is contained in the strongly rhythmically driven middle movement, amusingly entitled 'Impetuous Impromptu', where he exploits pedal *glissandi* together with 'the buzzing effect so often produced by mistake when a fingernail comes in contact with a vibrating string'.[28] 'Caoin' and 'A Dream of Ballyfarnon' are the most distinctively Irish in character, but suggest the world that Carolan travelled within, rather than employing direct quotation of Irish airs. Carolan's locality is referenced in the title 'A Dream of Ballyfarnon', and Boydell describes the movement in his programme notes:

> Musically, it is very simple, consisting mainly of a singing, folk-like melody; though this is set in an atmospheric context created by a shimmering misty glissando played by a xylophone stick.[29]

In the earlier manuscript draft, the title for this movement is missing and instead Boydell seems to be considering a number of options that are written on the side of the score: 'Dream', 'Morning Mist', 'Autumn dream' and the eventual title 'A Dream of Ballyfarnon'.[30]

In the interview with Charles Acton for *Éire-Ireland*, Boydell addresses the subject of the composer writing within a national environment, which is particularly pertinent given this work's tribute to Carolan and its reference to the eighteenth-century travelling harper tradition:

> By living in a community and by living in a country with certain types of scenery, certain types of traditions, a certain type of atmosphere, he absorbs that atmosphere so that it affects his creative personality. The important thing is that if one is writing absolutely honestly, then the things that one has absorbed by being part of that community will come out in one's writing. And surely it is better to use a reasonably international language, so that one can make a contribution from one's own corner of the world to the international language of music, rather than taking a short cut.[31]

Martin Adams highlights the national aspect of the work in a review of a performance that I presented at a Mostly Modern Series concert at the Bank of Ireland Arts Centre in 2003. In this programme I was exploring 'works for concert harp by composers who embrace their respective country's indigenous music traditions'.[32] The programme combined three works: *A Pack of Fancies*, Takemitsu's *Stanza II* (which is suggestive of the Japanese koto) and Javier Alvarez's *Acuerdos por Diferencia* (evoking Mexico's vibrant harp practice). Martin Adams writes:

> Sibelius was right, as were all the composers in this programme. The creation of national character in music does not depend on folk song... Brian Boydell's *A Pack of Fancies for a Travelling Harper* (1970) is among a handful of that composer's

works which refer to Irish traditional music. Carolan, to whom it is a tribute, becomes a living figure, not through the juiced-up quotation of existing melody, but through the inventive use of folk music's characteristics. As always, craft, shape and timing are paramount.[33]

This also draws attention to an important stylistic issue in Boydell's compositional output: that the composer does not often overtly draw upon Irish traditional music but, when he does, it is the essence of the traditional air rather than quotation.[34] However, this work has an unmistakable distinctive Irish voice.

As mentioned earlier, Brian Boydell speaks of the difficulties of writing for the pedal harp in terms of an extensive harmonic language. Examination of the final manuscript and an earlier manuscript draft indicates his careful consideration of the harp's pedal mechanism. Contained in the Brian Boydell Archive at Trinity College Dublin is a postcard with a handwritten diagram of the harp pedal arrangement, together with the instrument's range, presumably used as a tool through the compositional process.[35] The manuscript copies indicate that the pedalling indications are included from the start, ahead of many expressive markings, with each pedal movement detailed throughout the score. In each movement he mainly utilises the intervallic and harmonic possibilities within a fixed seven-note pitch set, which corresponds to a fixed harp pedal setting. However, within these mainly ternary structured movements, the greatest harmonic shifts, and resulting pedalling, are reserved for the most part for the middle contrasting sections. He exploits the semitone within these seven-note pitch sets, therefore ensuring a chromatic feeling to the work that is employed both dissonantly and colouristically. There is a strong sense of tonal centre to each movement, which also outlines the semitone: F for movements 1, 2 and 5, and up a semitone to F♯/G♭ for movements 3 and 4. However, the pitches of this tonal centre semitone (F/F♯) are also strongly featured in the melodic material for movements 1, 2 and 5, providing structural cohesion to the work. This leads to an economic motivic and harmonic language, which is an aspect explored by Michael Dervan in his review of a performance by Denise Kelly in a concert to celebrate the composer's 80th birthday on 25 March 1997:

> Odd as it may seem, the *Pack of Fancies for a Travelling Harper* of 1970 can now be heard to embody something of the mood of minimalism if not the actual mechanism, an association evoked elsewhere through a fondness for ostinatos and dreamy repetition.[36]

PERFORMANCE HISTORY AND RECEPTION

A Pack of Fancies did not receive the same strong endorsement as the Quintet from Charles Acton on the occasion of its premiere by Una O'Donovan on 13 January 1971. In a review with the headline 'Fine harp playing by Una O'Donovan' that appeared the next day, we find a rather reticent reception to the new work:

> Recently, however, Professor Brian Boydell has used a television programme about his 20th-Century Music festival to inform the nation that he feels 'so violently' against music criticism in Ireland that he 'could not safely talk about it' on the air[.] After that anything that one might write about Professor Boydell's new work for harp solo might be open to misconstruction and it therefore seems wiser simply to record that it received its first performance at Una O'Donovan's harp recital at lunch-time yesterday.[37]

It was not until 1976 and Una O'Donovan's recital at the Royal Dublin Society (RDS) that Charles Acton provides his assessment of the actual composition. In this recital on 1 March 1976 Una O'Donovan performed a substantial programme including works by Spohr, Tailleferre, Pierné, Hindemith and Fauré. As any harpist will attest, this was a significant programme of major works for the instrument; however, Charles Acton writes: 'Interestingly, Professor Boydell's five short movements were the most exciting item of the night, with their strong contrasts, well devised harmonic clashes and a general feel of music with guts.'[38]

In the review for Caitríona Yeats' RDS recital in 1980 Charles Acton includes a qualification of his assessment of the work and suggests revising it as a four-movement sonata by removing the fourth movement, 'A Dream of Ballyfarnon'. He considers this movement worthy as a stand-alone work, but overlong in the context of the work as a whole: 'Without it, the work would be an extremely attractive and romantically individual sonata, while the "Dream" might well be an independent piece in its own right.'[39] Interestingly, it is this movement that is most often performed independently. The complete work received another favourable mention by Acton when performed a few months later by the same performer in an RTÉ concert of Brian Boydell's chamber works, commenting that 'Caitríona Yeats's totally authoritative playing of the harp work (written at the time of the Carolan tercentenary) shows it to be a work of great substance.'[40] In the review there is further disappointment expressed about the lack of international reception for the Quintet. This work later received an international performance in Stockholm, as part of a series of concerts promoting works by Irish composers in 1985.[41] Charles Acton's desire for a commercial recording of the Quintet[42] – an important factor in any work reaching a wider international audience – has now been realised with a recording on the RTÉ lyric fm label (release pending).[43]

The correspondence between Brian Boydell and Derek Bell provides a valuable early assessment of *A Pack of Fancies* by another established performer:

> I must say it is lovely to have a work in contemporary idiom which is not a hectic concerto for solo pedals with harp accompaniment! I have played the pieces over to-day for some fascinating lunch-time sight-reading, and I like them very much indeed. Nos. two, four, and five are my favourite ones at the moment.[44]

He then speaks of possible performance opportunities and requests if he can programme individual movements, mentioning opportunities with the Ulster Soloists, the University and BBC. Boydell responds, interestingly contradicting Charles Acton's idea from 1980 of the work being recast as a sonata: 'By all means take movements out of context if you wish (It's not a Sonata – so it doesn't matter – you could possibly devise pairs or threes).'[45] To date, no evidence has been found of any such performances.

In Ireland the work is well established as a major concert work for the instrument and it often features in third-level student degree and competition recital programmes, particularly the fourth movement, 'A Dream of Ballyfarnon'. A selective list of performances, from its premiere in 1971 to 2018, can be found in Table 2:

Year	Performer	Venue/Festival	Town/City, Country
1971	Una O'Donovan	Dublin Festival of Twentieth-Century Music	Dublin
1976	Una O'Donovan	RDS	Dublin
1977	Valerie Aldrich Smith	The Association of Irish Composers, St Catherine's, Thomas Street	Dublin
1980	Caitríona Yeats	RDS	Dublin
1981	Caitríona Yeats	RTÉ Concert: A Special Concert of Works by Brian Boydell, National Gallery of Ireland	Dublin
1982	Denise Kelly	NCH	Dublin
1987	Andreja Malîr	John Field Room, NCH	Dublin
1987	Andreja Malîr	Black Abbey, Kilkenny Arts Festival	Kilkenny
1988	Andreja Malîr	Embassy of Switzerland	Dublin
1994	Caitríona Yeats	Cairde na Cruite, Number 29	Dublin

1997	Denise Kelly	Brian Boydell 80th Birthday Celebration, John Field Room, NCH	Dublin
2000	Andreja Malîr	John Field Room, NCH	Dublin
2001	Geraldine O'Doherty	John Field Room, NCH	Dublin
2001	Clíona Doris	Music Network Musicwide	Omagh
2002	Clíona Doris	St Ninian Festival, Whithorn	Whithorn, Scotland
2003	Clíona Doris	Music Amongst the Mosaics Festival	Timoleague, Co. Cork
2003	Clíona Doris	Music Network Musicwide	New Ross
2003	Clíona Doris	Clonard Monastery	Belfast
2003	Clíona Doris	Mostly Modern Series	Dublin
2003	Clíona Doris	Down Arts Centre	Downpatrick
2004	Clíona Doris	Trinity College Chapel	Dublin
2005	Clíona Doris	Valvasorjeva kapela na Izlakah	Zagorje ob Savi, Slovenia
2005	Jean Kelly	Ninth World Harp Congress*	Dublin
2011	Clíona Doris	CMC Composers' Seminar	Dublin
2011	Andreja Malîr	St Patrick's College	Dublin
2012	Andreja Malîr	CMC Concert Series	Dublin
2013	Andreja Malîr	Curtis Auditorium, CIT Cork School of Music	Cork
2016	Clíona Doris	Creative Connexions Festival*	Sitges, Spain
2017	Clíona Doris	Brian Boydell Centenary Conference, RIAM	Dublin
2018	Clíona Doris	Dublin City University	Dublin

* Movement 4: A Dream of Ballyfarnon only

Table 2: *A Pack of Fancies for a Travelling Harper*, Selected Performances 1971–2018[46]

In addition, I recorded the work in 2002 for RiverRun Records[47] and it received a positive reception in a review by Andrew Achenbach for *Gramophone*: 'I particularly enjoyed Brian Boydell's sequence from 1970 entitled *A Pack of Fancies for a Travelling Harper*, a tribute to the blind Irish bard Carolan, its five movements are full of strong ideas and intriguing sonorities.'[48] *A Pack of Fancies* has obtained international reception through radio broadcasts and concert performances by Irish harpists, with perhaps most significantly a performance of 'A Dream of Ballyfarnon' at the Opening Concert of the Ninth World Harp Congress in Dublin in July 2005. However, the work has not yet achieved a wider performance reception from harpists without an Irish connection.

I have enjoyed exploring this work for nearly two decades, in performance, recording and teaching, and it continually provides much scope for interpretative re-evaluation. It is written very effectively for the instrument, as are all of Brian Boydell's harp works, and in this case with a distinct Irish voice reflecting Boydell's desire to 'make a contribution from one's own corner of the world to the international language of music'.[49]

EIGHT

HEAVENLY HARPS, HEAVENLY CLOTHS: THE MUSICAL COLLABORATIONS OF BRIAN BOYDELL AND GRÁINNE YEATS FOR IRISH HARP[1]

Mary Louise O'Donnell

The Irish harp is an instrument extremely limited in its technical possibilities. It also has an ancestry associated with hundreds of years of music that grew out from its limited potentiality. This is a challenge for the composer. I have tried to write new music for it which does not deny this genetic personality.[2]

In 1961 Brian Boydell commenced the composition of *Four Sketches for Two Irish Harps*, op. 52, the first of four works employing Irish harp(s),[3] with the others being *Three Yeats Songs*, op. 56a, *Musician's Song [Love is an Immoderate Thing]*, op. 56b, and *An Album of Pieces for the Irish Harp*, op. 88. The *Four Sketches* and *An Album of Pieces* were composed almost three decades apart and frame beautifully Boydell's compositions for an instrument that he found musically enigmatic.[4]

The Irish harpist Teresa Lawlor commissioned Boydell to write a selection of pieces for solo Irish harp in 1989.[5] When the commission was completed Boydell sent the manuscript to Lawlor with the following note:

Dear Teresa,
Here you are. What an impossible instrument you play! I enclose a full-size copy, which might be best to play from; and also a reduced-size one, which is in some ways much handier… Also, I am anxious to discuss any technical problems which I might have overlooked. You may well find a better way of doing things in some cases, in which case we could make suitable alterations… You will also notice that I don't think it a good idea to perform the whole lot together at the same time… well, all right, if the three groups are well separated by completely different things. But the continual sound of the Irish harp for 20 minutes or more would, I think, be a strain on the attention of any audience.

I did try some funny tricks – but in the end discarded them as not very effective. If only I weren't so recognisable, I would love to give a frightfully avant-garde recital on the Irish harp. I bet you I [would] get away with it!

I look forward very much to hearing your reaction to this quite painful parturition.[6]

In preparation for the composition of *Four Sketches* in 1961–2, Boydell borrowed an Irish harp to explore the technical and sonic capabilities of the instrument.[7] It was evident from this first encounter with a modern Irish harp that composing for the instrument would be a challenge. The instrument is chromatically limited.[8] Although there have been some attempts in recent decades to expand the chromatic potential of these harps – for example, the invention of chromatic cross-strung harps – very little concert repertoire has been composed to date that explores the Irish harp's potential as a solo instrument.[9] Until the 1960s the Irish harp was not considered to be an instrument suited to the performance of contemporary music and its repertoire was dominated by the compositions of Turlough Carolan, Thomas Moore and popular nineteenth-century Irish airs. The considerable number of works commissioned from Boydell and his contemporaries during the 1960s and early 70s remains the most significant body of contemporary music written for the instrument. *Four Sketches for Two Irish Harps*, op. 52, and *Three Yeats Songs*, op. 56a, which are the focus of this essay, were both written in the 1960s and were breathtakingly original at that time.

But what attracted Boydell to the Irish harp in the 1960s? After all, instruments that were incapable of realising his musical vision were of little interest to him and he openly despised the works of composers who married 'so-called Irish folksong, which had already been a good deal altered and tidied up, to Brahmsian or teutonic harmony'.[10] In an interview in 2005 Barra Boydell commented:

[I]f it weren't for Gráinne [Yeats], the Irish harp would never have entered my father's sound world. I think he had really little or no interest in Irish music. He slightly disdained it really, although he occasionally drew on it on a subconscious level... So in that context, the fact that he did write for Irish harp was definitely Gráinne's influence.[11]

Gráinne Yeats commissioned Boydell and many of his contemporaries to compose for Irish harp in various guises in the 1960s and 70s, and she was largely responsible for premiering these compositions and performing the works nationally and internationally.

Boydell and Yeats's first professional collaboration was in December 1958 when she was engaged as a soloist for performances of Handel's *Messiah* with the University of Dublin [TCD] Choral Society under the direction of Joseph Groocock and with Boydell playing oboe.[12] Yeats's performance was well-received but, perhaps more significantly for Boydell and Yeats, it initiated a professional relationship and a close friendship between their families that spanned four decades.[13]

Gráinne Yeats (née Ní hÉigeartaigh) was born in April 1925. Regarded as a pioneer in the harping world in Ireland in the latter half of the twentieth century, she was a harper, singer, teacher, arranger, historian, academic, a founder member of Cáirde na Cruite (Friends of the Harp), and is credited with reviving the centuries-old practice of wire-strung Irish harp performance. She studied history at Trinity College Dublin (TCD) and was an active member of the Historical Society where she met Michael Yeats, whom she married in 1949.[14] After her studies, she focused on piano and voice lessons at the Royal Irish Academy of Music (RIAM) but did not commence harp lessons with Sheila Larchet Cuthbert and Mercedes Bolger until the mid-1950s.

In 1959 Yeats, along with Cáit Cooper, Eilís O'Sullivan, Mary Boydell, Enid Chaloner, Hazel Morris, Dick Cooper, Leonard Jose (later replaced by George Bannister) and Tomás Ó Súilleabháin, became a member of the Dowland Consort.[15] This semi-professional vocal ensemble, founded and directed by Brian Boydell, performed regularly together nationally and internationally from 1959 to 1969, and it is likely that the Consort's longevity was largely due to the life-long friendships that were formed during this period amongst ensemble members. Yeats sang and played at the Consort's debut performance on 10 April 1959 in Dublin. She toured and recorded with the ensemble, and participated in numerous broadcasts on Radio Telefís Éireann (RTÉ) and BBC. When the Consort was awarded the Harriet Cohen International Music Award in 1966, Yeats was a member, but she also received an award in the solo instrumentalist category in that year. Although vocal music of the Renaissance dominated the programme at each concert, in the early years of the Consort's existence Boydell often included a section with three or four Irish songs sung by Yeats or Tomás Ó Súilleabháin with Irish harp accompaniment. In the Consort's performances Boydell endeavoured to recreate a relaxed atmosphere of domestic music-making.[16] He prefaced the performance of each item on the programme with some spoken background information on the composer and composition and provided a translation of the French, German and Italian texts. This informal approach to performance influenced Yeats and characterised her solo concerts from the 1960s onwards.

Boydell dedicated his *Shielmartin Suite*, op. 47, to Yeats in 1959, and he chaired many of her Arts Council-funded lectures on the history of the Irish harp at the Hibernia Hotel, Dublin in 1963. Most importantly, he introduced her to other contemporary composers who composed and/or arranged works for her. She, in turn, introduced these composers to the music of renowned harpers, such as Carolan, Cornelius Lyons and Thomas and William Connellan. Yeats's commissioning of contemporary works was a vital step in the evolution of music for the modern Irish harp in the 1960s. The instrument was enjoying an increase in popularity nationally and internationally largely due to Mary O'Hara, the figure who dominated the Irish harp tradition from the late 1950s onwards.[17] Although Yeats performed a repertoire similar to O'Hara, her performance style differed significantly. The frequent comparisons with O'Hara irked Yeats and this was undoubtedly a factor in her continuous efforts to push the boundaries of Irish harp performance by commissioning new works for the instrument.

Yeats, along with fellow harpist Mercedes Bolger, commissioned Boydell to write the *Four Sketches for Two Irish Harps* in 1961,[18] and they performed it at a seminal recital entitled 'My Gentle Harp' at the Eblana Theatre on 11 March 1962, along with newly-composed pieces *Lough Swilly Suite for two Irish Harps* by Ruth Mervyn[19] and *Two Arabesques* for solo harp by T. C. Kelly.[20] To say this evening was a defining moment in the history of the Irish harp in the twentieth century is not an exaggeration.[21] The premiering of works by contemporary Irish composers changed the perception of the Irish harp and introduced the instrument to audiences and composers who hitherto had shown no interest in it. In fact, when the *Sketches* were later performed as part of the RIAM's Recital Series on 29 February 1964, Charles Acton commented in his review: '[t]he first two in particular remain outstanding and a real pioneering contribution to a fascinating medium. They should be a spur and a challenge to such as Bodley, Ó Riada and Warren.'[22]

What made the *Sketches* so original? Quite simply, by treating two Irish harps as one fully chromatic instrument, Boydell extended the palette of pitches available to him. The two harps became a blank musical canvas that was stripped of any musical or cultural connections with Irish folk music or traditional harp repertoire played on wire-strung or modern Irish harps. Naturally, particular patterns or phrases played on an Irish harp suggest an Irish idiom, but this would, as Barra Boydell noted, 'have been something he used as an attractive sound, rather than for any other reasons'.[23] Boydell did not use extended performance techniques in the *Sketches* and did not fully exploit the chromatic potential of two Irish harps. Nevertheless, he succeeded in creating a work that liberated the Irish harp from the shackles of diatonicism and provided the Irish harpist with an alternative repertoire to the music of Carolan and Thomas Moore.

The first of the *Four Sketches* is in ternary form, and the A section is essentially a playful musical dialogue between the harps. The whimsical ornament in harp 1 (ex. 1 motif a) leads to a sustained chord centred on D. At bar 3, harp 2 plays a short contrasting figure in the bass part (ex. 2 motif b) that is repeated at bar 5 and leads into the opening theme (ex. 3) played on harp 1 in octaves; the doubling of a melodic line is a compositional technique that recurs in subsequent movements. Harp 2 then takes this theme but presents it with slight melodic variation. Harp 1 responds immediately with a new theme in octaves (ex. 4); harp 2 does not restate this phrase and opts instead to reiterate the opening theme. Throughout the *Sketches* harp 1 exposes and develops thematic material and harp 2 generally serves an accompanying role. In the middle section of this movement, however, the roles are reversed, allowing harp 2 to eschew temporarily its supportive role. Before the contrasting middle section commences, both harpists are reminded to change pitches in bars 17 and 18. The change in meter to 2/2 (from 4/4), the instruction to play *poco meno mosso*, variations in dynamic and tone colour and the steady rhythmic accompaniment, initiated by harp 2 (ex. 5) and sustained by harp 1 in bars 23–54, ensure that the B section contrasts effectively with the playful opening section.

Example 1: No 1 of *Four Sketches*, bars 1–2

Example 2: No 1 of *Four Sketches*, harp 2, bar 3

Example 3: No 1 of *Four Sketches*, harp 1, bars 6–7

Example 4: No 1 of *Four Sketches*, harp 1, bars 10–11

Example 5: No 1 of *Four Sketches*, harp 2, bars 19–22

The second *Sketch* provides a stark harmonic and rhythmic contrast to the first movement. Boydell employs a wider palette of pitches (ex. 6) and uses polymeter (2/4 against 6/8) to create an interesting rhythmic tension between the parts. The movement opens with a syncopated figure played in octaves on harp 2 centred around the notes E and G; this figure acts as a tonal pedal for most of the opening 12 bars (ex. 7). Harp 1 enters towards the end of bar 4 with a partial octatonic scale in demisemiquavers landing on E♭ and creating a dissonance with the syncopated figure in the second harp part. After three bars of silence harp 1 teases with another short flourish, but only enters in earnest at bar 14 with an incomplete octatonic scale (ex. 8) leading to the main theme. Moments of silence are used to great effect throughout the movement, particularly in the first harp part; they provide contrast between the parts but are also important points to change levers, e.g. bars 37–8.

Example 6: Lever settings for both harps at the start of No 2 of *Four Sketches*

Example 7: No 2 of *Four Sketches*, harp 2, bars 1–4

Example 8: No 2 of *Four Sketches*, harp 1, bar 14

The movement's main theme, which is introduced at bar 15 on harp 1, is built primarily around a series of open fifths (ex. 9). This frantic four-bar accented phrase, played in the harp's highest register, is followed by a short interaction between the harps and the return of a rhythmically modified version of the opening E–G figure in the bass part of harp 2. From bars 38 onwards, a steady, syncopated ostinato consisting of fourths and fifths in harp 2 forms the foundation for a tour de force passage in the first harp part that spans over three octaves. The return of the syncopated figure centred around E and G at bar 50 unifies the movement and the 14 bars of rising and falling *glissandi* between E_3 and G_5 that follow reaffirm E as the tonal centre of the movement. The dynamic level gradually fades and, following four harmonics on harp 1, the movement comes to an end on an open octave E in the bass part of harp 2.

Example 9: No 2 of *Four Sketches*, harp 1, bars 15–18

Considering the originality of the previous movements, No. 3 is disappointingly diatonic. The movement seems out of place in the overall work, probably because it was adapted from an existing piece, namely the *Dance for an Ancient Ritual*, op. 39a, which was published for solo pianoforte in 1959 (and which itself derives from the composer's *Megalithic Ritual Dances* of 1956).[24] Both harps are set in the key of E flat major and, apart from a few changes of levers from A♭-A♮ or E♭-E♮, there is little that challenges the performers. The movement opens with a four-bar introduction which establishes C as the tonal centre of the piece (ex. 10). The main theme is presented in harp 1 from bars 12–16 in octaves in the treble part and enunciated an octave lower in the bass part (ex. 11). Harp 2 accompanies the main theme but is given a brief opportunity to play a modified version of this theme from bars 19–22. The movement ends with references to the rhythmic motif used in the opening bars (ex. 10 motif c).

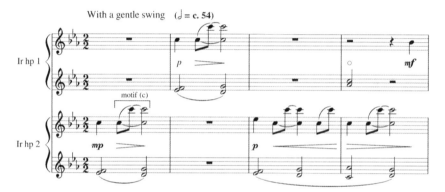

Example 10: No 3 of *Four Sketches*, harps 1 and 2, bars 1–4

Example 11: No 3 of *Four Sketches*, harp 1, bars 13–16

The performance marking for the final movement, 'with a very rhythmical swing – and rather skittish, *col lingua in guancia*' (tongue in cheek), indicates that this piece was intended as a musical parody. Harp 2 is set in C major and harp 1 has the following prescribed tuning (ex. 12). The opening second inversion major 7th chords in harp 2 establish this part as the rhythmic foundation of the movement. The main theme, played in octaves and with its distinctive dotted

Plate 1: Extract from completed score of *Magh Sleacht* (TCD MS 11128/6/MAGH SLEACHT/3, p. 89). (Photo Digital Collections. Courtesy of The Board of Trinity College Dublin)

Plate 2: Extract from draft score of *Magh Sleacht* (TCD MS 11128/6/MAGH SLEACHT/1, p. 7). (Photo Digital Collections. Courtesy of The Board of Trinity College Dublin)

Plate 3: Cue 1M2, *Yeats Country* (TCD MS 4951). (Photo Digital Collections. Courtesy of The Board of Trinity College Dublin)

Plate 4: Cue 1M3, *Errigal* (a) (TCD MS 4952). (Photo Digital Collections. Courtesy of The Board of Trinity College Dublin)

Plate 5: Cue 1M3, *Errigal* (b) (TCD MS 4952). (Photo Digital Collections. Courtesy of The Board of Trinity College Dublin)

Plate 6: Cue 1M1, *Errigal* (TCD MS 4952). (Photo Digital Collections. Courtesy of The Board of Trinity College Dublin)

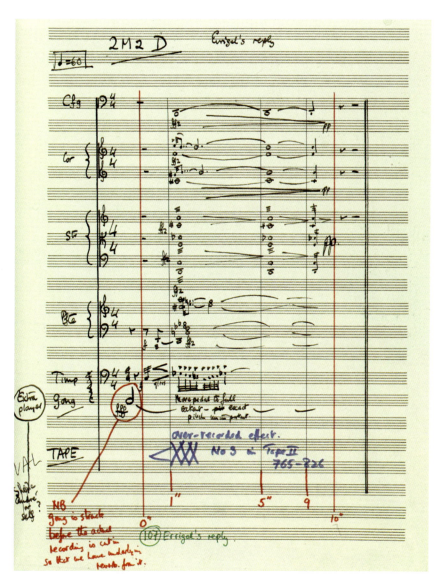

Plate 7: Cue 2M2D, *Errigal* (TCD MS 4952). (Photo Digital Collections. Courtesy of The Board of Trinity College Dublin)

Plate 8: Brian Boydell, *Atlas Approached* (1943). (Courtesy of Sean Barrett and Maeve O'Brien)

Plate 9: Brian Boydell, *The Return of the Wood* (1943)

Plate 10: Brian Boydell, *The Worm Hole* (1944)

Plate 11: Brian Boydell, *Gunnera* (1944?)

rhythmic patterns and triplet figures, enters on harp 1 at the end of bar 2 (ex. 13). The theme covers a range of almost two octaves and effortlessly floats above the steady, almost rigid, accompaniment in minims and crotchets in harp 2. Boydell develops rhythmic motifs from the main theme in bars 19–34 (ex. 13 motifs d, e and f). The main theme, with some modifications, returns at bar 34 (fourth beat) accompanied initially by offbeat syncopated chords in harp 2. At bars 52 and 55 there is an instruction for harp 2 to change two G♮s to G♯s to allow the piece to end on an E major chord (ex. 14).

Example 12: Lever settings for harp 1 at the start of No 4 of *Four Sketches*

Example 13: No 4 of *Four Sketches*, harps 1 and 2, bars 3–6

Example 14: No 4 of *Four Sketches*, harps 1 and 2, bars 53–6

The *Four Sketches* set the standard for the employment of the Irish harp as an instrument of art music for other composers. Critics who attended the premiere of the work in 1962 were astounded by the originality of Boydell's work and the sonic transformation of the Irish harp. In the *Irish Press*, the critic commented that:

> from the first commanding bar to the sardonic last, here was music that surprised and delighted the ear. . . To write for two Irish harps is surely as revealing an exercise of a composer's talents as to write for string quartet. Dr Boydell's inventiveness, his fresh and spritely ideas have never been better displayed [than] in the sketches.[25]

In the *Irish Times* Charles Acton lauded the work as 'a really important breakthrough' and was particularly impressed by the beauty and expressivity of the first and second movements, which 'not only show the Irish harp as a serious instrument for the art music of our time but have also called forth from Dr Boydell some of his very best work'.[26] Boydell had produced a work that successfully explored aspects of chromaticism on the Irish harp, albeit by combining two instruments.

In 1965 Yeats challenged Boydell to create a work that would push the boundaries of the instrument even further. To mark the centenary of William Butler Yeats's birth she commissioned him to set some of her father-in-law's poetry for soprano and Irish harp. Gráinne Yeats initially approached the English composer Peter Aston and mooted the possibility of writing a work based on Yeats's poetry. His composition *Five Songs of Crazy Jane* for unaccompanied soprano was regularly performed by Yeats at her solo recitals in the 1960s and 70s. Boydell's *Three Yeats Songs*, op. 56a, was musically far superior, technically more demanding for the voice and undoubtedly the most complex piece ever written for a singer/harpist. Yeats premiered the work on 24 March 1966 at the Abbey Lecture Theatre Hall, Dublin, and *Three Yeats Songs* was RTÉ's entry for the UNESCO International Rostrum of Composers in 1965. Although the composition was not awarded a prize, the Rostrum of Composers was an important forum to showcase the Irish harp as a viable instrument for contemporary composers.

Boydell frequently drew inspiration from the works of Irish poets and artists from early in his career. In the 1940s he composed *Five Joyce Songs*, op. 28 (1946) and collaborated with the poet/artist Thurloe Conolly on the song cycle *The Feather of Death*, op. 22 (1943). Boydell, however, had a particular fascination with and profound respect for W. B. Yeats's work. He based two of his earliest compositions on works by Yeats, namely the songs *Cathleen, the Daughter of Houlihan*, op. 4 (1936) and *The Witch*, op. 6 (1938). In 1965 he was commissioned by RTÉ to compose incidental music and an original song (*The Musician's Song*, op. 56b) for a broadcast of Yeats's play *Deirdre*.

Boydell had a very specific approach to setting Yeats's poetry, which he articulated at a lecture delivered to the Yeats International Summer School in 1969:

> I feel myself that in setting the poems of Yeats to music. . . it is necessary to preserve as closely as possible the original rhythm of the poetic words; and it is also necessary to reflect in the music the quite characteristic atmosphere inherent in the poems of different periods in his life, avoiding any possibility of imposing an alien feeling on poetry which has such a powerfully individual aura. As an example of this, I have myself, in setting some of the poems of the earlier period, attempted to convey a certain sense of timelessness – the unchanging, eternal quality of the Sligo landscape, which I feel to be reflected in the poems. This idea, along with a minimal distortion of word-rhythms, guided me in setting [Yeats's poetry].[27]

The three poems by Yeats that Boydell chose to set to music are from collections published over 12 years: 'Aedh Wishes for the Cloths of Heaven' from the collection *The Wind Among the Reeds* (1899), 'Red Hanrahan's Song about Ireland' from *In the Seven Woods* (1903) and 'A Drinking Song' from *The Green Helmet and Other Poems* (1910). It is not clear whether Gráinne Yeats suggested the poems to Boydell, or whether he chose the texts. In any case the three poems are meditations on the theme of love, both human and patriotic. The text is of primary importance in these songs. The harp accompaniment is subservient to the vocal part and although the composer explores the sonic possibilities of the Irish harp, its importance primarily lies in its ability to create a particular musical sound reflecting the timeless beauty of the County Sligo landscape so beloved of Yeats. At the beginning of each song, Boydell indicates a specific tuning for the harp in each octave; the remaining unavailable chromatic pitches are generally incorporated into the vocal part, thus facilitating complete chromaticism from the harpist/singer (ex. 15).

In 'He Wishes for the Cloths of Heaven' the poet wonders if love is a destructive force that merely destroys dreams. In the harp accompaniment the traditional playing position of the hands, i.e. right hand playing the melodic line and left hand playing chords, is reversed. The harp part opens with a two-note motif a diminished 3rd apart which forms an irregular syncopated ostinato in the lower line for 38 of the 54 bars that form the song (ex. 16). The motif creates a quasi-hypnotic effect that is temporarily interrupted in bars 12–13 and 25–30 when the music attempts to break away from the notes G♯ and B♭. Following a dramatic pause after bar 30 it seems as though the music has finally settled on a pitch. Five open A chords and one further chord over a B♭

132   *Creative Impulses, Cultural Accents: Brian Boydell's Music, Advocacy, Painting and Legacy*

bass prepare the listener for the most important phrase in the vocal line, 'But I, being poor have only my dreams' (ex. 17). The eerie two-note motif creeps back again under the phrase 'I have spread my dreams under your feet, tread softly because you tread on my dreams', and the song finishes as it began, in an atmosphere of unease and tension.

Example 15: Lever settings for 'He Wishes for the Cloths of Heaven'

Example 16: 'He Wishes for the Cloths of Heaven', bars 1–2

Example 17: 'He Wishes for the Cloths of Heaven', bars 31–8

The second song, 'A Drinking Song', appears initially to be an inconsequential piece. One might expect to hear a typical Irish drinking song, e.g. 'Preab san Ól', but from the opening bars of the accompaniment, it is clear that Boydell has no desire to present an idiomatic Irish piece in 6/8 time. The busy, layered harp part, with its dotted and syncopated rhythms, is peppered with diminished 4th and perfect 5th chords and hovers over a C bass note (ex. 18). It contrasts strongly with the short, but beautifully legato phrases in the vocal part, which rise and fall in an arc and culminate in a masterful example of word painting on the phrase, 'I look at you, and I sigh.' The song ends with a quick lever change to facilitate the playing of the final chord, an open C chord with added 9th.

Example 18: 'A Drinking Song', bars 4–6

Cathleen Ni Houlihan, the powerful mythic symbol of Irish nationalism, is the central character in the final song, 'Red Hanrahan's Song about Ireland'.[28] She can rekindle sacrifice-patriotism in the Irish people and unify all those with political and religious differences. Consequently, Boydell sets Yeats's poem about the protagonist in a dramatic, elaborate recitative style with the harp generally used to mark an important word in the vocal line or to fill moments of silence between phrases. The introduction to this piece initially formed part of the incidental music to a performance of *Deirdre* on RTÉ, but Boydell cleverly uses it here to create a complete contrast to the superficial joviality of 'A Drinking Song'. The two-chord motif used in the opening bar (ex. 19) recurs throughout the song and provides unity to a piece that otherwise lacks a particular form or structure. This piece could be described as tonally restless as, although the composer suggests that C or C♯ are the most important pitches until bar 30 (ex. 20), he assigns B the role of tonal centre for the remainder of the piece. Boydell uses a mixture of idiomatic and more unusual sound effects to heighten the intensity of the dramatic text. *Glissandi* and arpeggiated figures are frequently employed but in bars 26–7, on the line 'Our courage breaks like an old tree in a black wind and dies', the performer is instructed to 'sweep the palm of the hand longitudinally upwards over lower strings, and turn over towards upper strings with fingers outstretched.' This is the only extended instrumental technique employed by Boydell in any of his compositions or arrangements for Irish harp.

Example 19: 'Red Hanrahan's Song about Ireland', bars 1–2

Example 20: 'Red Hanrahan's Song about Ireland', bars 30–6

Boydell's *Three Yeats Songs* featured regularly at Yeats's concerts in the 1960s and 70s, in particular, in North America and Japan. Op. 56a and op. 56b (*The Musician's Song*) were combined, adapted and orchestrated by Boydell to become the *Four Yeats Poems*, op. 56, for soprano and orchestra, which was premiered on 25 February 1969 at the St Francis Xavier Hall, Dublin by Mary

Sheridan and the RTÉ Symphony Orchestra under the baton of the composer.[29] Unfortunately, the *Three Yeats Songs* have rarely been performed over the last three decades and this is largely due to the complexity of the work. When Boydell was asked to contribute a composition to *The Irish Harp Book* in 1969, he proposed five pieces that he thought would be suitable, amongst which were one of the *Four Sketches for Two Irish Harps*, an arrangement of *Tighearna Mhuigheo* and any one of the *Three Yeats Songs*. In his correspondence with Sheila Larchet Cuthbert, the editor of *The Irish Harp Book*, it is noteworthy that, in brackets beside *Three Yeats Songs*, Boydell inserted the word 'difficult': it is a challenging work for any singer/harpist, but it is a rare example of an imaginative composition that truly integrates the voice and harp as one instrument.

Boydell did not compose again for the harp for over two decades, until he was commissioned by Teresa Lawlor, with a grant from the Arts Council of Ireland, to compose *An Album of Pieces for the Irish Harp*, op. 88, consisting of six pieces: *Triptych I, II, III, Lament for a Legendary Queen, Pastoral Song* and *Eccentric*.[30] The work was premiered at the National Concert Hall on 23 April 1990 and was preceded by an introduction by Boydell:

> Each musical instrument has an individual character and personality of its own; derived mainly from its physical construction, the limitations of the technique required to produce sounds from it, and also its race-memory: or its association with the kind of music found suitable for it throughout its history... As a composer, I do not wish to dominate the personality of the instrument so completely that it becomes a puppet struggling against its own nature to make sounds not suited to its character.[31]

Boydell's attitude to the Irish harp and his approach to composing for the instrument had changed significantly from the 1960s. Composing for solo Irish harp was a challenge, but also a compromise. Without a second harp or voice to articulate his musical language he had to simplify his compositional style and produce a work that could not push the boundaries of contemporary music on the Irish harp any further.

Boydell's early works, however, are firmly embedded in a golden age of composition for the Irish harp. From 1961 until the publication of *The Irish Harp Book* in 1975, Gráinne Yeats regularly commissioned contemporary composers to write for Irish harp duo, Irish harp solo or voice to harp accompaniment. Joseph Groocock's *Three Pieces for Voice and Harp* and *Six Pieces for Harp* (1962), *Teach lán le Cruiteoirí* for pedal harp and four Irish harps (1963) composed by A. J. Potter, James Wilson's *A Woman Young and Old* for soprano and Irish harp (1966), Joan Trimble's *Introduction and Air for Two Harps* (1968) and *The*

Poet's Circuits for voice and Irish harp by Aloys Fleischmann, which was written for the 1972 Dublin Festival of Twentieth-Century Music, were all premiered by Yeats. This inspired period of musical creativity and innovation has yet to be surpassed in the history of the modern Irish harp tradition.

APPENDIX

Compositions for Irish Harp by Brian Boydell

Chamber Music
Four Sketches for Two Irish Harps, op. 52 (1962)

Solo Voice (accompanied)
Three Yeats Songs, op. 56a (1965), s, Ir hp
Musician's Song [Love is an immoderate thing], op. 56b (1965), s, Ir hp

Solo Instrumental
An Album of Pieces for the Irish Harp, op. 88 (1989)

Arrangements (no opus number)
Tighearna Mhuigheo/Lord Mayo (David Murphy), s, Ir hp (1966)
Caoine Phiarais Feirteara, Ir hp (1966)[32]
Molly St George (Thomas Connellan), s, Ir hp (1966)
Bumper Squire Jones (Turlough Carolan), s, Ir hp (1966)

PART II: BOYDELL AS CONTRIBUTOR TO IRISH MUSICAL AND CULTURAL LIFE

NINE

MUSIC AT TRINITY COLLEGE CHAPEL: THE INNOVATIONS AND LEGACY OF BRIAN BOYDELL

Kerry Houston

The appointment of Brian Boydell as professor of music at Trinity College Dublin (TCD) in 1962 marked a considerable departure from precedent with regard to the relationship between the professorship and the College chapel. All professors before Brian Boydell had strong connections with the church and some were organists of the Dublin cathedrals. This strong alignment of the professorship at Trinity with organists and church musicians underlines Boydell's appointment as professor of music as an important turning point and a break from a tradition that had been such a strong strand in TCD's identity. As Boydell was not a church musician his approach to the musical establishment he inherited at the College chapel is particularly interesting and somewhat controversial.

Evidence of musical activity in Trinity College chapel survives from an early date, but the first formal choir was not established until 1762. The first professor of music was appointed in 1764.[1] However, the awarding of degrees in music at TCD predates the establishment of the professorship. The first of these was earned in 1612 by Thomas Bateson (c.1570–1630), organist of Christ Church Cathedral from 1609–30.[2] His anthem *Holy, Lord God Almighty* is probably his exercise for this bachelor of music degree.[3]

The first professor of music, Gareth Wesley [Wellesly] (Lord Mornington – professor 1764–74) had been a pupil of Ralph Roseingrave (organist of both Dublin cathedrals).[4] The post remained vacant after Mornington's resignation until the appointment of John Smith (1797–1861) in 1845, who remained as professor until his death. Smith was succeeded by Robert Stewart (1825–94), who also continued in harness until his death. Smith and Stewart were employed at both Dublin cathedrals and both wrote considerable amounts of church music. After Stewart's death the professorship went to Ebenezer Prout (1835–1909). Although Prout did not hold a cathedral position, he was an organist and indeed a founding member of the Royal College of Organists. His compositional output is strong in sacred music. Prout was a non-resident professor at TCD as he held teaching posts in London at the Royal Academy of Music and the Guildhall School of Music. He is best remembered today for his edition of Handel's *Messiah* (1902), which was the most widely used version in England and Ireland until the publication of Harold Watkins Shaw's edition in 1959.[5] After Prout's death he was succeeded by another who lived in England, Percy Carter Buck (1871–1947), who was professor from 1910 to 1920. Buck had been organist of Worcester College, Oxford (1891–4), Wells Cathedral (1896–9) and Bristol Cathedral (1899–1901) before becoming the director of music at Harrow School. His tutor *The First Year at the Organ* is still used widely.[6] When Buck resigned from TCD he was succeeded by Charles Kitson. Like Prout and Buck, Kitson was a non-residential professor. However, Kitson had lived in Dublin in the decade before his appointment at TCD when he was organist of Christ Church Cathedral (1913–20) and professor of music at University College Dublin (1916–20). He left Ireland in 1920 to join the teaching staff of the Royal College of Music in London. In the same year he was appointed professor of music at TCD.[7] When Kitson resigned in 1935 he was succeeded by George Hewson (1881–1972). Hewson had been organist of St Patrick's Cathedral, Dublin since 1920 and organist of the chapel at TCD from 1927. After retiring as organist of St Patrick's and TCD in 1960, Hewson retained the professorship at TCD until 1962. He was succeeded as organist of both St Patrick's Cathedral and Trinity College chapel by his assistant, William Sydney Greig (1910–83). Indeed, Greig may have seemed a likely candidate to succeed Hewson as professor, but he did not hold a doctorate.[8]

Brian Boydell was brought up in a protestant environment (his father was a Moravian, his mother from a Church of Ireland background), but he himself was an atheist. This placed him on uncertain ground when suggesting changes to the long-established practices in the College chapel; however, he recognised the chapel as a conduit for the advancement of his vision for music at TCD. Boydell had a strong desire to move the College away from its almost umbilical-cord and centuries-old connections with the cathedrals.[9] Boydell's activities as a singer and choral director undoubtedly motivated the importance he placed on singing as a vehicle for music education. He saw that one way in which he could improve music education at TCD was through the establishment of an independent choral foundation at the College chapel to replace the existing one that utilised cathedral musicians. Boydell's vision was to have a choir consisting of staff and students of the College. His experience at Cambridge where he had held a choral scholarship seems to be the model he utilised. At Cambridge Boydell had become a friend of Boris Ord, who was director of music at King's College and also director of the Cambridge Madrigal Society.

The musical establishment in the College chapel that Boydell inherited was one whereby music on Sunday mornings was provided by the senior boy choristers and the vicars choral of St Patrick's Cathedral.[10] A relic of this establishment may still be seen in the College chapel where the music stands in the front rows are designed for the height of teenage boys, while the stands in the back rows are of adjustable elevation to suit the heights of adult men. These musicians sang without a conductor, which must have seemed strange to Boydell given his experience at Cambridge. The organists in the chapel used the organ rather than hands to 'conduct' their singers.

The repertoire in the College chapel in the early 1960s would not have been to Brian Boydell's taste: it was almost entirely of Victorian and Edwardian extraction. Much of this repertoire had already fallen out of use in English cathedrals, but St Patrick's (and Christ Church) preserved it for much longer. This seems to be a result of a strong desire to continue 'tradition'. There was virtually no contemporary music being performed in the College chapel at this time.[11]

With William Sydney Greig, Hewson's successor as organist at St Patrick's, firmly established as organist in the College chapel (where all services were held according to the Rites of the Church of Ireland), Boydell was not in a strong position at the time of his appointment as professor in 1962. However, he had some luck in that many in TCD were unhappy with the long-established practice of the choir leaving the College chapel before the end of service in order to arrive in time to sing at the morning service at St Patrick's. The fact that they left before the sermon seemed to have been a particular ground for annoyance. This played into Boydell's hand and therefore he gained support for a new choral arrangement that would both remove the grievance of the choir leaving the service early, while also fulfilling Boydell's desire for a choral establishment more securely based in the College and independent of the cathedrals.

The change in arrangements seems to have been a unilateral decision from TCD rather than a negotiated divorce with St Patrick's. St Patrick's Cathedral Board

> noted with surprise that it had received no official notification or explanation of the decision to change the time of service in Trinity College Chapel on Sunday morning in such a way as to make it impossible for the choir and organist to attend.[12]

Clarification was sought from the Regius professor of divinity at TCD, Professor Hugh Frederic Woodhouse,[13] who responded by asking if the cathedral choir could continue to attend at the new hour of 11 a.m., to take effect from 1

January 1968. Woodhouse and others at TCD knew that this request was completely impossible and would sever the links between the cathedral and the College chapel. It would have been a likely expectation that Woodhouse would have become a canon of St Patrick's Cathedral during his tenure at TCD. However, this incident did not further his cause – a prebendal stall was not forthcoming. This rather unseemly divorce struck a raw nerve as the historic institutional links were strong.

As far back as the 1870s the Guinness Choir Scheme at St Patrick's included the provision of £10 a year for the purpose of furnishing exhibitions at TCD.[14] A new agreement between St Patrick's and TCD was drawn up in 1927 setting out the provision of music in the College chapel by members of the cathedral choir. St Patrick's pledged to provide singers for matins in the College during term time on condition that the singers could be at St Patrick's by 11 a.m.[15] TCD increased the payment to the six senior boys to £30 per annum and the agreement was not to be changed 'without a year's notice on either side'.[16]

The provision of one year's notice was not adhered to when TCD unilaterally decided to change the agreement in 1967. As with so many arguments involving church musicians, there were financial implications. St Patrick's increased Greig's salary by £100 as compensation to him from loss of earnings at TCD when he ceased to be organist. Arthur Moyse, one of the vicars choral who had sung in Trinity College chapel for 17 years, asked the cathedral board to intervene and assist him in acquiring a pension from TCD. This request generated considerable correspondence. TCD refused to provide a pension and made an opening bid of an ex-gratia payment of £25. After appeal, this was increased to £75.[17]

Despite the circumstances of this change of a long-standing arrangement, relations between Hewson, Greig and Boydell did not seem to suffer. Indeed, as their musical interests were quite different, it is unlikely that Boydell would have had much occasion to interact with either Hewson or Greig. Greig certainly does not appear to have held any grudge against TCD – he proudly wore his Trinity College Association tie on a daily basis. It seems that Brian Boydell managed to avoid being involved in the tense relationship that this divorce caused between TCD and St Patrick's. One of the singers in his Dowland Consort, George Bannister, was a long-serving vicar choral at St Patrick's.

This rather unceremonious departure of St Patrick's singers from the College chapel required a new choral foundation to provide music at liturgies in the chapel. The hand of Brian Boydell, reflecting his Cambridge experience, may be seen in the new arrangements, which consisted of a director of chapel music, an organ scholar and choral scholars. This is the position that continues to this day with the addition of a student conductor (this post was added in 1989). While Brian Boydell had a great sense of vision for music at TCD, he admitted frequently that he was not always the best judge of character. The appointment of Nigel Burton as the first director of chapel music and lecturer in music was somewhat problematic (despite Burton's considerable talent and drive in his role as director of chapel music). Burton was a 'High Tory' and occupied rooms in the Front Square of TCD where a portrait of Queen Elizabeth II was clearly visible to anyone who passed by his window. Upon the election of Margaret Thatcher as leader of the British Conservative party, Burton held an impromptu late-night celebration in the College chapel. His political and social views made him a somewhat divisive character in the College chapel and in the music department.

Burton was meticulous in his attention to detail in the performance of music in the chapel. Copies of his heavily annotated scores for use by the choir are retained in the chapel choir library. His research interest focused on the music of Arthur Sullivan, and this is reflected in the wide-ranging dynamic markings in the music in the chapel choir library. His interventions are particularly interesting in Tudor repertoire where his musical directions might be considered unconventional to say the least.

Brian Boydell's Dowland Consort specialised in Renaissance repertoire. He included considerable amounts of sacred music, and indeed the repertoire at the Consort's inaugural concert in 1959 included William Byrd's *Mass for Five Voices*. Barra Boydell has commented that the consort's performances were free of 'any taint of the precious or mannered characteristics which too often marked performances of early music at that time'.[18] Recordings of the Consort support Barra's comment and indeed Brian Boydell would perhaps have approved of the somewhat romantic interpretations suggested by Burton's markings in the copies of early music held in the chapel choir library. However, as Brian was not a practising Christian he only attended services in the College chapel on very rare occasions. Nigel Burton did not favour all of the tunes in the Irish Church Hymnal of 1960 (which had been edited by George Hewson). There are many instances of alternative tunes from English hymnals being pasted into hymn books still in the library of the College chapel. Burton worked with his organ scholar and had regular meetings to discuss choices of music.

Burton left TCD in 1979 and the post of director of chapel music remained vacant until the appointment of Kerry Houston in 1995. Boydell may have seen the alignment of chapel duties with a post in the music department as one that he did not wish to repeat. Indeed, he may have seen his role with regard to the chapel choir complete after his influence in the formation of the new choral foundation. He may have been frustrated by the lack of adequate financial support and by the fact that there was a strong denominational element in the makeup of the choir, which sang at Church of Ireland services only.

It is interesting to note that Brian Boydell did not compose any music specifically for use in the College chapel, despite his interest in music in the chapel in the early years of his professorship. Boydell had been a student of Herbert Howells, who is often seen as a quintessential Anglican church musician.[19] Yet, he was not drawn to religious texts, which may explain the lacuna of sacred repertoire in his output. His small sacred output includes *I will hear what God the Lord will speak* (Psalm 85). This anthem was commissioned by St Patrick's Cathedral, so any bad feeling about the severance of the choral arrangements in the College chapel and the cathedral were not directed at Boydell (or any that were had been forgotten by 1988 when this anthem was composed).

Despite the eccentric views of Nigel Burton, the recasting of the musical establishment in the College chapel achieved most of Boydell's vision. There are sung liturgies twice weekly in College term time and the choir attracts students from many disciplines in the College – many former organ scholars and conductors of the choir have pursued very successful careers in Ireland and abroad.[20]

Brian Boydell did not restrict his interest in the College chapel to the choir – he also exercised his attention on the chapel organ. While Boydell never described himself as an organist, he received some organ tuition from Meinhard Poppen during his stay in Heidelberg in 1935.[21] His wide-ranging musical interests included the study and performance of early music, undoubtedly influenced by his choral scholarship in Cambridge. His founding of the Dowland Consort in 1959 was a very forward-looking development for its time and was a precursor for a lively early music scene in Dublin in the 1970s and 1980s. The organ in the College chapel at the time of Boydell's appointment as professor was most unsuitable for the performance of early music or baroque music. This was a catalyst for Boydell's campaign for a radical approach to recasting the existing instrument.

The earliest surviving reference to an organist at TCD is from 1675 when a certain Thomas Patrickson is described as the 'present organist'. What his duties would have been is unclear (and what sort of organ existed is also unclear). It seems that there was no formal choral establishment at that time. The original College chapel was replaced by a second chapel consecrated on 5 October 1684. An organ was provided for this second chapel by Lancelot Pease. He was appointed a lay vicar at Christ Church Cathedral in 1667 having worked in London and Chester before his arrival in Ireland. The contract for his organ of 1684 for the College chapel, a single manual instrument with eight stops, has survived. This was enlarged by John Baptiste Cuvillie [Caville] in 1701 and it seems that the chair division was added then.[22] When the third (and existing) chapel building was consecrated in 1798, a new organ was provided and the Pease/Cuvillie instrument was moved to the Public Theatre (Exam Hall).

The new organ for the College chapel was the work of Samuel Green and was characteristic of the period, noted for its sweetness and delicacy of tone. Rapidly changing taste in style resulted in Green's instrument being abandoned in the mid-nineteenth century, with a new organ being built by William Telford. The original Green case was retained to accommodate Telford's organ.[23] This instrument underwent many restorations and 'improvements' including work by Hill and Son in 1879 and Magahy of Cork in 1930. These works rendered the instrument rather characterless as each change diluted the original tonal plan and resulted in a rather sprawling monster with a mongrel voice.

When work was required on the organ in the 1960s, Brian Boydell was instrumental in a more radical approach. He did not favour a repetition of pumping more oxygen into a dying instrument but rather argued for an almost completely new instrument. It may be that the displacement of the choir of St Patrick's Cathedral made it easier for him to advocate for an instrument that was not primarily designed for the accompaniment of Anglican church music. Indeed, it resulted in what is a most unsuitable instrument for the accompaniment of Anglican church music, requiring quite inventive use of registration by the organists who accompany the Church of Ireland services in the College chapel today. One of the strands of Brian Boydell's historic research on music in Ireland focused on organs and organ builders, so he had a particular interest in this project.

The services of the prominent English organist and organ consultant Ralph Downes were utilised for the 1960s work on the chapel organ. Downes was a noted performer of the organ works of J. S. Bach (the existing organ in the College chapel was most unsuitable for the performance of this repertoire). Downes had recently embarked on controversial and uncompromising projects in London at the Royal Festival Hall (with organ builders Harrison & Harrison) and the Brompton Oratory (with builders J. W. Walker).

Downes's design for the new organ for the chapel at TCD was a rather extreme example of the neo-classical revival in English organ building taking place at that time. The Green case needed to be expanded (this was accomplished rather crudely) to incorporate Downes's three-manual organ with a sizeable pedal division.[24] The great organ has a substantial *plenum* rooted at eight-foot tone, while the chair and swell *plena* were at four-foot pitch.[25] The swell is essentially a *brustverk* and, although enclosed, the position of this division makes the level of expression relatively restricted except when the manual is used without coupling. The sole reed on the swell is a strident Cremona that organ consultant Ian Bell has described as 'rather like a shark in a goldfish bowl'.[26]

Downes had limited experience in dealing with tracker action when he embarked on the TCD project. Indeed, in his autobiography *Baroque Tricks*[27] Downes states that following the rebuilding of Gloucester Cathedral organ he would turn to tracker action (although the Royal Festival Hall and TCD projects both had tracker action). Downes's design resulted in a rather heavy and unresponsive action in the organ at TCD; organ builder Trevor Crowe, who maintained the organ for many decades, has suggested that the layout of the tracker action indicates that electric action may have been envisaged originally and that there was a change to tracker at a late stage of the development of the project.

Ralph Downes presented the opening recital on the new instrument on 28 February 1969. The programme book indicates the registrations used for each piece. These varying combinations display the versatility of the new instrument and its ability to capture a vibrancy appropriate for Baroque repertoire. Music critic Charles Acton described the organ in his review of the opening recital as 'perhaps a puritan and high-thinking instrument rather than a sensuous one to touch the heart'.[28]

This new organ at TCD made quite an impact in Dublin as there was no other instrument of this style in the city. It was used for a series of recitals presenting the complete organ works of J. S. Bach and was undoubtedly the best instrument in the city suited to the music of Bach at the time. The organ was also the chosen instrument for the first three competitions of the Dublin International Organ Festival, which was founded by Gerard Gillen in 1980 (now Pipeworks).[29]

Kenneth Jones was commissioned to undertake minor work in the late 1970s, which seems to have been aimed at taming the more extreme elements of Downes's design. I remember Brian Boydell telling me that when he commented on some of the more strident elements of the new instrument he was rebuffed in no uncertain terms – 'that was how it was meant to sound.' Jones's minor rebuild tamed the 16-foot trombone on the pedal division that many considered to be out of proportion to the rest of the instrument. It also replaced the four-foot reed on the pedal with a very strong mixture (which does not blend with the rest of this division). Indeed, the pedal division is one of the least satisfactory as the 16 flute is not quite strong enough while the eight- and four-foot ranks are rather too present. An independent pedal division along the lines of the German Baroque has not been satisfactorily achieved. Curiously, Jones also removed the swell *celeste*, which was one of the few concessions to romanticism in Downes's design.

Brian Boydell retained his keen interest in the organs in TCD after his retirement as professor and he continued to serve on the College Organ Committee. When plans were being formulated for the quatercentenary of TCD in 1992, the organ committee investigated the possibility of providing an exciting new instrument for the Public Theatre (Exam Hall). The organ committee wrote to Provost William Watts proposing a new instrument to be ready to celebrate the quatercentenary.[30] While emphasising the importance of the 1684 organ case, the committee underlined that:

> the instrument that it houses today does not match up to the splendour of the case. While it does contain a few good nineteenth-century Telford stops, it largely dates from a rebuild in 1961. It is poorly balanced and of limited scope, and overall is of little musical significance.[31]

The committee consisted of Peter Boyle (chair), Brian Boydell, Martin Adams, David Grayson and Kerry Houston (organ scholar). The committee was proposing a new organ in the existing case with an estimated cost of £55,000. Sadly, this initiative did not come to fruition, but Brian Boydell would have been delighted with the restoration of both the organ case and a largely new instrument in the Public Theatre that was completed by specialist builders Goetze and Gwynn in 2018.

Boydell also had a central role in exploratory investigations to bring the original 1798 Green organ back to TCD from Durrow, County Laois. I remember a visit to Durrow in 1992. I travelled in Brian's car and enjoyed one or two of his *Gitanes* cigarettes on the journey down as we were discussing strategies for this project. While travelling back to Dublin the cigarettes were supplemented by some glasses of whiskey in Morrisseys's spirit grocer in Abbeyleix. We found the Green organ largely unaltered in St Fintan's Church but in a poor state of repair with only a few stops speaking. I remember vividly Brian's excitement of what we could make work as it was pretty close to the sound that would have been heard in the College chapel almost 200 years earlier. The minutes of the organ committee meeting of 19 October 1993 report that the committee had concluded that it would not be practical to incorporate the Green organ into the cases in either the chapel or the Exam Hall. Indeed, the new(ish) organ in the chapel was too recent to be considered for major alterations. However, the minutes also record that 'the cinema on Pearse Street, or another building in the area, might be acquired by College in the not-too-distant future and it might be suitable for such a venue.'[32] This acquisition never happened, but the visit of Brian Boydell and the interest shown by TCD in the organ in Durrow proved to be a catalyst for the gradual restoration of the organ in St Fintan's. This was led by the rector, Revd Canon

Patrick Harvey, with pragmatic use of grants and very imaginative planning from organ builder Trevor Crowe. This instrument is now in much better condition and suitable for recitals as well as church worship. Along with the organ cases in the Public Theatre and the chapel at TCD, this is one of the most important surviving artefacts for the history of the organ in Ireland.

Brian Boydell's imaginative and pioneering work with regard to music in Trinity College chapel is testament to his polymath character as is displayed in other essays in this volume. Despite not being a practising Christian, Brian saw how music in the College chapel could be made more accessible to students and staff at TCD, and he established a more modern choral foundation that continues today. If Brian Boydell had been a practising Christian, he would have undoubtedly been a 'broad churchman'. His passionate interest in the history of music in Dublin in general and in organs in particular is reflected in his drive to have a new organ in the College chapel; and although his initiative to provide a new organ in the Public Theatre was not achieved in his lifetime, this has since been completed and is a further testament to the great vision that Brian had for music at Trinity College, in Dublin, in Ireland and on the international stage.

TEN

BRINGING TO LIFE THE SPIRIT OF AN AGE: BRIAN BOYDELL AND MUSICAL LIFE IN EIGHTEENTH-CENTURY DUBLIN

Ita Beausang

Musicology was only one of Brian Boydell's multifarious musical activities. In an interview in 1970 with the *Irish Times* music critic, Charles Acton, he acknowledged the diverse choices that he had made:

> All my life I have been torn between various different things. At the beginning I was torn between science and music and even now between musicological research and composition – to say nothing of teaching and a lot of other things. But I have always shied away from the one-track specialist.[1]

As professor of music at Trinity College Dublin (TCD) from 1962 to 1982 Boydell travelled on many tracks. In addition to composing, conducting, teaching, and administrative duties, he conducted musicological research on a variety of topics and published articles from 1947 to 1995.[2] Boydell's writings while he was professor of music at TCD presage his later preoccupation with music in eighteenth-century Dublin.[3] They include three articles, the BBC publication *Four Centuries of Music in Ireland* (1979), which he edited, and numerous entries for *The New Grove Dictionary of Music and Musicians* (1980).

When he retired from TCD in 1982, Boydell had more time and space to continue his research and writing. From 1984 to 1995 he published eight articles and contributed two chapters to *A New History of Ireland* (1986), in addition to entries in *The New Grove Dictionary of Musical Instruments* (1984), *The New Grove Dictionary of Opera* (1992), *The New Grove Dictionary of Music and Musicians* (2nd edn, 2001), and *Die Musik in Geschichte und Gegenwart* (1999–2007). His landmark books, *A Dublin Musical Calendar 1700–1760* (1988) and *Rotunda Music in Eighteenth-Century Dublin* (1992), were not merely products of post-retirement but, as he states in the Preface to *A Dublin*

Musical Calendar, they were the culmination of his immersion for many years in musical life in eighteenth-century Dublin:

> This calendar represents an attempt, after about thirty years of research, to make available for the first time a carefully documented record of all the main events and personalities in Dublin musical life during the period 1700–60.[4]

With his scientific training from his Cambridge days, Boydell's approach to research was systematic and highly organised.[5] The eighteenth-century print and manuscript sources that he consulted include contemporary newspapers, not many of which have survived from the first three decades of the eighteenth century, directories, commentaries by writers of the time and the previously unexplored archives of institutions such as the Rotunda and Mercer's Hospitals.

A Dublin Musical Calendar opens with an introductory essay that provides the historical backdrop to the capital's social and musical life during the period, placing the information in context and 'bringing to life the spirit of an age when Dublin's cultural reputation was second only to London's in these islands'.[6] The reader is made aware of the fashionable sophistication of a colonial governing ruling class, during a period of peace and prosperity after the Williamite war (1688–91). Statistics are provided about Dublin's population growth, while the split is noted between Gaelic and Anglo-Irish, and between Protestant and Catholic. This sense of place permeates all Boydell's writing, together with a keen observation of the people who occupy the space: audiences, visiting performers, composers and native musicians.

Most of the concerts were held by musical societies for charitable purposes; their profits were used for the founding and maintenance of eight Dublin hospitals. Boydell states that the oratorio choirs of the mid eighteenth century mostly consisted of cathedral singers, and seldom exceeded 24 voices. He calculates that during the 1749–50 season there were 33 performances of 16 large-scale choral works, including 2 first performances. However, he speculates that, compared to modern performances, the standard achieved was 'doubtless rather haphazard'.[7]

There are many entertaining anecdotes in the essay, such as the Irish harper who was secreted by Mrs Delany (wife of the Dean of Down) in the shrubbery of her garden at Delville House, Glasnevin, to entertain her guests.[8] Or Mr Charles, 'an Hungarian, the famous French Horn who has been allowed by the best Judges to be the most excellent in Europe for that instrument',[9] who arrived in Dublin in March 1742 when Handel was in residence, and literally stole a march on the composer by advertising a performance of 'the Overture in Saul with the Dead March, compos'd by Mr Handel but never performed here before'.[10] For a concert in Smock Alley Theatre in May, Mr

Charles provided what Boydell describes as one of many examples of rather astonishing musical arrangements, announcing that 'with his Second he will perform the Water Musick in which he will be accompanied on the Kettle-Drum by Mr Kountze'.[11]

Boydell places the *Dublin Musical Calendar* in its historical context with a list of important events at the end of the seventeenth century. The 60 years from 1700 to 1760 are divided into 7 sections, beginning from 1701 to 1719 and ending from 1755 to 1759. There are six comprehensive appendices, incorporating the music trade, concert venues, societies and charitable bodies, personalia (twenty-five pages in alphabetical order of musicians active in Dublin 1700–60), an index of music performed or published in Dublin during the time, and a summary of periods or seasons. The *Dublin Musical Calendar* is enhanced by 32 illustrations and a map of musical venues in Dublin c.1750. Additional information and explanatory notes are added to many of the entries. Such painstaking research might result in a certain tedium for the reader, but Boydell explains in the Preface that 'the time-consuming research required to discover details of identity or life-span has not been pursued in those cases where the information is considered unimportant in the context of this work.'[12]

On 18 November 1741, the *Dublin Musical Calendar* records the arrival in Dublin of 'Dr Handell' from Parkgate, the port near Chester. On 14 December Handel is selling tickets in his house at Abbey Street for his 'six musical entertainments'. A second series of concerts between 17 February and 3 April 1742 is listed, and on 13 April the first performance of *Messiah* is recorded with the comment, 'Details of this notable occasion are amply covered elsewhere and are not repeated here.'[13] However, Boydell includes a newspaper notice that appeared in advance of the second performance of *Messiah* on 3 June: 'In order to keep the Room as cool as possible a Pane of Glass will be removed from the top of each of the Windows.'[14]

Open-air concerts were also very popular in Dublin. In 1748 Dr Bartholomew Mosse, founder and first master of the Dublin Lying-in Hospital, leased a plot of land in Great Britain Street, now Parnell Street, and opened the New Gardens there to raise funds for the hospital that he had opened in George's Lane in 1745. The musical entertainments and fireworks displays held in the Gardens during the summer months are compared by Boydell to Ranelagh and Vauxhall Gardens in London. He gives a colourful account of vocal and instrumental concerts held on fine evenings three times a week, including details of the refreshments available. There was no alcohol for sale but reference in the minutes to 'rowdy and unseemly behaviour in the Gardens' suggests to Boydell that many gentlemen carried hip flasks.[15]

By 1757 Dr Mosse had built the new Lying-In Hospital on the Great Britain Street site; the Round Room or Rotunda from which the hospital later took its name opened two years later. Boydell estimates that over 2,000 concerts for the hospital's benefit were held during a continuous period of over 40 years. Accounts from the Register for each year from 1760 to 1784 are preserved in the Rotunda archive, which records full details of receipts and expenditure, artists' fees, box office sales for individual concerts and band expenses.

The Rotunda archive also provided Boydell with the research material for his second book, *Rotunda Music in Eighteenth-Century Dublin*, published in 1992, for which he sounds a note of caution in the Preface:

> Being convinced that serious musicological studies should not assume false academic dignity and avoid the oft humorous context of a performing art so affected by the vagaries of fashion, an attempt has been made to provide narrative that is readable and entertaining.[16]

Boydell's chronicles of music and musicians in Dublin from 1745 to 1791, gleaned from primary sources in the Rotunda archive, are both readable and entertaining. His unerring ability to recreate the atmosphere of eighteenth-century Dublin is balanced by meticulous research and methodology. The personalities of the time become alive on the pages, from the visionary Dr Bartholomew Mosse and the composer Lord Mornington, first professor of music at TCD and a governor of the Rotunda Hospital, to the visiting singers, conductors and concert promoters.

The lists of band members and their salaries in 1758, and again almost 30 years later in 1783, provide fascinating evidence of employment conditions for instrumental musicians. In 1783, the second violins in the band include Robert Field, father of John (born 1782) who would become one of the most famous Dublin-born composers. Another of the musicians, Frederick Seafort, appears to have changed from playing the oboe in 1758 to the violin in 1783, prompting a comment from Boydell, who was himself an oboist, that 'perhaps his teeth began to give trouble as he grew older'.[17]

Boydell's enjoyment of the research process is evident throughout as he recounts episodes such as the tensions between Niccolo Pasquali and Thomas Sheridan that turned the opening concert of the 1750 season, for which 'a numerous and polite audience had gathered', into a fiasco.[18] In the chapter entitled 'Sirens', reminiscent of *Ulysses*, Boydell gives vivid accounts of the celebrated female singers from London who performed in Dublin theatres and at the Rotunda concerts, together with tables of the fees paid and comparative incomes of the period. The male singers, with a few exceptions, attracted smaller fees and less publicity. From 1763 many well-known Italian singers arrived after the introduction of Italian opera to the Dublin theatres. Boy trebles who were choristers at the cathedrals were also in demand at the concerts.

From 1767 the availability of the Rotunda Round Room enabled concerts to be held during the winter and gave opportunities for oratorios and operas to be presented. The hall was hired out for benefit concerts, assemblies, balls and Sunday Promenades, although the latter incurred strong protests from the Society for Promoting Religion and Virtue, which persuaded the governors to discontinue 'All Species of Publick Entertainments of any Kind whatsoever on the Sabbath'.[19] Boydell comments wryly that the governors took the best part of three years to comply with the demand since by doing so they stood to lose a yearly income of nearly £1,000 from the Sunday Promenades.

The period 1769–75 marked six years of expansion for the Rotunda concerts. The governors, realising their value as a source of funding, appointed a committee of four 'Gentlemen of Approved Taste', all amateur musicians, to oversee the musical entertainments. In 1775 Boydell reports the announcement of 'a favourite concerto. . . on a new Italian Instrument never before heard in this Kingdom & which imitates the female Voice in the highest Perfection',[20] which he speculates could be the form of tenor oboe developed in England in 1750 known as the *Vox Humana*.

An even more unusual announcement was for 'a new Concerto on the Teagoto by a celebrated Performer lately arrived here', which Boydell identifies as a tárogató, a Hungarian version of the shawm, a shrill unjointed instrument played with a double reed. Having heard 'the harsh and piercing sound produced by a modern reconstruction of the tárogató', he concluded that it was 'hard to imagine that the concerto provided a very pleasant experience'.[21] It is tempting to imagine Boydell's scientific interest in the violinist and conductor Michael Arne, who appeared as a solo organist at the Rotunda in 1775 and spent some time conducting alchemical experiments in Clontarf in search of the philosopher's stone.[22]

Unlike the abundance of financial details in the Rotunda archive, Boydell found it disappointing that there was very little information there about the music performed during the first 20 years of the Rotunda concerts, apart from some newspaper advertisements for special occasions. However, towards the end of the 1776 season a new policy was adopted and programmes for concerts were regularly published in newspaper advertisements, which enabled Boydell to analyse 71 detailed programmes and a dozen incomplete ones for 6 seasons. He also categorised repertoire and changes in musical taste, and compiled three tables based on his analysis of over 2,400 concerts promoted by the hospital. The five appendices to the narrative of *Rotunda Music in Eighteenth-Century Dublin* contain the complete findings of this mammoth research. His exemplary use of sources is a model for the theory and practice of musicology.

In 2005 Harry White wrote that Brian Boydell would probably have disdained the word 'musicology', whose 'connotations of scholarship and detached, archival enquiry would have offended his resolutely engaged and pragmatic sense of music history'.[23] In all his writings Boydell's reconstruction of music in eighteenth-century Dublin is reinforced by the historical and social framework. His scholarly legacy endures today in his unparalleled contribution to the cultural history of music in Ireland.

ELEVEN

A VOICE FOR IRISH ART MUSIC: BRIAN BOYDELL AND THE MUSIC ASSOCIATION OF IRELAND

Teresa O'Donnell

Join the Music Association of Ireland and help to add a new voice to the chorus of nations.[1]

Brian Boydell was a founder member and first chairman of the Music Association of Ireland (MAI), founded in 1948. The MAI contributed considerably to the musical life of Ireland, particularly in its educational initiatives and its efforts to create a musical infrastructure for composers. Boydell was a dynamic force in the Association for the first two decades of its existence and spearheaded many MAI initiatives such as the Composers' Group and the joint publication scheme of previously unpublished works by Irish composers with the Cultural Relations Committee (CRC). With the support of composers such as Aloys Fleischmann, Frederick May, Edgar Deale and Joseph Groocock on the MAI's first council, it is axiomatic that the standing of the composer and the performance of their works would be foregrounded in the MAI's policy and activities. Although these composers differed in their desired level of disengagement from Irish folk music or idiom, it was Boydell's vision of removing Irish contemporary music from its parochial setting and placing it in an international context that mostly prevailed in the MAI. Through an examination of various MAI activities initiated by Boydell, I will assess his contribution to the MAI and to the creation of an infrastructure for Irish composers.

ESTABLISHMENT OF THE MUSIC ASSOCIATION OF IRELAND

The genesis of the MAI lay in a discussion among a group of friends, Brian Boydell, Edgar Deale, Frederick May and Michael McMullin, about the standing of music in Ireland and their concerns for its future. Boydell noted that attempts to encourage music at all levels in society were unfocussed and in urgent need of a 'more unified purpose'.[2] He stated that they were 'trying to do something for Irish musical life equivalent to the inspiring excitement that had resulted from the stimulus of fresh ideas in the visual arts'.[3] The quartet was later joined by other friends, colleagues, academics, professional and amateur musicians and singers, composers and educationalists to form the National Music Association at a meeting on 30 March 1948 (changed to the Music Association of Ireland at its next meeting). The MAI set itself six objectives: to further musical education; to improve conditions for composers and musicians generally; to work for the establishment of a national concert hall; to submit recommendations on musical policy to the authorities concerned; to encourage the formation of musical groups, societies and choirs throughout the country; and to organise popular lectures, concerts and recitals and awaken a musical consciousness in the nation.[4] The MAI's first council included Brian Boydell (chairman), Michael McMullin (honorary secretary), Olive Smith (honorary treasurer), Edgar Deale, James Delany, Brendan Dunne, Aloys Fleischmann, Joseph Groocock, Anthony Hughes, Madeleine Larchet, Nancie Lord, Frederick May, Terry O'Connor, Joseph O'Neill, Dorothy Stokes and William F. Watt.

The MAI came into existence at a time when Ireland was beginning to progress toward modernisation. The election of the first inter-party Government in February 1948[5] was indicative of the numerous changes that occurred in Ireland in the post-emergency period:

> The country, it seemed, had been gazing at its own reflection since independence and many were becoming weary of the image. There was a new-found idealism which declared that the country would have to take her place among the nations, to face outside influences rather than seek to exclude them.[6]

Ireland gradually turned away from the previous government's conservative and protectionist economic policies in favour of more progressive, open policies, embarking upon an ambitious 'building programme of houses and hospitals costing £120 million'.[7] The MAI was ready to embrace this progressive, outward-looking attitude and it benefited greatly from two significant events, namely Bodkin's *Report on the Arts in Ireland* (1949), which echoed much of the MAI's discontent expressed in its policy document, and the ensuing establishment of the Arts Council (An Chomhairle Ealaíon) in 1951, which kept 'the arts at arm's length from political interference'.[8] Finally, it appeared Ireland had a government that was willing to 'go forward in policies concerning the Arts' and negate years of apathy.[9] The MAI was well positioned to reap the rewards of this transformation in attitudes. With its strong council of well-known musicians, composers and pedagogues, its aim 'to make music a part of the education of every citizen' appeared to be a viable mission.[10]

MAI INITIATIVES

The MAI council moved swiftly into action with the honorary secretary, Michael McMullin, compiling a substantial policy document, *Memorandum: Music and the Nation*.[11] The memorandum consisted of four parts: Introduction, Music in General Education, The Music Profession, and Conclusion, and sought to address Ireland's 'backwardness' in classical music and to proffer radical reforms.[12] The recurring theme of Ireland's musical 'backwardness' is symptomatic of early MAI rhetoric and even after McMullin's departure from the MAI, this rhetoric continued; thus, one can conclude that it pervaded general MAI policy and was not just the view of an individual. A number of sections of the memorandum were submitted to government departments: Part III: 'Broadcasting', 'The Orchestra' and 'The Training of Musicians', were submitted to the Department of Posts and Telegraphs (July 1948), and Part II: 'Music in General Education', was submitted to the Department of Education (December 1949). These submissions together with correspondence and meetings with government departments stressed the need for government to take responsibility for the arts and to seek 'expert musical opinion' in order to avoid both 'absolute dictatorial power in musical matters' and 'narrow individual policy'.[13]

On 25 October 1948 a deputation from the MAI consisting of Boydell, Deale, McMullin and Dunne met with the Minister of Posts and Telegraphs, James Everett, and the department's secretary, León Ó Broin, to discuss a number of pressing issues, including the need to create a permanent director of music at Radio Éireann (RÉ), distinct from the position of conductor of the Radio Éireann Symphony Orchestra (RÉSO); the appointment of conductors for a period of two years; the establishment of a music advisory board; the necessity to promote concerts more widely; the commissioning of new works by Irish composers; the employment of suitably qualified sound engineers; and, most importantly, the resumption of the public symphony concerts at the Capitol Theatre, Dublin. The MAI's recommendations to the Department of Posts and Telegraphs received a favourable response in contrast to its submission to the Department of Education. Within a few weeks of the meeting, MAI members were informed of the outcome of the discussion in a four-page report. Ó Broin agreed with all recommendations in the relevant sections submitted from Part III of the Memorandum, except the suggestion that an independent advisory group be established to advise the Minister, since an advisory committee, which included Fleischmann in its membership, was already in existence.

The language employed in the MAI's Memorandum and in discussions with government departments reflected a trenchant criticism of RÉ by the MAI. Richard Pine has observed that officials in RÉ viewed the MAI with suspicion and vice versa, naming Boydell, Anthony Farrington and Olive Smith as its most vocal critics. He stated that RÉ considered those involved in the MAI as a clique of Anglo-Irish who were distrustful of the Irish government and RÉ's ability to manage the RÉSO and to carry out an effective music programme. Pine recalled a conversation with Gerard Victory, who recounted to him an incident at the offices of RÉ at the GPO at which Boydell banged 'the unattended reception desk with his walking stick "in the manner of an Anglo-Irish squire trying to attract the attention of the natives"'.[14] Though Pine doubted Victory's recollection of the incident, he argued that it reflected the mistrust between both sides. A further explanation for the tension was proffered by León Ó Broin, who suggested that the MAI's criticism possibly stemmed from Boydell's failure to secure the position of either RÉ's music director or assistant music director and May's failure to succeed in his application for the position of temporary music director.[15] Regardless of the source(s) of the mistrust, if the MAI wished to work closely with the government to develop a cohesive plan for music, overt criticism was not advisable.

Despite an appeal for subscriptions, the Memorandum was never published. McMullin defended his approach, admitting that 'certain sections already written have been criticised as too Utopian. . . calling for reforms, that are much too radical and beyond hope of realisation. . . if one demands more, one is more likely to attract attention.'[16] Boydell and other members of the MAI were keen to distance themselves from McMullin and believed he went too far in his criticism of the musical status of the country. Interestingly, many of McMullin's observations were echoed in the writings of Boydell and in numerous contributions in Aloys Fleischmann's tome, *Music in Ireland: A Symposium* (1952).

This period, the early 1950s, experienced a phase of lively exchanges on the future of music in Ireland, particularly in *The Bell*. An article written by Boydell, 'The future of music in Ireland' (1951), declared music in Ireland to be in a 'shocking state'.[17] His article provoked reactions from three other contributors, namely Aloys Fleischmann (MAI council member), P. J. Malone and Joseph O'Neill (MAI council member). In his response Fleischmann described Boydell's observations as unwelcome, unfounded and 'a trifle ungenerous'.[18] He pointed out that, although progress was slow, much had been done to improve the status of music and listed many positive initiatives introduced in the past few years to further the appreciation of music, namely: the establishment of the Advisory Committee on Cultural Relations (1949) and the Arts Council (1951), and the Bach bicentenary festival organised by the MAI. He also mentioned the popularity of RÉ's school concerts at regional venues.[19] In the second response to Boydell's article, P. J. Malone stressed the importance of a musical education for children, as they represented future audiences; he urged the Department of Education to take into account the recommendations made in the Irish National Teachers' Organisation [INTO]'s *A Plan for Education* (1947) and suggested that local authorities should be responsible for the development of music at community level.[20] The last contributor, Joseph O'Neill, noted that music was not viewed as a viable career as there were limited employment and performing opportunities for those who wished to make music a full-time occupation. Commenting on career opportunities in general at this time, O'Neill questioned how 'many musicians in Ireland are earning £1,000 a year? Perhaps one or two after a lifetime of work. A first-class performer on a stringed instrument might obtain employment in Radio Éireann Orchestras, where he would earn about £400 a year.'[21]

The MAI defended Boydell's article in a letter to the editor of *The Bell* on 17 January 1951, arguing that Boydell's courageous article boldly expressed what Irish people had privately felt for many years and gave 'a much more acute picture of the condition of music in the country than was given by one of your correspondents in your November issue, who stated that music was in the healthiest state of all the arts in Ireland.'[22] The letter rehearsed characteristic MAI rhetoric regarding Ireland's backwardness as a musical nation, stating that Dublin had no concert hall and that, outside Dublin, there was 'literally no music taking place'.[23] The MAI employed Ireland's independence as a means of convincing Irish people of their responsibility to address the country's 'lack of musical culture'.[24] Considering the predominantly Anglo-Irish make-up of the organisation, this strategy of apportioning responsibility or blame on Irish people rather than on Ireland's former colonisers (as had been previously customary) is a novel approach by the MAI. Its arrogance in equating Ireland as being 'of no consequence whatever so far as music is concerned' and in implying that the Irish were an uncultured people is outrageous and perhaps explains why Fleischmann, Malone and O'Neill were critical of Boydell's initial article.[25] Despite their differences, Boydell, the MAI and various commentators shared a desire to create a musically educated audience.

'Though the proper foundations for a musical nation can only be laid eventually in the education of children, adult musical education is probably equally important in the intervening stages.'[26] The area of adult education was a priority for the MAI and, in order to build up a musically educated audience, it proposed in its sixth objective 'to organise popular lectures, concerts and recitals and to awaken a musical consciousness in the nation'.[27] Within months of its formation, the MAI was invited by Ruaidhrí Roberts, honorary secretary of the Workers' Educational Organisation (Irish Trade Union Congress) to provide weekly music appreciation lectures at the People's College Adult Education Course (sponsored by the Irish Trade Union Congress). Michael McMullin assumed the role of director of the series and immediately set about devising a course of music appreciation lectures and, in consultation with Boydell, compiling a comprehensive recommended reading list. Boydell delivered the inaugural lecture of the series in October 1948, entitled 'Three ways of appreciating music: The distinction between good and bad music' and also delivered the concluding lecture in December 1948 entitled 'Brief analysis of St. Anthony Variations by Brahms'. Extracts from Boydell's last lecture of the series survive in the MAI Archive (albeit on the verso of a draft letter to the People's College); he described Brahms as:

> [a] great figure who welds together the new discoveries in the use of instruments, in the use of new and colourful harmonies in the classical forms of Beethoven's middle period. The mood is that of the most profound qualities of the Romantic spirit – cast within the solid structure of classical design, with an exquisite degree of workmanship.[28]

Éamonn Ó Sé, who attended all lectures in the first series, wrote to Boydell expressing his gratitude to him for sharing his 'vast knowledge with a working-class man from Pearse Street'.[29] Ó Sé recalled how one of the brothers at the Christian Brothers School, Westland Row, Dublin often spoke of his admiration for Brahms but, as a school boy, Ó Sé admitted that he could not fully appreciate the music:

> Now, as an older man with a bit of learning under my belt I opened my heart to Brahms, whom you described in your talk as 'a truly great composer'. I was glad to hear that I was not alone in my ignorance and I enjoyed your comment about George Bernard Shaw's failure to recognise Brahms' genius while Shaw worked as a music critic in London in the 1890s.[30]

The first series of lectures also featured a number of other lecturers including Michael McMullin, Brendan Dunne, Liam Ó Laoghaire and Thomas May. They spoke on a range of subjects from analysis of Beethoven's Symphony No. 5, to national expression in music and a history of European music. Boydell was undoubtedly the most experienced lecturer of the group, having broadcast radio programmes on music appreciation, contemporary Irish music and popular classics for RÉ from the mid-1940s and later as music appreciation lecturer for the Vocational Education Scheme under the auspices of the Royal Dublin Society. Attendance at the lectures numbered between 30 and 40, which pleased the MAI and the People's College. However, venues (Thomas Ashe Hall and Women's Workers' Union Building, Fleet Street, Dublin) proved unsuitable for various reasons and Boydell suggested relocating to the Royal Irish Academy of Music, which had access to numerous pianos and other facilities. Another melting point for Boydell and McMullin was the lack of remuneration for the lecturers, noting that 'this would not be asked of any other professional person, and least of all tradesmen and craftsmen represented by the Trade Unions themselves.'[31] The matter, however, was eventually resolved and a cheque of £17.17.0. was sent to the MAI.[32]

Though Boydell and McMullin worked together on numerous aspects of the People's College lecture series, there was growing tension between the two men and other members of the MAI council. Verbal evidence, corroborated through interviews, suggests that McMullin was considered by Boydell and a number of council members to be too radical, somewhat of a loose cannon, 'a would-be dictator' and too readily critical of the musical establishment.[33] McMullin sent a notice calling a general meeting on 10 January 1950 owing to the lack of a quorum at the previous three meetings of the council. Boydell noted in his diary, 'Michael is certainly fed up with the whole thing, since it didn't turn out to his liking viz. as a society to 'down' [Fachtna] O' Hannrachain, and to publish his memorandum. This notice seems designed to wreck any future the MAI might have.'[34] Boydell foresaw a split in the organisation and set about managing the crisis; he requested to see Deale's correspondence with McMullin and opined that Deale's replies to McMullin 'should be strong enough to disturb even a lizard like M[ichael]'.[35] He also organised a meeting of Aloys Fleischmann, Edgar Deale, Frederick May, Joseph Groocock and Olive Smith on 7 January 1950 to plan for all eventualities. Francis J. Kelly acted as chair at the general meeting on 10 January and Boydell reported his relief that the council was 'very well-behaved, and in spite of evil omens, a major row was averted'.[36] McMullin was eventually replaced by Francis J. Kelly as honorary secretary.

At a meeting of the MAI council on 29 March 1950, it was decided to organise a series of concerts and lectures to honour the bicentenary of J. S. Bach's death. Boydell and Groocock acted as musical advisors and Olive Smith was chief organiser of the festival. The Bach bicentenary festival took place between September and November 1950 and was the first major project undertaken by the MAI. By organising a guarantee-against-loss fund and encouraging members to purchase tickets in advance, the MAI sought to save on unnecessary advertising expenses. The first concert on 29 September 1950 at the Metropolitan Hall, Abbey Street, Dublin, featured Bach's *Mass in B minor* performed in front of an audience of nearly 1,000 people by the RÉSO, conducted by Otto Matzerath, Cór Radio Éireann, the Culwick Choral Society and two UK-based players of trumpets in D. In the weeks leading up to the concert the MAI requested that the Irish National Anthem, *Amhrán na bhFiann* not be performed by the RÉSO at this concert as the MAI believed the playing of the anthem did not suit the occasion. As it was customary for the orchestras of RÉ to perform the anthem at the beginning of their concerts, the radio authorities informed the MAI that they 'were [only] willing to provide the orchestra on condition that the performance was preceded by the National Anthem.'[37] Neither side was willing to relent until, as Boydell later recounted, 'Edgar Deale thought of the perfect ploy by quietly remarking [at a meeting]... "Isn't it funny that we cling to so many British customs, such as playing the National Anthem before a concert." The opposition blushed and the anthem was not mentioned again.'[38] Boydell and the MAI expressed delight in their triumph over RÉ officials and referred to the event as 'Victory over the Anthem Day'.[39] Would the MAI still have had such an aversion to the national anthem had one of its own members arranged the piece?

This concert was followed by a second concert on 20 October that featured the Clontarf Choral Society and the RÉSO led by MAI council member Nancie Lord and conducted by Sixten Eckerberg. The programme included two cantatas: *Thou Guide of Israel* [BWV 104] and *The Sages of Sheba* [BWV 65], Suite No. 3 in D major and Brandenburg Concertos Nos. 3 and 4. A number of ancillary concerts and lectures took place at various venues in Dublin, including Boydell's lecture, 'The cantatas and orchestral works of J. S. Bach' on 9 October. Boydell stated that Bach 'was neither a conservative nor a revolutionary – for he distilled from these two opposing streams those procedures that would further his expressive purposes.'[40] Boydell admired Bach's combined use of newly-invented and 'dying' instruments according to the emotion he sought to express in his music. He noted Bach's ability to use a wide range of sources, secular and religious, German, French and Italian, old and new, and opined that if Bach were alive at the time of the lecture he would probably have embraced American Jazz music.[41] Nevertheless, Boydell emphasised that Bach was not unoriginal or even a plagiarist, rather that he perfected and purified every idea and unified 'all the diverse streams into the flood of wonderful music that came from his unceasing pen'.[42]

In his Tuesday Review broadcast of 24 October 1950, Boydell admitted that the order of the two choral and orchestral concerts should have been reversed, stating, '[a]fter the overpowering experience of the B minor Mass, last Friday's concert was bound to be a bit of an anti-climax.'[43] Despite this, Boydell was proud of what he and the MAI had staged, in particular the fact that the audience had the opportunity of hearing 'some of the greatest music that has ever been written for perhaps the first time in Ireland'.[44]

Preparations for the festival did not always run smoothly and Boydell recounted three major obstacles that threatened the life of the festival. Firstly, having identified suitable soloists for the B minor Mass, Boydell discovered that they were engaged for another festival the day after the Dublin concert. Secondly, specialist players of the D trumpets were in high demand during the Bach bicentenary celebrations. Finally, and most worrying for Boydell, was the discovery in early June 1949 that no harpsichord of a suitable standard could be located for purchase or hire in Ireland. As Boydell later observed, '[n]ow we can't get away with the excuse that the harpsichord is an extinct instrument – and it is sheer ignorance to say that a piano does the job just as well.'[45] Olive Smith, as a last resort, contacted the journalist Quidnunc in the hope that he might highlight the MAI's plight. In his column 'An Irishman's Diary' in the *Irish Times*, Quidnunc wittily made a plea for an instrument that could be used in Bach's *Mass in B minor*. It read, 'If you are one of those soulless scoundrels who is at present using great-aunt Agatha's harpsichord as a repository for the assegais carried home in triumph from the Zulu by great-uncle Egbert, I am requested to bid you desist at once. Extract the assegais.'[46] He recommended that great-niece Millicent, 'the talented one', should test the standard of the instrument and, if her playing sounded as it should, 'then telephone 83968 at once; ask for Mrs Lyall Smith and say to her: "Sleep in peace – your quest is ended – when do you wish to pick up a harpsichord in playable condition?"'[47] Sadly, the plea was not successful but the free publicity was appreciated. Eventually a harpsichord made by Dublin maker Ferdinand Weber *c*.1770 was located at the National Museum of Ireland. John Beckett played the instrument or, as Olive Smith stated, he 'coaxed the instrument along' for both performances.[48]

The Bach bicentenary commemoration was a nexus for the fledgling MAI; it emboldened the organisation to host similar events. Most importantly, the MAI was invigorated with the belief that there was a public demand for a national concert hall in Dublin and that this could be realised soon.[49] Though Olive Smith was the main driving force for 30 years in the agitation for a concert hall, Boydell was also involved in the campaign. He opined that we 'cannot expect our musicians and musical audiences to enjoy the fruits' of far-sighted arts policies 'in buildings more suitable for badminton or the spectacles of Hollywood'.[50] In 1969 Boydell corresponded with Minister for Finance, Charles J. Haughey, regarding the delay in building the Kennedy Memorial Hall, which Fianna Fáil had committed to build in a statement released by An Taoiseach, Seán Lemass, in January 1964. He praised Haughey for the great encouragement he had given 'to those who have the cultural well-being of this country at heart by demonstrating through your enthusiastic championship of the arts that our government really cares about our achievements in this field.'[51] Boydell was also approached by the architect, Raymond McGrath, to use his influence as a member of the Arts Council to exert pressure on his colleagues so that the 'project is not to be mothballed and forgotten'.[52]

'FOLK MUSIC... THE CURSE OF PRESENT DAY COMPOSITION IN IRELAND.'[53]

Undoubtedly, Boydell's greatest contribution to the MAI lies in his efforts to create a musical infrastructure for Irish composers and composition, independent of the prevailing nationalist sentiment and firmly posited in an international context. With eminent composers such as Boydell, Fleischmann and May on the MAI's first council, the plight of the composer, the performance and publication of their works and the creation of an audience for contemporary music was assured strong support for its endeavours. The challenge of expressing a national identity in compositions reflected a dilemma facing many composers in the nineteenth and early twentieth centuries, not only in Ireland but elsewhere in Europe and North America. While a number of Irish composers employed folk idioms in their works, a significant number of European composers captured the character of their native country without employing folk melodies or motifs. MAI council members, such as Boydell and May, had no desire to engage with Irish folk music or idiom and, consequently, the MAI became increasingly focused on promoting contemporary Irish composers with an international rather than a national stylistic outlook. Fleischmann was also conscious of the necessity to locate his compositions firmly in a wider international context but differed significantly from Boydell and May in the use of Irish idioms in compositions. In the case of the MAI it was Boydell's singular vision of contemporary Irish composition (discussed by other authors in this collection) that prevailed. The MAI's search for cultural authenticity was perhaps a little over-ambitious considering the time of its formation and the limited number of composers who could compose in this style. Nonetheless, its efforts prepared the way for the younger generation of Irish composers who embraced international influences and employed the techniques of the avant-garde.

MAI COMPOSERS' GROUP

Early activities of the MAI focused on the establishment of a musical infrastructure for composers, where financial security, artistic freedom and social acceptance could be secured. It wished to unite musical creativity, offer creative and organisational support to composers, promote the work of contemporary composers, encourage the training of young composers, provide opportunities for the performance and publication of contemporary works and generate interest in contemporary Irish music. To this end, the MAI contacted the International Society for Contemporary Music and the Committee for the Promotion of New Music to establish links with international organisations. However, with limited resources the MAI was unable to make meaningful connections with either organisation. Nevertheless, the formation of the CRC in early 1949 heralded a new era for arts policy in Ireland and the beginning of state-funded cultural infrastructure. The MAI benefited from this development and afforded it the opportunity to publish the works of contemporary Irish composers through a joint copying scheme. This scheme was eventually completed in 1953 and it laid the foundations for the establishment of the Composers' Group, which was founded in 1953. Boydell was the first chairman of the Composers' Group with A. J. Potter as chief organiser. The focus of the Group was on the performance, publication and recording of recent works by Irish composers. One of its earliest activities was to arrange four lunchtime concerts in November and December 1954 at the Graduates' Memorial Building, Trinity College Dublin (TCD); the series and compositions performed were praised by audiences and critics alike. Boydell's *Divertimento for Three Music Makers*, String Quartet no. 1 and *Five Joyce Songs* were performed at the final concert in the series on 3 December at which he also played the oboe. The Composers' Group arranged informal concerts and record-listening sessions (from Boydell's private audio collection) at the homes of various members.[54] Such gatherings allowed members to examine each other's work and the works of other contemporary composers free from the unwelcome criticism of 'narrow-minded Irishmen and nationalists, who, like the Germans in the years before the war were blinded by their unbalanced fervour.'[55] Boydell's membership of the Echo Club at Cambridge University, a group that met to listen to gramophone recordings and to discuss various compositions, including their own, undoubtedly influenced this similar gathering.

To create awareness of contemporary Irish compositions at home and abroad, the MAI made representations to An Gúm (Government Publications) to expand its catalogue of Irish composers and also wrote to the Feis Ceoil and An t-Oireachtas suggesting that they submit winning compositions to An Gúm. However, only limited progress was made in this regard. In 1956 the Decca record label (New York) requested the Composers' Group to compile a list of six contemporary Irish compositions for two records under the title *New Music from Old Erin*. The two LPs were recorded by the RÉSO under the baton of the Croatian conductor Milan Horvat and produced by an American, Simon Rady. By all accounts the experience of the recording did not run smoothly, though it did provide members of the RÉSO with an opportunity to earn 'extra money outside their routine contract'.[56] In his memoir Boydell recalled an incident during the recording when Rady accused the clarinettist of providing the orchestra with a flat A during tuning. The clarinettist, Michele Incenzo, replied, 'I have-a a certificate from my *professore* in Napoli: my *clarinetto* plays a perfect 440 A!'[57] Rady, whom Boydell described as a brash individual, responded by sending the wind section home but they returned for the afternoon session 'with their tails between their legs'.[58] The final selection – *Megalithic Ritual Dances* (Boydell), *Music for Strings* (Bodley), *An Sparainín*, *The King's Cave* and *I'll Travel to Mount Nebo* from *Suite of Irish Airs* (May), *Variations on a Popular Tune* (Potter), *Three Pieces for Strings* (T. C. Kelly), *Dirge for Ossian* and *MacAnaty's Reel* (John F. Larchet) and *Irish Suite* (Arthur Duff) – was notable for the prominence of Irish airs and dance tunes reworked into a classical idiom. Notwithstanding the fact that these works were suggested by members of the Composer' Group, this was not the type of music the group wished to promote and the disc was never released in Ireland. It is important to note that the title of the record and the depiction of a traditional thatched cottage from rural Ireland on the record cover 'blatantly' targeted the Irish-American market. Music critic Ian Fox described the sleeve as 'the most awful sleeve ever given to a disc of modern music' but noted that 'the record itself is well worthwhile.'[59] Despite these justifiable criticisms, the recording brought awareness of Irish contemporary music to an international audience, thus fulfilling one of the Composers' Group's objectives.

Boydell resigned as chairman of the Composers' Group in 1966 and was replaced by Seóirse Bodley. 'In many ways, he was a true successor of Boydell and his unique voice in Irish music delivered a long-awaited disengagement from the folk-music trap.'[60] The Composers' Group's most successful activity was the Dublin Festival of Twentieth-Century Music (1969–86) with Bodley as festival director. The festival attempted to provide a broad range of twentieth-century orchestral, chamber and solo music with a particular focus on works by Irish composers, and was supported by leading Irish composers.[61] RTÉ's director of music, Gerard Victory, arranged for the availability of the RÉSO for performances and Boydell arranged for the use of the Examination Hall at TCD as a regular venue. The inaugural festival (5–10 January 1969) was well attended and performances were critically acclaimed. Most importantly, the festival realised the objectives of Boydell and other members of the MAI's Composers' Group in providing a platform for national and international contemporary music and fostering an awareness of contemporary music. The MAI was now the vanguard for contemporary music in Ireland.

On 29 January 1987 the MAI organised a concert to celebrate Boydell's 70th birthday at the John Field Room of the National Concert Hall, Dublin

(NCH). The programme comprised his String Quartet no. 1 (1949) performed by the Degani Quartet, *Five Mosaics* for violin and harp or piano (1972), *Mouth Music* (1974), 'When from My Love' from *The Carlow Cantata* (1984), *Three Geological Glees* (1981) and *The Small Bell* (1980). The concert was recorded by RTÉ. In his review of the concert Michael Dervan commended the String Quartet but was decidedly unimpressed by other performances on the night.[62]

Although Boydell resigned from active involvement in the MAI council and the Composers' Group, he always maintained his links with the organisation and was not shy expressing his dissatisfaction at decisions taken by council members, in particular, the connection with the Training and Employment Authority commonly known as FÁS (An Foras Áiseanna Saothair) in the 1990s. In a letter to Marion Doherty, MAI chair in 1993, Boydell voiced his disappointment at the type and standard of work now being undertaken by the MAI. He complained about the lack of detail in, and poor quality of, the MAI Monthly Diary, highlighting that in its infancy, the MAI had produced superior monthly bulletins with limited finances and basic typing skills. Nonetheless, such observations did not affect Boydell's standing within the organisation, and in 1993 he was made an honorary life member of the MAI.

When the MAI celebrated its golden jubilee in 1998, its chairperson, Eibhlín Ní Chathailriabhaigh, wrote to Boydell seeking advice on how best to honour the occasion. An anniversary dinner was hosted at the Oak Room of the Mansion House and a gala concert was held at the NCH on 10 October 1998, featuring Bernadette Greevy, John O'Conor, the Enchiriadis Treis Choir and Gerard Gillen. Boydell's comments in the programme for the gala concert are particularly noteworthy and capture his pride at what the MAI had achieved to improve art music in Ireland and, in particular, how its initiatives grew into or influenced many of the independent, professional organisations that exist in Irish musical infrastructure today. I would like to conclude with an extract from Boydell's reflections on the pioneering achievements of an organisation that he founded:

> There is no doubt that the most significant achievements in the development and organisation of musical endeavour during the second half of this century have been due to the MAI.
> When I look back over the fifty years during which it has been so enthusiastically active, there is a great feeling of satisfaction and pride at having been one of the founders and, for many years, an active Council Member, of a movement which focused positive endeavour to create so many of those organisations which are responsible today for such a vibrant musical scene in the country.

The country concerts led to Music Network; the Composers' Group led to The Association of Irish Composers and the Contemporary Music Centre; Schools Concerts are still actively organised by the MAI. Many Festivals of Contemporary Music grew out of their biennial Festivals of 20th Century Music; and the existence of the National Concert Hall. . . owes much to the hard work and persuasive lobbying which formed the main thrust of our endeavours for many years.[63]

TWELVE

EVERYONE'S MUSIC: THE RHETORIC OF ADVOCACY IN BRIAN BOYDELL'S EARLY BROADCASTS FOR RTÉ RADIO

Barbara Dignam

We are celebrating fifty years of Irish broadcasting – fifty years during which we have seen the most significant and all-embracing step towards the establishment of mass communication that civilisation has experienced – an enlargement of our means of communication with even broader implications than the invention of printing.[1]

Throughout this current volume and previous publications, Brian Boydell is most often referred to in his capacity as composer, musicologist, performer, teacher, advocate and painter. With the exception of brief mentions in writings by Pine (2005; 2002), Kehoe (2017) and Klein (2004), very little has been documented on Boydell as broadcaster, although, especially during the 1950s and 1960s, it was through his radio broadcasts that he was best known to a wider public.[2] In considering a small, but not insignificant, selection of Boydell's early contributions to radio broadcasting in Ireland, this essay posits that they constitute a composite representation of almost all facets of his extraordinary benefaction to musical and artistic life. In engaging frequently with listeners across the airwaves, Boydell acts as mediator, agitator, promoter, instructor, presenter, entertainer, and above all, musical companion.

Boydell's contribution to radio is immense. Over the course of five decades commencing 1945, he delivered over 1,000 broadcasts ranging from series on assorted topics including composers and their works, instruments, music in Ireland and music history, to concert interval talks, celebratory events and miscellaneous contributions to radio magazines and book review shows.[3] Recordings of some broadcasts are stored in both the Radio Telefís Éireann (RTÉ) archive and the extensive Brian Boydell Archive at Trinity College Dublin (TCD); however this essay focusses solely on select typed and hand-edited typescripts from the TCD collection. These comprise radio scripts produced either for series or one-off programmes at Radio Éireann (RÉ)/ RTÉ including those focused on orchestral instruments or the piano for RÉ's Children's Hour; a weekly discursive piece, 'Topical Notes for Tuesday Review'; a musicological series 'Crossroads in the History of Music'; programmes on composers (Bach, Handel, Haydn, Mozart, Sibelius, etc.); new music from around the world (America, Latin America, Europe) and music festivals; and a variety of music appreciation programmes such as 'Everyone's Music' and 'Collector's Choice'. Also included in the collection are scripts relating to the broadcasts he gave for the BBC and for the CBC in Canada.[4]

The intention here is to allow the typescripts to 'speak for themselves': not only do they serve as valuable historical, cultural and musicological artefacts illustrating cultural developments in the life of the emerging Republic, but they also reveal Boydell's fervent convictions and philosophies about such developments, or lack thereof, explicitly as they related to music in cultural life. The scripts are taken at face value with cognisance of their original context, and so they will not be interrogated for inherent biases such as Boydell's obvious preference for art music or his aversion to 'the plague of light music'.[5] Instead, in highlighting Boydell's rhetoric of advocacy, this essay will celebrate his significant contribution to public awareness and discourse. The utterances on each page do not need to be heard for their meanings to be appreciated, although it may be posited that Boydell's delivery would have further illuminated the text. In exploring the rhetoric embedded across typescripts, this essay will uncover the key messages of advocacy to which Boydell consistently returned, drawing upon idiosyncratic textual content in highlighting his unique mode of communication and the joy that he expressed for listening to music and music-making when advocating for the importance of both. Given the enormity of his contribution, it is not possible also to explore the breath of musical material that he introduced; this text can only serve as an introduction to the topic but it is hoped that it will spark further interest into this less explored facet of Boydell's remarkable life.

RADIO BROADCASTING IN IRELAND AND TALKS ON MUSIC

> Broadcast talks. . . designed to assist the ordinary member of the public in an appreciation of music, are commonplace today; but before the war they were unheard of in the programmes of RÉ.[6]

In the early 1940s, as Boydell notes above, broadcast talks dedicated to music appreciation and aimed at the general public in Ireland were non-existent. Listening to the BBC series 'Music for the Ordinary Listener' most often presented by Walford Davies sparked his interest in creating a similar series for RÉ.[7] He later recalled having to persuade the then director of music Captain Michael Bowles of the advantages of offering RÉ listeners something similar.[8] Bowles eventually agreed and Boydell was engaged for a four-part experimental series, 'Everyone's Music', commencing 6 June 1945 at 7 p.m.[9] Interestingly, Boydell also felt compelled to argue against the proposed title for the series, 'Music for the Amateur', as he explains in the opening segment of the programme:

> EVERYONE is potentially an amateur musician... the [a]rt of listening to music... is just as important as the art of playing an instrument, and needs just as much cultivation... I didn't want to address these talks to amateur instrumentalists (which is what the title might have suggested).[10]

Such comments illustrate that from the outset, Boydell was intent on reaching a broader cohort of everyday listeners in order to 'sow the seeds of consciousness' rather than solely conversing with those regularly participating in music practices, although as it will become clear, he also strongly advocated for the importance of engaging in amateur music-making.[11] Boydell envisioned 'Everyone's Music' as a set of four arguments, scripting it in the form of a 'two-hander' play to resemble an ongoing dialogue with 'a casual member of the public' (played by his friend Thurloe Conolly) who bursts into the radio station with the explicit intention of challenging Boydell's 'rather stuffy academic manner' and pulling him down from his 'unassailable position as the preacher [on] the pulpit'.[12] However, as Boydell reminisces, this 'dramatically arresting beginning' didn't quite go to plan thanks to the dutiful Garda stationed outside the GPO who blocked Conolly's passage thereby forcing Boydell to improvise an entirely different script.[13] Handwritten and typed notes attached to the subsequent programme's typescript illustrate that he reused this material during the second 'argument', and although never broadcast as intended, the text of 'Everyone's Music No. 1' still serves as an important commencement for an illustrative discussion of Boydell's rhetoric. It is also an initial example of the entertaining manner in which he attempted to entice his audience to 'plunge into a new field of enjoyment'.[14] More on this later.

While music contributed significantly to RÉ's output schedule, Boydell became the first broadcaster to produce comprehensive programmes that intended to unlock the elements and structures of musical works for the purpose of experiencing 'one of the greatest pleasures in the art of living'.[15] Indeed, by the time he was well-established on the wireless in the 1950s, the country was experiencing what O'Neill has called 'the indisputable golden age of Irish radio', where most households owned a radio set whether or not, as Boydell frequently quips, they had purchased the appropriate licence.[16]

DOING THE SCRIPT

Similar to his diaries or correspondences, Boydell's broadcast typescripts constitute standalone cultural documents; further, they exemplify the professionalism with which he prepared for each broadcast, the importance he placed on crafting purposeful messages, and the musical illustrations he selected to present. It is clear from the precise layout of the scripts that they were not intended as guideline notes, although one can speculate that ad-libbing occurred from time to time. Boydell systematically prepared his scripts and rehearsed them in advance: as his son Barra recollects, the 'noun "script", so often uttered, took on quite a significant meaning in my early life!'[17] It seems that Boydell was unique in this regard, as in 'those early days of broadcasting nobody bothered much about the necessity of providing a typescript before the broadcast (which of course was always "live").'[18] Where needed, edits were usually made by hand and included directions on reading pace ('not too leisurely', 'with fairly fast reading'), timings of musical extracts and spoken text, the band and side of records for ease of operation, notated melodic and rhythmic content to play, sing or clap, etc. All scripts are identifiable from their detailed titles (broadcast, series, date, time) with later scripts becoming more sophisticated due to the insertion of broadcast numbers and red ink for highlighting.

THE RADIO VOICE AND VOICING ON THE RADIO

The rhetoric of advocacy in Boydell's typescripts is twofold, illustrated through emotive expressions, declarative statements, and visual analogies: on the one hand, his language clearly sets out to agitate his audience with the explicit intention of declaring his concerns about music and musical life in Ireland; on the other, he endeavours to educate and advise in the hope of engaging and enticing the listener. These approaches frequently cross paths. The tone of his rhetoric differs depending on audience, topic, programme type and the corresponding role that Boydell plays in the process, be that educator, agitator, narrator or informer. He purposefully exploits the power and immediacy of radio in communicating with the mass public, at the same time speaking to discrete listeners, initiating a personal relationship and offering them opportunities for individual agency and growth.

The focal theme underpinning his advocacy across all typescripts is his fervent belief in the criticality and value of music appreciation, what he calls intelligent listening for the obtainment of a richer, 'fully-lived life'.[19] Stemming from this is his contention that engaging with amateur music-making, group-singing and chamber music concerts is of vital importance in establishing sustainable cultural norms within one's local community, consequently impacting the developing cultural character of the nation.[20] He argues for a nationwide adjustment in attitudes and cultural behaviours, adamant that music education policy needs explicit reform and he attributes collective responsibility to those in educational roles to foster the next generation of concert-goers and performers. Coupled with this, he advocates for the provision of adequate supports and structures for those involved in building a fully-functioning national music identity ready to situate itself within the wider European cultural context. Such arguments consistently appear across his broadcasts in different guises, framed most often as issues to which he offers solutions and, depending on the context of the broadcast, he pragmatically engages in translating these ideas into practice through dialogue and activity.

The central tenets of his arguments align with the sentiments and aims of the Music Association of Ireland (although often pre-dating the MAI), however the fundamental difference is the immediacy of delivery. Boydell could speak uninterrupted, openly and directly to his audience. As Adorno notes, 'the listener has the impression that in a way he is present at the broadcasting event. There is no gap between the time in which something is happening and the time in which one is listening to it'.[21] Boydell's arguments are complexly interwoven and symbiotically shape his rhetoric, which make them equally enlightening and problematic to explore. What follows is a selection of prevalent examples extracted from series or one-off broadcasts dating from 1945 through 1955 (with a few exceptions) and with particular emphasis placed on his 'Topical Notes for Tuesday Review'. Nowhere was Boydell's advocacy more prolifically and pointedly articulated than in this series that provides his most colourful use of rhetoric. Over the course of 97 broadcasts between 27 June 1950 and 30 December 1952, Boydell lays out his personal and professional positions on all matters musical in Ireland, from the epistemological to the concrete.[22]

NOT YET A MUSICAL NATION

[T]he cultural assets of a country are those by which it is in the long run assessed.[23]

Underpinning much of Boydell's discourse around musical life in Ireland is his advocating for the attainment of a more cultured nation – particularly in the 1940s and 1950s when Ireland was still an emerging country:

> The cultural attainments of a country, which I believe (rightly or wrongly) to be ultimately the most important, are measured not only by the quality of the creative

work produced by its artists, but also by the general level of appreciation of the arts amongst the ordinary people. We in Ireland have a very long way to go before we reach the standard of – say, pre-war Germany, where the great composers were considered to be figures of rather greater importance than film stars and race horses. . . a task which will have to be begun in the schools – but everything which encourages the appreciation of music, helps to raise the cultural standard of the country.[24]

Boydell speculates that Ireland needs to become less insular in order to carve out its distinctive cultural place within Europe, asserting that the responsibility for creating a more 'musically cultivated community' and engendering a modern cultural identity should rest with local government, the newly-formed Arts Council and educational authorities, but that such bodies should realise that 'Music DOES NOT PAY FOR ITSELF in. . . shillings and pence, but in spiritual terms.'[25] Drawing on the position of the MAI, he lists all that is required to support this development including a national concert hall – noting that Dublin was the only European capital without one – appropriate spaces for performances across the country, a professional symphony orchestra outside of RÉ to entice international performers to come to Ireland, a national conservatoire to train younger musicians for professional life and the publication of more musicological works, which he contends is the duty of universities. Knowing that this list alone may not entice any movement, especially from those he sees as suffering from cynicism 'arising from a mood of detachment', he pits the current state of Ireland's cultural supports against several European counterparts, quoting figures from Fleischmann's article in *The Bell* on the future of music.[26]

He later reflects on the apparent prejudices of certain cohorts of society whose intolerance threatens 'the healthy development of the musical consciousness which is awakening',[27] and warns that every precaution must be taken so that musical development is 'not stunted', criticising the 'general apathy of the press towards the art of music', many of whom in his opinion are in denial of the existence of musical activity in Ireland, instead giving over substantial column space to 'events in London'.[28] He is particularly aggrieved with the *Irish Times* 'Review of the Year' 1950:

> I don't think we quite deserve to be publicised abroad as a country in which no music takes place at all. . . Complete pages are given over to the theatre, the plastic arts, broadcasting and every other kind of activity; but no mention what[so]ever is made of the art of music. . . I do think it disgraceful that such a biased account of our artistic achievements and activities should be so widely publicised. . . could it be perhaps that the editor dislikes music or musicians – or both?[29]

MUSIC APPRECIATION AND THE FATAL DISEASE OF DISILLUSIONMENT

> The main object of these talks is to banish the prevalent idea that good music is a luxury for people of superior intelligence.[30]

From early on, Boydell was adamant that the public should 'take the necessary step up' to become intelligent listeners who 'understand its language'.[31] The aptly titled 'Everyone's Music' (1945) sets the scene for Boydell's championing of the value and benefit of appreciating 'good music', which he defines as 'some universal or emotional concept, experienced by the composer and expressed by him through the medium of sound.'[32] He purposefully confines his definition 'to the CONSCIOUS expression of HUMAN beings' to steer his listeners towards 'the emotional beauty of ORGANISED sound' rather than noises emanating from singing telegraph wires.[33] Both his choice of words and their capitalisation point to his explicit intention to focus on human consciousness in articulating not only the beauty behind the music he has selected for the series, but also in stressing a need for the development of a greater public awareness of art music alongside a capacity for listening to and communicating about music more perceptively:

> The Appreciation of music, or art of some kind, is something without which we cannot claim to be anything more than animals; for perhaps the most important attribute of human beings is their ability for the expression and appreciation of what we call Art.[34]

He later posits that an intelligent listening public would be more positively disposed towards supporting live concerts, thereby treating what he contends as the 'fatal disease of disillusionment' that had infected the spirits of organisers, professional promoters and amateur societies.[35] Understanding his privileged position on the wireless, Boydell sets out to aid the treatment of this malady through giving voice to these entities in promoting events and advocating for increased audience participation, as well as educating current and future audiences about the works to be performed.

He remarks in 'Everyone's Music No. 1' that the rising popularity of the Dublin symphony concerts series was signalling, at least within the capital, a societal shift away from predominant notions that classical music was beyond the grasp of every citizen. In the knowledge that he was speaking to the public *en masse*, he quickly notes that such concerts could not possibly 'answer the arguments of those who would like to appreciate good music, and find a lack of knowledge and understanding in their way'.[36] It is this shortfall that Boydell attempts to address in these programmes, consistently framing his arguments in terms of active participation in music appreciation – 'It is no good just HEARING music passively, you must ACTIVELY listen to it' – and within the contexts of the benefit to well-being that listening intelligently will bring to the everyday lives of ordinary listeners and the life of the country. He sees listening as the first step to future participation in music-making and concert-going, and he offers to act as guide, educator and translator; but it is the manner in which he interacts with his audience that is most striking.

He outlines three types of listener to whom he will direct his arguments over the course of the series. So that Boydell may speak appropriately to each, they are embodied within Thurloe Conolly's scripted questions, opinions and declarative statements, to which Boydell may directly challenge their antagonism, apathy or misunderstandings. The first, and least problematic, listener might be termed a nervous novice who has 'been wondering for a long time whether they would brave a symphony concert', and who Boydell feels 'just need[s] a little push' from his mediating hand.[37] A little more difficult to argue with is the prejudicial 'poseur', the 'stick-in-the-mud' who insists that they '"know what they like" and feel that musicians are trying to force a nasty medicine down their throats'.[38] This listener is content to consistently consume a sonic meal of 'stagnant slime' owing to their fear 'of meeting something new which they don't understand' and Boydell cleverly employs the analogy of old ladies who still shake their umbrellas at motor cars because they are afraid of change and development; the world they are familiar with has been disturbed. Boydell wants to disrupt their listening behaviour further in the hope of transfiguring this medicine into something more palatable so they might share his enjoyment of music.

The final, and possibly most troublesome, listener is the one suffering from outright apathy, a member of the 'lazy public' who buys into the 'all-too-popular idea that music is a pleasant [and] soothing background for sausages and mash'.[39] Upon Conolly's suggestion that music is a relaxation, Boydell exclaims:

> O horrible heresy! That is an attitude which makes me weep!...If you are content to sit back and let the superficial sound of music titillate your senses, you are nothing more than an automatic machine... Turning on the wireless during tea-time conversation is not listening to music; even if you do stop now and then and say "That's a lovely little bit"... you have to <u>listen intently</u> to hear the detail and the dramatic development of a piece.[40]

All three listening personalities appear in altered states throughout Boydell's broadcasts like recurring musical themes punctuating his narrative and, in attempting to convince them of the benefit of alternatives to their current behaviours, Boydell consistently returns to real-world analogies and relatable musical materials. When addressing the novice for example, who is unsure about 'all this form and fugue business', seeing it as overly-academic and unnecessarily distractive, Boydell argues to the contrary that form exists in all things in the universe and that a Bach fugue, such as the final movement of his Brandenburg Concerto No. 4 in G major, can just as easily be understood and appreciated as a well-known round like 'Three Blind Mice', but only when one learns how to analyse the signposts in the music subconsciously, 'to recognise [the] landmarks which announce a period of contrast' in the same manner that we can naturally distinguish night from day, season from season and the different elements of a meal.[41] Such signposts to both contrast and repetition, he argues, provide 'something to hang on to' thereby allowing us to 'appreciate the movement as a large-scale dramatic design', after which we can 'FORGET all about the dry academic aspect of it'.[42]

In delineating the sonata structure of Mozart's Symphony No. 40 in G minor, Boydell employs the analogy of a dramatic play. He anthropomorphises the first and second subjects as characters, giving us the opportunity to familiarise ourselves with the essential elements of their identities, the rhythmic ideas and melodic content inherent to each theme. Humour ensues when Conolly suggests that these characters are akin to Shakespeare's Macbeth and Banquo, to which Boydell retorts that unfortunately 'in the next section Banquo, our "second subject" is murdered – and we can't afford to lose him as far as a symphony is concerned!'[43] This analogy becomes Boydell's 'tried and tested' means for explaining Sonata Form and he returns to it in other broadcasts such as 'Symphonic Music for the Young Listener', during which he attempts to entice young novice listeners to explore Beethoven's 7th Symphony, 'the 1st symphony that I ever got to know', employing the metaphor of nature to illustrate melody, timbre and form respectively:[44]

> With the radio and the gramophone, music is today part of our everyday surroundings, and its sound could be nearly as familiar to us as the song of the birds, or the colour and shape of the hills.[45]

His use of relatable language illustrates his consciousness around speaking appropriately to his different audiences to ensure musical elements are more easily remembered.

CHAMBER MUSIC CONCERTS, AMATEUR MUSIC-MAKING, AND THE 'CULT OF THE VIRTUOSO'

> As the crowd gaped in wonder. . . it began to forget that music was a form of artistic expression [that] should be part of everyone's <u>personal</u> experience. . . The time has come now, I think, when the pendulum is due to swing the other way – though we will all have to <u>do</u> something about reversing its direction.[46]

For Boydell, chamber music is 'one of the highest forms of the art, since music is found here in its purest form' and his philosophy of ensemble playing centres on developing one's 'spirit of cooperation and give-and-take. . . essential to life itself'.[47] He sees the 'musical health of a community' as measured solely 'by the activity and vitality of the ordinary amateurs who scrape away in quartets or in amateur choral orchestral societies', and not by 'those who must make music day after day'.[48] The rhetoric in Boydell's early broadcasts relating to chamber music or amateur music-making in Ireland tends to pendulate between agitation by what he sees as a lack of willingness by the public to either attend chamber music concerts or participate in 'subjugating their personalities in the service of [amateur] music-making', to elation from learning on his travels around the country giving talks and corresponding with radio listeners, that there was in fact quite a lot happening particularly in communities outside the capital.[49]

Such discussions become a regular feature in his 'Topical Notes'. He also dedicates an entire one-off broadcast, 'The Amateur in Music', to the topic where he argues that a tumultuous shift in perspective has occurred over several centuries since 1600, from the expansion of musical language and techniques bringing with it a move away from the collective towards the individual, to the introduction of 'canned music', i.e. gramophone records, and having 'great masterpieces. . . ready to hand on the wireless. . . available with the turn of a knob'.[50] He charts this 'distortion of a natural musical development', most notably referencing Paganini and reciting the tale of his standing atop a piano in Dublin so that 'the gentleman who had walked from Sligo to witness the event could <u>see</u> the incredible things he was doing.'[51] The underlining of 'see' signals Boydell's disapproval of privileging visual spectacle over auditory beauty. His main gripe with Paganini is the undeniable, and in Boydell's opinion destructive and long-lasting, influence that he had on the art of performance, reducing it to:

> the circus ring, where it was degraded before a gawking public, who were only too easily persuaded that it was a sign of inspired musicianship to be able to execute

extravagant technical acrobatics on an instrument which has no more connection with music than a clown playing a trombone on a one-wheeled bicycle.[52]

This trope of the acrobatic specialist musician whose sole purpose is to entertain rather than enlighten is littered throughout this broadcast and in 'Topical Notes', thus illustrating Boydell's utter distaste for the superfluous display of pyrotechnics by professional musicians solely for the purpose of entertaining popular taste.[53] Ultimately, he hypothesises, this 'cult of the virtuoso' has impacted the 'ordinary educated person today [who] derives far less enjoyment from music than he could do',[54] perpetuating a consumerist approach to music and a lazy climate of listening 'too much and too carelessly', ironically asserting that:

> Today we have a superficial acquaintance with a repertoire so vast that few can assimilate it. . . I am quite sure that our forebearers extracted more ultimate enjoyment from the art than the knob-twiddlers of today. . . the wireless and the gramophone are in fact a mixed blessing. If a prize is too easy to win, we fail to appreciate its true worth.[55]

Another contemporary issue he addresses is what he sees as the growth of 'celebrity concerts' particularly in the capital, where 'the purely musical interest is. . . sacrificed for celebrity glamour.'[56] He concocts a whimsical and witty story for his final 'Tuesday Review' of 1950, a colourfully caustic tale of the Marquis and Marchioness of Stepaside and their 'charming young family of debutantes' who frequently occupy the front row of the opera circle 'to worship at the shrines of Bellini, Rossini, Puccini, Piccini, Respighi, Paganini, Lily, Killarni and Mimi':

> The Lady Sophie had draped a bassoon-blue shawl of Traviata taffeta over her bare white shoulder, with a daintily executed semibreve embroidered in chromatic style nestling beside her heart; symbolising the falling phrases of Isolde's love-death. The Lady Norma is more classically-minded, and was adorned with a ternary chemise of Mozart-mauve, set off by a rich white sash which had been trimmed with falling sequences made to resemble dainty staccato semiquavers. Her eldest sister. . . enrobed herself accordingly in Brahms-brown flannelette towel-cloth, on which had been sewn a florid Borodin bustle. . . Their mother [wore] nine yards of Wagnerian velvet. . . The marquis himself. . . looked strikingly dignified in [a] giraffe-skin waistcoat. . . Paganini pink will be the colour for 1951 – You mark my words![57]

In contrast, Boydell regularly reports on the flourishing of amateur music-making – a string quartet in Galway, brass band, amateur orchestra and light opera society in Tipperary, another amateur orchestra in Cloughjordan, and a music-listening club in Waterford for example – and makes particular mention of the educational and advocacy approach of the Dublin Orchestral Players (DOP), of which he was conductor from 1943 to 1966:

> The orchestra fulfils several aims which are vital to the future of music here. . . young instrumentalists can obtain that experience of playing in the body of an orchestra. . . portions of the rehearsals are given over to students who wish to gain experience in conducting an orchestra. . .[58]

He also endorses a new periodical called *Music World* (established 1951), which attempts to reach not only professional musicians but also the amateur, promoting James Plunkett's article 'Playing for Pleasure' as an appeal to the ordinary person to make music at home.[59] Singling out the chamber concert series presented by the violinist Francois d'Albert at the Hibernian Hotel, Boydell hopes that this 'truly gargantuan series' will be supported by Dublin audiences as 'it would be a shame to shatter [d'Albert's] energetic idealism' given that he had not been in Dublin long enough to catch the 'fatal disease of disillusionment' mentioned earlier.[60] He also commends d'Albert's 'courageous step' in asking audiences to come for the music and not the performers, professing that 'it is for this reason that I take a very poor view of any concerts which do not advertise the programme.'[61] Despite this positivity, Boydell becomes increasingly concerned with the fate of the amateur musician in Ireland and with locating an appropriate venue for chamber music in the city.[62] In a latter-year interview ('In my time', 1981) he suggests that the standard of performance was becoming so high that it was 'edging out amateur enthusiasm'.[63] He urges all musicians to:

> recognise the tremendous importance of doing everything possible to nurture the small, though healthy glow of enthusiasm for music making in the home: an enthusiasm which is still afire despite the fire-hoses of radio, gramophone and pre-digested entertainment which can be turned onto this smouldering fire in every home today.[64]

He beseeches the everyday listener to make an effort to move beyond the 'vulgarity and effects' of opera and symphony concerts, asking: 'isn't some effort needed in order to attain real enjoyment in all things?'[65] Taking a pragmatic approach, he requests that his listeners encourage children to take up an instrument as 'the very best training for the enjoyment of music as an intelligent listener'.[66] This echoes his message in 'Pianoforte Music for the Young Student' where he advises young musicians to immerse themselves in good music rather than 'meaningless finger exercises of frusty old teachers who have nothing to say', reiterating that 'music is first and foremost a MEANS OF EXPRESSION – a way of telling a story. . . not merely an accomplishment, like learning to be an acrobat or a conjurer.'[67] Boydell's sentiment perhaps reflects his experiences as a young pianist at Cambridge where the 'very stiff training of the Solomon School' broke his spirit to the point that he lost his nerve, ceased playing in public and eventually gave up on the piano as a 'virtuoso instrument'.[68]

Boydell attests that not all people who once studied singing or who have an interest in playing with others are confident or skilled enough to enter Feiseanna or perform in public; he also recognises the difficulty in bringing people together and provides the following suggestion:

> Wouldn't it be a great idea if there were some way of bringing musicians such as these together? – such as, perhaps, a central list on which would appear the names and addresses of those who wish to meet others with a view to making music.[69]

His proposal bears fruit and in less than three weeks, he announces that:

> Messrs. McCullough's have very kindly agreed to keep a book in their premises for this purpose. . . it is hoped to expand the idea into some kind of a club for the practice of amateur chamber music.[70]

A DRASTIC REVOLUTION

> The most fruitful place in which to sow the seeds of this consciousness is of course in the minds of young people. . . our concert audiences of the future are now the children in the junior schools.[71]

Boydell is adamant that the lack of an appropriate and sustainable musical education is a fundamental barrier to 'establishing a musical tradition in the nation' and by not fostering in our young people an interest in playing music and listening intelligently, we are damning ourselves for the future.[72] He even postulates that 'we should be ashamed of ourselves.'[73] In arguing for the effective development of a cultured society, he challenges the traditional views of educational authorities and their policies, requesting that they 'throw off that damp and all-too-comfortable cloak of relying for our honour and glory on what happened many hundreds of years ago'.[74] Instead, he calls for 'a drastic revolution' in which 'every child in every school should be made aware of the beauties of music.'[75] In this regard he echoes Larchet's call in 1927 for every school to own a 'cheap gramophone. . . as an aid to the collective development of musical skill, taste and culture'.[76] He criticises primary-level educators for doing 'very little to indicate to the coming generation that such a thing as music exists' let alone 'educate their pupils in the nature and meaning of music itself' and launches a particularly scathing attack on schools of music that he contends show little regard for maintaining high standards of valuable repertoire, instead programming student concerts 'filled with items such as "Violin solo by Dorabella Jenkins" and "Group of songs sung in Welsh by somebody else"'.[77] To his mind, this will breed yet another generation of prejudicial posers and apathetic audiences.

Boydell's role in driving this revolution is a didactic one: he engages directly with young audiences through his dedicated broadcasts during 'Children's Hour' and his involvement with the now well-documented RÉ Schools Concerts, providing regular updates on such in his 'Topical Notes', eager to roll out this series to all schools in Dublin:

> I have had the great pleasure of taking charge of two of these concerts, and I was very struck by the obvious enjoyment and attentiveness of the young audience. I am quite sure that these concerts will have a most healthy influence on the future musical life of the country.[78]

For Boydell, the benefit of interacting with young listeners lies in their inherent openness, their 'complete lack of prejudice' not having heard a sufficient volume of music 'to have formed a fixed opinion of what music <u>ought</u> to sound like'.[79] This absence of preconceived notions, he explains, triggered an unexpected reaction in schoolchildren in Carlow to the performance of a movement from Bartók's Third String Quartet where the children were visibly moved, enthusiastically applauding the 'strange, and possibly incomprehensible modern sounds'.[80] Drawing on this attitude, Boydell attempts in his 'Music For All' series to persuade his young listeners 'not to generalise too rashly about music which [they] have not thoroughly explored'.[81] Later, in 'Music and Communication', he implores all listeners to practice equality of judgement; that is, not to evaluate a Mozart symphony against a folksong or consider one form of music like extemporised jazz as being a more valid musical expression than classical music.[82] He is particularly keen to foster a sense of enjoyment and fun for those learning music and informs the young piano student of the benefits of 'playing duets [to] teach yourself better than any other way, to read music'.[83]

An excellent example of his use of effective storytelling and word play occurs in his 'Symphonic Music for the Young Listener':

> This symphony of Beethoven's is often played on the wireless – and so we can compare it to a plantation of trees which a boy I know used to pass by on his frequent journeys to visit a friend in a neighbouring village.[84]

The boy is representative of the general listener who has not yet learned to engage with music in depth. Boydell tells the listener that the boy passed by without ever noticing the details inside the wood all 'because he had never learned to use his eyes' until the tree-creeper birds were pointed out to him by a man who 'loved the countryside [and] knew the ways of birds and wild animals' and then the more he began to do so, the more he learned to explore for himself.[85] The 'man' is clearly Boydell, who is ready to be the listener's guide and teacher:

> Well I am going to bring you inside the symphony, which you may so often have passed by, and I will show you some of the interesting things inside it which you may never have looked for. . . the boy in the wood learned to use his eyes, and he began to make discoveries for himself. I will try to help you to use your ears so that you too will make your own discoveries in this, and many other symphonies.[86]

A REVELATION OF BEAUTY?

Since its establishment, RÉ/RTÉ has presented itself as the foremost public service broadcaster in Ireland.[87] In engaging people in dialogue around music – Irish and international art music in particular – and around other arts and cultural life in Ireland, Boydell fulfilled this function by offering his unique 'services' to the general public via his broadcasts. In this way, it may even be argued that he was practicing what is now understood as 'public' musicology.[88]

Broadcasting provided the ideal mechanism for Boydell's advocacy in promoting the value and importance of music appreciation, addressing ongoing issues around engagement including amateur music-making and national music education policy, broadening listeners' awareness of the breadth of music in existence that they may otherwise have been precluded from experiencing, and sharing his enthusiasm for communicating about music and the joy he expressed as emanating from this 'revelation of beauty'.[89] Could it be argued that Boydell, a Renaissance man and an unwavering advocate for music for all in Ireland, was himself the revelation of beauty? It seems fitting to leave the last word to Boydell:

I leave you with one last thought. . . I was talking once with a young Italian composer who writes very advanced music which is far beyond my own comprehension. When I spoke of my own desire as a composer to communicate and give pleasure to a reasonably large proportion of the musical public, he shrugged his shoulders and said: 'Evidently you in Ireland still believe that life is worth living'. . . but so much great music can entertain <u>and</u> bring enlightenment at the same time – perhaps almost secretly: for who can deny that being in the presence of greatness or beauty does something to us which few can put into words?[90]

THIRTEEN

RACING DEMONS: BRIAN BOYDELL AS PAINTER

Peter Murray

When Anne Crookshank was appointed to the newly established position of professor of art history at Trinity College Dublin (TCD) in 1966, she found a university rich in eighteenth-century portraits of clerics and professors, but with little in the way of twentieth-century art. Crookshank set about remedying this, forming a 'Committee of Taste' that included, at various times, geographer professor Joe Haughton, historian Jocelyn Otway Ruthven and professor of genetics George Dawson. A leading member of this committee was Brian Boydell, who had been appointed professor of music in 1962. An energetic advocate of the Modernist movement, Boydell's recognition of the need for TCD to engage with new art forms stemmed in no little way from his own early work as a painter, before he decided to devote his life to music.

During Boydell's time at TCD, the College, under the leadership of George Dawson, commissioned architects Ahrens Burton and Koralek to design a new arts building, and at the same time began to build up a fine art collection that included sculptures by Henry Moore, Alexander Calder and Pomodoro, and prints by Picasso, Matisse and Rouault. This group of outward-looking, friendly and enthusiastic academics characterised Trinity in the 1970s, as the College itself became a more socially-inclusive institution. Dawson's rooms in 'The Rubrics', a red-brick terrace within the College, were enlivened with African sculpture, while the new dining hall contained prints by William Scott and others. Crookshank's maxim for teaching was that lecturers should not bore their students, and this certainly also held true for Boydell in the music department. While Kitson's rules on harmony were still widely considered standard teaching aids at the time, Boydell abhorred Kitson's approach to the teaching of harmony and admitted to preferring rules imposed by his own ears.

Born in Dublin in 1917, Brian Boydell is best known today as a composer of tonal music for orchestra, chamber music including string quartets, and compositions for harp and voice. Appointed professor of singing at the Royal

Irish Academy of Music in 1944, a post he held for eight years, he was afterwards professor of music at TCD, until his retirement in 1982. In 1959 he founded the Dowland Consort, and he also conducted the Dublin Orchestral Players. A prolific broadcaster and writer, his energies and personal charm won him many friends. Even when bewildered by the contemporary nature of his musical compositions, critics and audiences, with a few exceptions, accorded him respect and recognition. His creative output however was far from fanciful, and today Boydell is regarded as one of Ireland's leading composers of the twentieth century. It is worth recalling that in the early 1940s he was also a talented artist, producing paintings and drawings inspired by Surrealism.

On the outbreak of World War II in 1939, Boydell was obliged to abandon his studies at the Royal College of Music and return to Dublin. Although he briefly joined his father's maltings business, working in the research laboratory, he left soon after to become a painter and composer, supporting himself by working part-time as an art and science teacher at St Columba's College and taking his Bachelor of Music degree at TCD. Culturally, these were interesting years in Ireland. During the 1930s the government had pursued an increasingly isolationist and xenophobic policy, culminating in Ireland's neutrality in the Second World War, a period known as The Emergency. From 1939 onwards however, there was an upsurge of interest in the visual arts, due not least to the policy of neutrality, which attracted refugees from the continent, including creative talents, conscientious objectors and others opposed to the war. Up to 1940 progressive art in Ireland had been moderate in character rather than radical, and was largely led by women artists, many of whom were members of the Society of Dublin Painters, founded some 20 years earlier. Exhibiting the work of Mainie Jellett, Paul Henry, Stella Frost, Mary Swanzy, Hilda Roberts, Lilian Davidson and others, the Dublin Painters gallery promoted Modernist art in Ireland.

Although the Modernist styles adopted by these artists were not particularly revolutionary, they were nonetheless marginalised from the mainstream Royal Hibernian Academy (RHA), dominated as it was by male artists, notably Maurice MacGonigal, James Sleator and Seán Keating. Greeting the experimental art styles of the Dublin Painters with indifference or disdain, the academicians saw themselves as 'professional', and regarded their female counterparts as semi-professional or amateur. Such discrimination was not confined to Ireland: in Paris, up to 1897, women were not admitted as students to the École des Beaux Arts; women were obliged therefore to study in private schools, such as Académie Julian. By the 1920s there were many independent academies in Paris, and when Mainie Jellett and Evie Hone travelled there to pursue their art studies, they enrolled in the studio of André Lhote. In a treatise on landscape painting, Lhote summarised his theories:

> Contrary to the belief of the layman, the essential of art is not to imitate nature, but *under the guise of imitation* to stir up excitement with pure plastic elements: measurements, directions, ornaments, lights, values, colours, substances, divided and organized according to the injunctions of natural laws. While so occupied, the artist never ceases to be subservient to nature, but instead of imitating the incidents in a paltry way, he *imitates the laws*.[1]

He went on to describe how

> Minds trained in the study of natural forms. . . know that natural plastic manifestations: whirlwinds and waterspouts, shell or plant structure, etc., contain in them the most felicitous proportion of those exciting and reassuring elements . . . It was by no means an unreasonable thing on the part of the moderns to listen to the teaching of the Africans and Polynesians.[2]

After studying with André Lhote, Jellett and Hone went on to become the pupils of Albert Gleizes, whose style of Synthetic Cubism was based on a codification of Lhote's principles. Such precepts, absorbed by Boydell through his studying with Jellett after her return to Ireland, were to inform his early paintings, which are characterised by stylised abstractions, based on natural forms. As well as being a founder member of Abstraction-Création, Jellett exhibited in the Salon des Indepéndents and the 1925 exhibition 'L'Art d'Aujourd'hui'. She and Evie Hone showed their Cubist paintings in Dublin in 1924 to a generally hostile reception. The extent to which Boydell studied under Jellett is not recorded; he and his wife Mary were also collectors of her work: in October 2017, Adam's auctioneers sold *Western Landscape Study*, a Cubist work by Jellett dating from 1940, which came from the Boydell's collection. The cultural milieu within which Boydell moved included not only the Cubism of Jellett and Hone, but also the avant-garde choreography of Erina Brady. During these years, the influence of British progressive artists such as Victor Pasmore and Barbara Hepworth was introduced to Ireland by Norah McGuinness, a member of Lucy Wertheim's London Group before her return to Ireland in 1939. Among the refugees who settled in Ireland were several progressive British and European artists who formed themselves into the White Stag Group. Working in this relatively safe haven, they held several exhibitions in Dublin. However, apart from launching the career of just one progressive Irish artist, Patrick Scott, their presence does not seem to have had a lasting effect. While not a member, Boydell was associated with the White Stag Group, but his decision to abandon painting in favour of music marked the end of that thread of artistic influence.

In 1942 the RHA's rejection of *A Spanish Shawl*, a moderately avant-garde painting by Louis le Brocquy, led to a public debate about official opposition to new forms of art. Inspired by the vibrancy of the White Stag exhibitions, in 1943 a group of artists, led by Melanie le Brocquy, Norah McGuinness and Mainie Jellett, founded the Irish Exhibition of Living Art (IELA). Held at the National College of Art in Dublin in September of that year, the first IELA exhibition included nearly 200 works of art. Owing to the destruction of their original premises on Middle Abbey Street in 1916, at this time the annual exhibitions of the RHA were also held in the College of Art, in Kildare Street. Presumably Maurice MacGonigal must have been tacitly supportive of this initiative, as he was professor of painting at the College at this time. Seán Keating participated in the first IELA exhibition, his *Tip Wagons at Poulaphouca* (Collection ESB) receiving critical praise. The IELA, of which Norah McGuinness was to remain chairperson until 1972, demonstrated that there were many artists working in Ireland outside of an academic-realist tradition. The initial exhibitions included works by Ralph Cusack, Nano Reid, Patrick Scott and Gerard Dillon, the Fauvist inspiration of Norah McGuinness, the Cubist styles of Doreen Vanston and Mainie Jellett, the Surrealism of Colin Middleton and Nick Nicholls.[3] Sales at the IELA inaugural exhibition were surprisingly brisk; as the war progressed, people found they had little opportunity to spend money on imported goods, and so were pleased to buy paintings and sculptures instead. Commenting on the Society of Dublin Painters and the IELA, the critic Brian O'Doherty wrote:

> All this took place outside the official Dublin art world, represented by the pleasant body of men who make up the Royal Hibernian Academy. The Academy controlled. . . the National College of Art, where the teaching was and is, splendidly irrelevant to its students' needs. The floating complex of dealers (Waddington was joined by the Dawson Gallery in 1944 and by the Hendriks Gallery in 1956), artists and collectors thus had no access to the institutions. . . Jellett's failure to give Irish art a firm cubist underpinning (apart from the work of Nano Reid) is easily understood. A suggestive form of painting with a particular atmospheric complexion, a product of the interaction of the artists and the audience created by and for their art in the forties and fifties, gathered force.[4]

Brilliant academically, Brian Boydell was also an individualist. Part of a group of students, artists and musicians, whose Bohemian lives intertwined and overlapped in the Georgian houses around Baggot Street and Merrion

Square, in the 1940s he threw himself into projects with characteristic enthusiasm and often a disregard for personal safety. During World War II, when petrol was rationed, he used his scientific skills to convert his Sunbeam car to run on wood gas, attaching a charcoal burner to the back of the vehicle. The sight of a bearded Boydell, racing through the empty Dublin streets in this exotic machine, belching smoke, inevitably attracted the attention of the authorities, who assumed that, not least because of his eclectic circle of friends, he was somehow involved in international espionage and intrigue. In fact Boydell was studying and working hard, but also enjoying life in a Dublin that had suddenly become culturally diverse and cosmopolitan. His friends at this time included medical students Tony Reford and Philip Seaton, who were converting a coach house at 16 Haytesbury Lane into a mews residence. At parties in the mews, people sat on the floor and talked late into the night. Boydell recalls Seaton acquiring a gypsy caravan, and parking it in the yard below, emulating Augustus John in his search for a perfect Bohemian existence.[5] Regular musical evenings were held at Heytesbury Lane, the musicians including Boydell, Edward Oldham, Paul Egestorff and others. Oldham, who had a flat in Pembroke Road, was naval attaché in the British Embassy, a sensitive posting during the war years. Egestorff, a pupil of Mainie Jellett, was an accomplished Modernist painter who lived with his wife Edie at nearby Morehampton Road. A particularly lively member of the Heytesbury Lane circle was Nigel Heseltine, son of British composer Philip Heseltine, aka 'Peter Warlock'. It was rumoured that Heseltine had moved to Ireland to avoid serving in the British army. While in Dublin, his collection of poems *A Four-Walled Dream* was published and in 1942 Boydell set one of the poems, 'The Lamenting', to music (see Aylish E. Kerrigan's essay elsewhere in this volume). In partnership with the actor Sheila Richards, Heseltine also produced a series of new plays at the Olympia Theatre. Ralph Cusack painted the scenery, and Boydell was given his first professional job as composer, writing and performing incidental music for these productions. Boydell also composed incidental music for Frank Carney's play *The House of Cards*, with both Boydell and Edgar ['Billy'] Boucher as pianists. The set painters for this production were Anne Yeats, Ralph Cusack and Thurloe Conolly. It is clear that by this time, Boydell was moving away from painting and increasingly concentrating his creative energies on music. This decision may have been prompted in part by difficulty in obtaining art materials. Due to war restrictions canvas was in short supply; Conolly used compressed board called 'Masonite', covered with gesso, for these sets. The sets were afterwards cut up and used as supports for paintings by Conolly. Boydell's paintings are for the most part on recycled canvas; he may have been unwilling to compromise in his choice of materials although many artists used board at this time.

In his memoirs Boydell recalled another house that became a focal point for Dublin's artists, 25 Lower Baggot Street, where the flat on the first floor was occupied by a Swiss-German named René Buhler and his wife 'Zette' – the painter Georgette Rondel.[6] Buhler lived off his wits, giving French and German lessons and selling vacuum cleaners. In the flat above were the White Stag painter Stephen Gilbert and his wife, Canadian-born sculptor Jocelyn Chewitt. The Buhler flat was apparently the scene for an occasional *ménage à trois* with artist Nick Nicholls also taking up residence. Buhler was regarded with suspicion by the police, not least because he was thought to be having an affair with the wife of a government minister. At this time Boydell was living with a friend Lionel Kerwood at Imaal, a house he rented in Rathfarnham. He recalled spending one night, when his car would not start, sharing René's bed, and was apparently thereafter listed in police records as a possible 'dangerous homosexual'.[7] An occasional lodger was the gay Surrealist poet and Communist Roger Roughton, noted for his habit of wearing a bowler hat in bed. Roughton's suicide, in April 1941, cast a shadow over the artistic community in No. 25.

In 1944, even though Boydell's interests were tending more towards music, he continued to participate in the visual arts activities of the White Stag Group. Led by Basil Rákóczi and Kenneth Hall, this loose affiliation of artists was also based in Lower Baggot Street. Boydell's involvement came about through his friends Thurloe Conolly and Ralph Cusack, but he was also on good terms with the architect Noel Moffett and his wife Margot, who organised the White Stag Group's 1944 Exhibition of Subjective Art, held at 6 Lower Baggot Street. In this exhibition Boydell showed *Atlas Approached* (1943–4, pl. 8), a fantastical landscape, as well as *The Return of the Wood* (1943, pl. 9). The critic Herbert Read had agreed to come to Dublin to give a talk at the opening; however, as Boydell recalled, because of Read's known Communist sympathies, he found it difficult to get permission to travel to Ireland, and so his speech had to be read by Margot Moffet at the opening.[8] At this time Boydell was preparing for the recital of his chamber music at the Shelbourne Hotel. He was also about to get married to Mary Jones, a student of his who sang at the recital, and who assisted him in looking after visitors to the Subjective Art exhibition. Brian and Mary visited the Aran Islands on their honeymoon in June 1944, where Boydell worked on several paintings, including *The Worm Hole* (pl. 10), inspired by Pol na bPeist, a natural rectangular rock pool on Inis Mór. Like many of Boydell's paintings there is a theatrical quality to this work. He represents the pool not as rectangular but as circular, and more like a stage set rather than a naturalistic landscape, while the surrounding rocks are equally stylised, as if constructed of lath and canvas for a theatre production. As with Boydell's music, *The Worm Hole* is also an exercise in tonal harmonies, of greys and light ochres. *Abandoned Engine Works* (1944) depicts a turret-like structure in a deserted landscape, with the remains of a wooden building in the foreground. Earlier works from this period, such as *The Return of the Wood*, inspired by an old mill in woodlands, or *Laurel Tangle, Kilcool* (c.1943) are slightly nightmarish scenes, characterised by dancing tree limbs. Indeed most of Boydell's paintings are based on plants and landscapes; his trees writhe and mutate into surreal entities. In *Gunnera* (c.1942, pl. 11), a semi-abstract depiction of the giant-leafed plant *Gunnera tinctoria* to be found in many Irish gardens, the giant veined leaf forms a circle, closing in around the red flowers.

While accomplished, these canvases are not entirely resolved and led to Boydell's decision to forgo visual art in favour of a career in music. On 30 January 1944 Thurloe Conolly's Surrealist song cycle *The Feather of Death*, with music by Boydell, premiered at the Shelbourne Hotel on Stephen's Green (see Philip Graydon's essay elsewhere in this volume). The work was scored for baritone, flute and string trio. Conolly recalled:

> I enjoyed writing words for a short song cycle, while Brian worked on the score at the piano. Much of my writing at that time was influenced by Eugene Jolas, André Breton, James Joyce, Gertrude Stein and others in the quarterly review *Transition* where *Finnegan's Wake* first appeared as 'Work in Progress'.[9]

Around this time, Kerwood's place at Imaal was taken by Thurloe Conolly, who was later to marry Boydell's sister Yvonne. Evenings at Imaal were often devoted to Surrealist Expression in the form of drawings and texts, sometimes with one author, but generally written as collaborative exercises. The more inventive and scatological the narratives, the more they were enjoyed by those participating. A certain competitive element crept into the proceedings as the group strove to produce ever more outrageous and disgusting texts: Boydell describes it as a convenient form of rebellious catharsis for his group, who had quite recently 'broken free from a polite and civilised upbringing'.[10] However, these scripts were of their time, echoing the literary extravagances of Myles na gCopaleen in the *Irish Times*, the free-ranging expressiveness of Jack Yeats's 1938 novel *The Amaranthers* and Samuel Beckett's *Murphy*, published that same year.

Boydell was keenly interested in Modernist literature; at Cambridge he befriended the poet John Berryman, who visited Ireland in April 1937, hoping to meet W. B. Yeats. The evenings at Imaal led to the slightly tongue-in-cheek formation of a vibrant but short lived 'Rathfarnham Academy of Surrealist Art'. Boydell and Mary were also part of the Dublin Marionette Group, with Mary manipulating the puppets and making costumes, while Brian provided music and read the speaking parts. Their Surrealist play for marionettes, *Revelation at Low Tide*, was put on at the Peacock Theatre in November 1944, the characters including Kryptomena and Pencille, who lived in sea shells; Mr Crankbox, the Hollow Monitor and the 'Inhabitants of the mud flats'.

Photographs of evenings at Imaal show the group of friends entertaining themselves with Surrealist performances and whimsical entertainments. But their paths in life were beginning to diverge. After Boydell and Mary married they moved to a new house at Cabinteely, and the Academy of Surrealist Art, with its irreverent and iconoclastic outpouring of creativity, gradually dispersed. While Conolly concentrated on his work as a visual artist, Boydell was turning to music. Although he continued painting throughout the year and exhibited at the Living Art Exhibition during the autumn, Boydell came to the conclusion that he could not devote the time needed to develop his ability as a painter. Towards the end of 1944 he made the decision to devote his energies to music, and put away his canvas and brushes. However, while opting for music, he had no wish to confine his life to a single track. Motor sport was still an enthusiasm, and with petrol once again becoming available, he was able to enjoy driving his Brescia Bugatti. After moving out of Imaal and setting up house in Cabinteely, one lively chapter in Brian and Mary's lives came to an end, and another one began, now devoted more fully to music.

FOURTEEN

LISTING THE PAPERS OF BRIAN BOYDELL (TCD MS 11128): AN ARCHIVIST'S PERSPECTIVE

Ellen O'Flaherty

The papers of Brian Boydell were donated to the Library of Trinity College Dublin (TCD) by his immediate family. The Library was one of the obvious repositories for the collection given Boydell's long and close association with the College. The bulk of the papers was transferred in early 2001, just a few months after his death in November 2000. Further smaller transfers were made in 2005, 2006, 2011 and 2014.

To mark this important donation, in November 2002 a reception was held in the Long Room of the Old Library, where some of Boydell's manuscript scores were placed on display. Afterwards, the Dublin University Choral Society performed his work for voices and orchestra *Under No Circumstances* (op. 85, 1987) in the East Theatre.

The material in the collection was originally contained in 31 'banker's' boxes, and comprises correspondence, photographs, diaries, administrative documents, radio broadcast scripts, talks and lectures, research notes, music scores (mainly in manuscript form), cassette tapes and glass lantern slides.[1] The collection reflects many aspects of Boydell's life: as composer, academic, advocate, broadcaster, teacher, husband, father and friend.

The collections in the Manuscripts & Archives Research Library are divided into two sections: manuscripts (MSS) and College Archives, otherwise referred to as 'muniments' (MUN). The manuscripts section includes cuneiform tablets, papyrus fragments, early Irish manuscripts, medieval books of hours, estate papers, the papers of Irish politicians and literary figures, and various other objects and items. The collections development policy is based on building on existing collections' strengths, as well as acquiring important papers and manuscripts relevant to the history of the College. The College Archives consist of administrative, legal and financial records of the College: student records; the records of departments, faculties and offices within College; legal documents, including the foundation charter, statutes, leases and deeds; accounts and other financial records; photographs, maps and plans; student society records; and the papers of College officers who have made a major contribution to the academic or administrative life of TCD.

Although Brian Boydell had a long association with the College, completing his MusB degree in 1942 and MusD in 1959, and later as professor of music, it was decided that the collection would be treated as a 'manuscript' collection, given that the contents of the papers relate to much more than his relationship with TCD. They cover his early years, including his musical education; his time at The Dragon and Rugby schools (1927–35); his university education at Clare College, Cambridge (1935–8); his involvement with various musical groups and associations; and his career as composer and broadcaster, as well as many other aspects of his life and work.

Apart from being aware of Boydell as a composer and his connections with TCD, I knew fairly little about him before I began to catalogue his papers. Sometimes, an archivist's relative ignorance of the subject of a collection is an advantage. If the cataloguer has a particular interest in the subject, the process of listing the papers could be delayed. It could also be argued that the archivist would have an unfair advantage over outside researchers in terms of access to the material: an archivist's job is to facilitate access for others, and to provide entry points to the collection by means of the production of a comprehensive descriptive list. To this end I carried out basic background research on Boydell and became familiar with his life and work mainly through the papers themselves. My job was aided by a 'box list' of the papers, which had been compiled prior to the transfer of the collection to the Library.

In terms of intellectual divisions, the collection was considered as having three main components: the 'papers' element, containing correspondence and text-based documents (predominantly in single-sheet format); the musical scores (also paper-based, and mainly handwritten); and material in other formats, including cassette tapes, photographs, glass lantern slides, scrapbooks and appointment diaries. The section divisions are listed below:

TCD MS 11128/1 – General Papers
TCD MS 11128/2 – Correspondence
TCD MS 11128/3 – Diaries
TCD MS 11128/4 – Scrapbooks
TCD MS 11128/5 – Photographs
TCD MS 11128/6 – Lantern slides
TCD MS 11128/7 – Cassettes
TCD MS 11128/8 – Music scores

The 'papers' element of the collection posed the biggest challenge in terms of the volume of material, as well as the diverse nature of the documents and the subjects they covered. This section was divided in two: 'General Papers' (TCD MS 11128/1) and 'Correspondence' (TCD MS 11128/2). The latter contains informal communications – in the form of letters, postcards, cards and telegrams – between Boydell and his family, friends and acquaintances, and covers various topics, although music dominates. The 'General Papers' section also contains some correspondence, but of a more formal nature, as well as various other types of documents. It covers a vast range of subjects, including Boydell's education in schools and universities in Ireland and the UK (reports, correspondence, books, concert programmes, menus and certificates); his musical education (certificates and reports); musical groups in which Boydell was involved, for example, the Dowland Consort, the Dublin Orchestral Players and the Dublin Oratorio Society (administrative documents, correspondence, concert programmes and publicity material); radio broadcasts (scripts on musical topics for radio shows on Radio Éireann and the BBC); Boydell's own music (correspondence with publishers and recording companies, and concert programmes); his membership of musical and arts organisations, such as the Music Association of Ireland, the Association of Irish Composers, the Arts Council, and Aosdána. There are also documents relating to talks and lectures he gave to music societies around Ireland, and to his participation in music festivals and competitions in Ireland, the UK and Canada.

The contents of each of the sections give an insight into Boydell as friend, teacher, composer, husband and father, and this is particularly evident with regard to 'General Correspondence'. Further sub-division was necessary within this section, resulting in identified correspondents (TCD MS 11128/2/1), unidentified correspondents (where just a first name or no name is given: TCD MS 11128/2/2) and 'other' (TCD MS 11128/2/3). The latter includes letters to and from family, students and 'fans'. The lists are arranged alphabetically either by the surname or first name of correspondents. It is clear from the volume of extant letters, which number over 2,000, that Boydell had many friends and acquaintances and was a prolific letter writer. The date range spans many decades, from the 1930s to the 1990s. Correspondents include school and university friends, other musicians, members of his family and various other friends and acquaintances. He often made copies of his own letters, and their presence give a more complete picture of the relationship he had with his correspondents, as the researcher is provided with two sides of epistolary conversations. Although the use of electronic communication in the form of email could have been available to Boydell in the final years of his life, he never adopted the use of computers (including email).[2] While the possibilities that electronic records present to archivists are exciting, they are also very challenging in terms of preservation, arrangement, storage and description. Therefore, the analogue nature of the contents of this collection has made its processing relatively simple, compared to hybrid collections of a similar nature and subject, which contain emails, scores created with music notation software, and other electronic files.

One of the qualities that distinguishes an archival collection catalogue from a general library catalogue is its hierarchical nature. The highest level of description in an archival catalogue relates to the collection in general and the lower the level the more specific the description becomes. In other words, the descriptions proceed from the general to the specific. The most detailed description would be that applied to an item such as a letter, which may belong in a file, which in turn may belong in a file series or another intellectual grouping. For example, within each of the eight main sections of the collection there are various sub-sections, which may further be divided into sub-sub-sections containing individual files or items.

With regard to depth of description the attempt was made to give as much information as possible so that individual items and groups of documents would be as discoverable as possible by researchers. However, not every single document is described at 'item level', and nor does it need to be. Many of the sections of the catalogue contain descriptions of files or groups of documents with a common subject. In the case of 'General Correspondence', the correspondent and date of each letter are identified, but a description of the contents is not given. Each document does need to be read however, as it is sometimes necessary to 'close' (i.e. make unavailable for consultation) some items for a period of time because of the personal or sensitive nature of their contents. Closure would generally be applied to correspondence emanating from others. These people, when writing to Boydell, probably did not envisage their letters being open for general scrutiny in an archive or library. There are also copyright implications for documents created or written by others. While the recipient of a letter (in this case Boydell himself) owns the physical document, it is its creator/writer or his/her estate who retains the copyright.

Within the 'General Papers' section, the volume of documents and the range of subjects demonstrates that as prolific as Boydell was in letter-writing, he was equally productive and active in so many other areas of his life, both personally and professionally. Sub-sections within this section include 'Early Education', 'Performing Groups', 'Music Organisations', 'Broadcast Scripts', 'Festivals and Adjudication', 'Talks and Lectures', 'Scholarly Research', 'Awards and Honours', 'Hobbies and Leisure' and 'Family and Domestic'. The sub-section 'Broadcast Scripts' contains over 300 typescript copies of scripts for his radio programmes on musical themes broadcast on what was then Radio Éireann (later Radio Telefís Éireann) and the BBC (see Barbara Dignam's essay elsewhere in this volume); 'Talks and Lectures' contains around 50 drafts of lectures that he delivered to musical societies around the country; and 'Scholarly Research' includes several files of research notes on music and the music trade in eighteenth-century Ireland.

In archival science there is also a principle called 'original order' whereby – where possible and practicable – the archivist should maintain the order of documents in which the creator arranged them. Sometimes the archivist must impose a certain amount of artificial arrangement for the purposes of producing a comprehensible descriptive list. In the case of Boydell's collection there are elements of both original order and imposed arrangement. Another archivist might have arranged the papers in a different manner. For example, all the documents relating to a particular piece of music (correspondence, concert programmes etc.) could have been listed with the original handwritten music score(s). Instead, all of the scores are listed in one section, while the concert programmes are listed in another, and the correspondence is listed in several different sections, as described above.

An interesting aspect of Boydell's career was his role as adjudicator at music festivals and competitions both in Ireland and abroad. As well as adjudicating frequently throughout Ireland and occasionally in England, he travelled to Canada twice in the 1950s. These visits are documented in two scrapbooks and a file of newspaper cuttings (TCD MS 11128/1/14/132–4 in the 'Adjudication: music festivals and compositions' sub-section of 'General Papers').[3]

There are several other scrapbooks in the collection. Some contain documents relating to events and activities in which Boydell was involved – including concerts of his compositions, membership of performing groups, lecture series, etc. – in the form of newspaper cuttings, correspondence, concert programmes and photographs. The latter are to be found in one of the main sections of the descriptive list: 'Scrapbooks' (TCD MS 11128/4). Another is in the sub-sub-section 'Dowland Consort', in the 'Performing Groups' sub-section of 'General Papers' (TCD MS 11128/1/5/3).

The collection also contains documents relating to Boydell's hobbies, which included angling, photography, archaeology, wine appreciation, gardening and classic cars: 'Hobbies, leisure and social engagements' (TCD MS 11128/1/24). Some of this material is loose: for example, a fishing register, car log and various items of correspondence. More items are to be found in some of the scrapbooks in the top-level section 'Scrapbooks' (TCD MS 11128/4) described above.

The foregoing discussion illustrates that the process of arrangement in the description of an archival collection is not a straightforward one; sometimes documents are grouped together according to format, and at other times they are associated with other documents relating to a common subject.

At the time of writing, the descriptive list of the papers has not yet been added to the online catalogue of the Manuscripts & Archives Research Library (MARLOC).[4] Once this has been accomplished the hierarchical structure should become clearer to researchers.[5] One of the reasons for the delay is the fact that the musical scores have not yet been fully catalogued. This section of the collection ('Musical Scores', TCD MS 11128/8) contains for the most part the draft and final versions of parts and full scores of Boydell's musical compositions, the majority of which are in manuscript form. While there is a full list of these works, they have yet to be arranged and numbered. Untitled and/or incomplete scores will have to be identified, and insertions, such as letters, programmes and other documents will be removed and inserted into other sections of the catalogue, with relevant cross-referencing provided. In the meantime, researchers are given access to the musical scores, but the references for each are, by necessity, still provisional.

Like the scores, the slides and tape cassettes (TCD MS 11128/6 and TCD MS 11128/7 respectively) are also yet to be fully catalogued, although Boydell has provided enough descriptive information relating to these for individual items to be relatively easily identified and made available to researchers, and ultimately to catalogue. The cassettes contain recordings of Boydell's radio broadcasts, with the glass lantern slides including images taken by Boydell in France and Canada, as well as photographs from his father's travels in the earlier part of the twentieth century, and some commercially produced slides. Due to the format of the items in these sections it would be advisable to create surrogates for access, and in the interests of the physical preservation of the originals.

Ideally, some of the material within the collection would be digitised and available online (subject to copyright and other rights restrictions) to facilitate researchers who cannot travel to Dublin to consult Boydell's papers. While digitisation of archives is often hailed as a solution to the problem of access, it must be remembered that such activity must always be accompanied by proper metadata. In turn, metadata can only be created in the context of a collection that has gone through at least a minimal amount of archival processing. Otherwise, context is lost.

This essay has provided a brief survey of the collection contents and the process of archival cataloguing. It is hoped that the catalogue of the Boydell papers in its near complete state has helped researchers understand the collection, and will continue to facilitate access to its contents in the future.

FIFTEEN

AUTHORITY, ADVOCACY AND ACTIVISM: MUSIC IN IRISH LIFE AND CULTURE

Niall Doyle

As a practitioner rather than an academic, I would like to set out my own appreciation of and reflection on Brian Boydell and some aspects of his remarkable contribution to music in Ireland. What I have to say falls broadly into three parts. The first is a reflection on Brian Boydell's achievements as one of the greatest advocates, activists and achievers in music in Ireland in the twentieth century and the debt we owe him (and so many others) on that score. In the process I would like to offer a personal view of what it was that enabled him to be so particularly effective in that regard. In tune with that spirit I would also like to cast a slightly cold eye on aspects of art music in Irish cultural life at present and highlight what I think are some issues that should be of concern to all of us who care about music and opera in Ireland. Finally, looking forward, I would like to issue some challenges to individual members of the various academic and practitioner music professions (and to their institutions). Broadly, this is to take a lead from Brian Boydell's example and to harness professional expertise and standing in more effective ways to lead, influence and make important change in music in Ireland. In the process I will suggest one area where this might profitably be done in the near future.

THE 'GREAT MAN' OF MUSIC

After a brief career as a tuba-playing primary school teacher, I came to study music in Trinity College Dublin (TCD) in 1983. I began as a 23-year-old, very inappropriately categorised 'mature' student, just after Brian Boydell had retired as professor of music. He was no longer in the department, but No. 5 Front Square, where the music department was housed, was still very much 'the house that Brian built' and his influence and spirit was everywhere. All the TCD student friends I played and socialised with before that time not only admired but absolutely loved 'The Prof'. On the various occasions I had met Brian during those years it was easy to see why. A 'great man' of music in Ireland, in person he was utterly unaffected, and took a warm, enthusiastic human interest in every young musician he met. It was impossible not to be affected and infected by his interest, encouragement and enthusiasm.

I got to know Brian a bit more in the 1990s when I was managing Music Network. I programmed and commissioned some of his music and, meeting him in the process, I got to know more of his contribution to Irish musical life beyond his composition, musicology and teaching. When we organised a ceremony in Dublin Castle in 1997 to mark his 80th birthday, then President Mary Robinson used a memorable phrase in her address to describe the Brian she had gotten to know in Trinity. She described him as a tireless 'wheeler-dealer for music' – someone who found out how things worked, and who strategically, persistently and effectively pulled the right levers to make positive change happen. Bringing a fully-functioning university music department into being, building it up, inspirationally moulding generations of music graduates while also making major contributions to Irish historical musicology and continuing to be a distinctive leading voice in Irish composition would have been remarkable achievements for two professional lifetimes.[1] But even all of that was not the full story of Brian Boydell's astonishingly productive professional life. Writing in *The Bell* in 1951 in an essay entitled 'The future of music in Ireland', he described music in Ireland as being 'in a shocking state'. Tellingly, he identified one of the reasons for this as being the tendency to 'do a great deal of talking in this country... but positive action seldom follows all the talk'.[2]

As is evident throughout his broadcasting, teaching and writing, Brian Boydell was an immensely powerful advocate for music and its place in Irish life. However, what particularly distinguished his exceptional contribution was that, while he certainly could and did talk about it, he never stopped there. Throughout his life he was an energetic activist in every musical dimension possible. His response to identifying a need for change, or a gap to be filled, or an opportunity to advance music in some way was, wherever possible, to act, to seize the initiative and to make a difference. He was a doer as well as a talker, and he 'wheeled and dealt' with a particular effectiveness.

He took on what was to be a long leadership as conductor of the amateur Dublin Orchestral Players in 1943, giving extensive live orchestral concerts of symphonic repertoire with them (including new Irish works), and bringing the orchestra into schools to play for children. This was some five years before Radio Éireann (RÉ) founded the state's only professional symphony orchestra.

He also began broadcasting on classical music for a general public on RÉ in the 1940s, something he continued into the television age with the arrival of Radio Telefís Éireann in the 1960s. In 1948 he was one of the founders of the Music Association of Ireland (MAI), a ground-breaking and at the time enormously dynamic organisation. It quickly made the first strides in 'organising' Irish composers and promoting Irish composition. It advocated for improvements in music education and organised orchestral school concerts and a scheme of music performances in schools. The MAI also began a long and vocal advocacy campaign for a proper concert hall to house the RTÉ Symphony Orchestra, an aspiration that was finally realised with the opening of the National Concert Hall in Dublin in 1981.[3] Professor of singing in the Royal Irish Academy of Music from 1944, he founded and directed the Dowland Consort in 1959. This was an enormously important performing group. It blazed a trail for early vocal music not just in Ireland but also in the UK as the period performance movement was first emerging there. The Dowland Consort can be seen too as a direct progenitor of the Consort of St Sepulchre and the Dublin Consort of Viols – important links in the evolution of a very fine Irish tradition of professional choral and instrumental period performance that continues to this day. Just before becoming professor of music in TCD in 1962 and persuading the College to support his vision of building up a dynamic teaching music department, he also began a remarkable period of 22 years of service as a member of the Arts Council. When all of Boydell's advocate/activist-achievements are enumerated, one can begin to appreciate the scope of his achievement and the enormous debt that classical music in Ireland in the twenty-first century owes to him on that score alone, and also to the other 'doers' of that generation.

Why and how he was so successful is an interesting question. Brian Boydell had, of course, great personal gifts. His intellect, his great humanity, his interest in people and society, his positive energy and his personal warmth and 'likeability' were all great assets as an advocate and a practical leader of change. However, he had two other very important professional assets in this as well, from which I think we in the various music professions can draw some valuable learning. He had a particularly deep and rounded understanding of music and its place and meaning in our individual and collective life. This I believe was rooted in the diversity of his musical practices – from composing, scholarship, performing, teaching and constantly communicating not just with music students, but also with a wider public. Particularly striking was an interview response he gave to his TCD colleague Michael Taylor who observed that he had 'been involved in a great many things'. His typically self-effacing response was:

> Some people attempt to do an awful lot of things and could be easily accused of dabbling and doing none of them perfectly, whereas others just go absolutely bang onto one thing and perfect it. Well, I am in the first category. I am a dabbler and I probably have never done anything as well as I ought to, but if I had my life again I would do exactly the same... I believe enormously in a broadness of experience.[4]

His own particularly broad and deep professional musical experience gave Boydell what we might call a great intrinsic musical authority. Equally, he had also acquired a large amount of extrinsic authority: his national reputation, public persona and status as a leading composer and artist, as a performer, as a revered professor of music and as a highly effective and likeable broadcaster and public figure meant that he also carried a real reputational authority not just in the professional music world, but beyond it too. He understood this and used it to great effect. When he spoke, people listened. Leveraging all of his authority with skill, energy and determination was, I think, central to his being a particularly powerful advocate for change and a highly effective leader and collaborator in making change happen.

MUSIC AND OPERA TODAY

I would like to skip now to today – to a post-Boydell era if you like – and briefly consider some current aspects of our classical music and opera 'ecosystem' and the place of classical music in modern Irish life. Let us firstly acknowledge that the world of classical music in Ireland, in general and in many particular ways, is considerably better than it was for much of the latter part of the twentieth century. We have more widespread and better instrumental music teaching than before. A major national music education initiative (Music Generation) is steadily rolling out across the country and has truly transformative potential. We are producing more music graduates and postgraduates than ever, more professional-standard singers and instrumentalists, and more aspiring composers than ever before are emerging each year from our universities and music colleges. We have professional orchestras, choirs and a wide range of performing groups playing to high standards. We now have our National Concert Hall and a range of other concert venues in the capital. We have an embryonic National Opera Company, and a significant number of festivals, general arts venues and music and arts organisations of various types promoting and developing music and the arts across the country – in some cases to very high standards indeed. The list goes on...

All of these are, I believe, producing and presenting more high-quality live-music-making than heretofore, and of course, in the background in the internet and digital age, we as audiences now have 24/7 easy access to an incredible range of recorded, broadcast and live performances of great music and opera. Two processes have been operating in parallel with, and underpinning, much of this positive change in Ireland. The first is more money, or, to be slightly less crude, increased public investment. With this increased public investment has come greater levels of professional music activity and, sustained over time, this has supported the rise of musical standards and opportunity. The second process, partly related to the expanded scales of operation made possible by more investment, has been a greater degree of specialist professionalisation in most fields of music. For the most part, professional performers dedicate themselves early and exclusively to performance careers, composers to composition, conductors to conducting, musicologists to musicology, teachers to teaching, etc. Even managers and administrators are now increasingly being produced through specialist arts management education. Greater professional specialisation is of course a universal trend in most disciplines. Music is no different, and broadly speaking this is a good thing, though it raises some issues to which I would like to return a little later. However, notwithstanding the many improvements and areas of excellence, there are some major issues and concerns. Many of these are deeply ingrained and should be of serious concern to everyone who cares about music and our musical life. Conscious that I am skating over the surface of some big and complex issues, I would nevertheless like to name some of these.

a) Education
While peak-of-pyramid music education improves constantly for the small numbers who can and do avail of it, at the base of the pyramid music in the more general formal education system is for the most part sparse, marginal and uneven in quality and impact. This has been highlighted time and time again over decades, but remains a fundamental issue that has never been adequately addressed.

b) Audiences
While we are investing in and are producing more music makers and music-making of high quality, there is a strong case that we are not effectively reaching, developing and growing audiences to match. The blame-game list of reasons is long, but whatever the causes, more and more composers and performers describe finding themselves struggling for elbow room to fish in a small and fairly static audience pond. This has obvious short-term consequences for them, but potentially very serious long-term consequences for public and political support and investment in an art form if it is perceived as becoming of increasingly marginal interest to the public. Public investment is necessary

for sustaining what economists might describe as commercially unviable 'cultural merit goods', but nonetheless relies in part commercially and to a considerable extent politically on a demonstrable degree of public valuing. To put it crudely, people need to turn up and consume music and opera in substantial enough numbers to persuade funders and political decision-makers that continued subvention is merited by public interest and appreciation. Achieving a healthy balance is not easy, but it is essential. As we invest in producing more great music and opera and more opportunities to hear it, it is critical that the Irish music profession as a whole does better at growing audiences too, if we are not to accelerate down a terminal slope of seeking more and more subvention to produce more excellent music for fewer and fewer people.

c) Place in Irish Cultural life
Coming from a weak enough historic position, the place of classical music in Irish life and culture may be in the process of becoming even more marginalised. This is a large and complex issue, and it is difficult to measure, but my contention is based in part on observation of mainstream media coverage and discourse as reflecting perceived societal interest, standing and public/political support. Admittedly this is an observational opinion rather than a research-supported thesis, but my strong sense is that western art music and opera receive a small and shrinking amount of arts coverage or commentary in Ireland, and I also have the impression that more 'serious' discussion of rock and popular music is filling that art music commentary and critical space.

d) Public investment
Finally, there is the question of the adequacy of public investment in music and opera. We could argue (and I do it a lot!) about whether music and opera receive a fair slice of the national arts investment pie, but to be frank, by far the more fundamental and relevant discussion in Ireland is the size of the public arts investment pie itself. While public investment in the arts has improved a lot since Brian Boydell's era, it remains minute as a percentage of our GDP by any meaningful international comparison. A recent post-budget statement from the National Campaign for the Arts puts it pretty succinctly:

> At 0.1% of GDP, Ireland's expenditure on Arts and Culture is at the bottom of the list of EU countries compared with an average of 0.6%, surely something no country can condone.[5]

The obvious questions arise about why these and other issues are, and continue to be so.

CHALLENGES

However, I would like to sidestep that very large debate and any of the frequent allocation of external blame for problems and responsibility for solutions. Taking Brian Boydell's own exemplary approach and lifetime of contribution as a framework, I would like to encourage a little music and opera community introspection, in the process issuing some challenges to members of different musical professions and institutions.

The first is to make a plea for a little less exclusive specialisation and separation of musical professions, and the development in all branches of musical practice of expert practitioners with greater breadth of musical experience and understanding. As well as making more fully-rounded composers, performers, scholars, teachers, policy-makers and even managers, this will, I believe, make for more authoritative and effective advocates and agents of change.

The second challenge is to consider whether it could be productive for the various music professions to interact and have considerably more constructive dialogue with each other, and with the wider community. One danger of our increasingly specialised and compartmentalised music profession is that a great deal of our professional dialogue now appears to take place within narrower, more discrete audiences of immediate peers. And whatever about what we might call 'inter-species-communication' within the music profession, real dialogue and engagement with the public is particularly rare. Without these dialogues, a sense of cohesive, common-purpose community is difficult to achieve and, without that, achievement of any major change is difficult, if not impossible.

A third challenge is for us to recognise and value both the intrinsic and extrinsic authority of the expert knowledge and public status of professional musicians, musicologists, composers, teachers (and managers), and to look at how we can leverage that more effectively to advocate for change.

Finally, to the fourth challenge, which is perhaps the most critical: are we prepared not just to talk, but to *act* individually, collectively and institutionally to make change happen where it is most needed to strengthen music in Irish cultural life? Taking action – even on a small scale – is the most powerful advocacy tool of all, and central to inspiring and effective leadership.

These are not just challenges for us as individual Irish musical professionals and citizens. There is even greater scope, and arguably greater responsibility, for a more connected and integrated advocacy and for change-making actions by music institutions. Shamelessly doing a bit of soap-box advocacy of my own in the process, for something I believe would be close to Brian Boydell's heart were he still amongst us, let me give just one example of where a perfectly feasible and potentially high-value change is waiting to be made.

Classical music and opera have consistently had particular difficulties in developing greater presence and traction in Irish cultural life, thought and policy throughout the twentieth century and to the present day. I am increasingly convinced that one of the major 'soft' issues underpinning this has been a lack of a general knowledge, understanding and belief that this has been a strong current in our national cultural history for over 300 years, a deep and rich element of our national heritage. Often tangled in the past with more binary ideas of national cultural identity, in the more historically and culturally pluralist awareness so evident in and after our national 1916 centenary commemorations, it seems to me there is a more receptive public environment for awakening that realisation than ever before. A great deal of excellent revelatory work has already been done by historical musicologists, from Brian Boydell's own pioneering research work to that by the editors and many contributors to the magnificent *Encyclopaedia of Music in Ireland*, and a host of others. Historical Irish music and opera is being brought to life in performance and recording by pioneering researcher-performers such as Peter Whelan and Una Hunt. Some remarkable amateur authors and archivist-collectors of historical material like the late Basil Walsh, his brother Derek, Richard Bonynge and Paddy Brennan have gathered and preserved a wealth of important historical material. Various collections in institutions and libraries here and abroad are also coming to light. Irish classical music and opera of the eighteenth, nineteenth and early twentieth centuries is a large, exciting and open field for Irish music scholars, musicians and, most importantly, for the public whose cultural heritage it is.

However, this is the tip of a large cultural iceberg, with most of it still locked away, preventing any broad public dissemination and making scholarly, professional and public access difficult. With the transformative digital documentation, linkage and dissemination possibilities now available this is not really defensible. Neither is the fact that as a nation, we have not acted to preserve, document and disseminate this major strand of our cultural history and identity, a neglect heightened by the attention we have given to other aspects of our cultural heritage. In terms of documenting and disseminating our cultural history, we have our National Library, a National Theatre Archive, a National Film Archive, a National Traditional Music Archive, and a National Dance Archive. Some of these are now employing digital technologies in highly effective ways and some partner with or are based at higher education institutions where the synergies with scholarship and teaching add significant value.

A dynamic, public-facing National Classical Music and Opera digital 'archive' or 'knowledge-hub' seems an obvious, yawning gap in the documentation and dissemination of our cultural history and development as a people.

I would also suggest that it is a relatively straightforward achievement. This is particularly so if done as a collaborative, inter-institutional, digitally-imagined project, perhaps with a host institution that can also avail of the obvious synergies of co-locating with specialist scholarship and teaching. I believe this is eminently achievable, and briefly wearing my current professional hat, I am happy to say that advocacy for such a development is now an explicit part of the Arts Council's recently published opera policy, and something that will be considered for incorporation into its next statement of music policy. This of course is just one of many areas in music and opera in which action is needed and leadership required; but it is, I believe, both an important and a relatively 'low-hanging fruit' and I would be very hopeful of seeing it happen in the near future.

I would like to finish by restating Brian Boydell's call to all involved in music and opera in Ireland. His centenary provides us with an opportunity to remember the exemplary contribution of a remarkable man, a particularly well-rounded musician of high expertise and deep understanding, a man who acquired a particular authority and leveraged it as an advocate for musical change and development. Perhaps more than anything else, in every sphere of his professional and artistic life, he was a man who led by doing. All who care about music and opera in Ireland have a role to play – individually, as institutions and in collaborative initiatives. In making our own small contemporary contributions to the history of music and opera in Ireland, the challenge we face is whether we can build on the legacy of Brian Boydell and his generation and take inspiration from their example of sustained advocacy and activism. In 1951 Boydell wrote about 'the great deal of talking' we are inclined to do. The challenge for us as we are faced with the many major issues currently facing music in Ireland is to emulate Brian Boydell and his many collaborators – to take and sustain the 'positive action' he not alone called for, but lived out to such great, lasting effect in his own musical life.

Notes

INTRODUCTION

1. T. W. Moody and W. E. Vaughan, *A New History of Ireland*, vol. IV (Oxford: Oxford University Press, 1986), pp 542–67; 568–628.
2. Harry White offers an extended critique of Boydell's musicology in '"Our musical state became refined": The musicology of Brian Boydell', in Gareth Cox, Axel Klein and Michael Taylor (eds), *The Life and Music of Brian Boydell* (Dublin: Irish Academic Press, 2004), pp 45–61, (p. 61).
3. Ibid., p. 45.
4. Emma Costello and Nicholas Carolan, 'Music Publishing and Printing', in Harry White and Barra Boydell (eds), *The Encyclopaedia of Music in Ireland* (Dublin: UCD Press, 2013), pp 707–10, (p. 708).

ONE

1. See for example, Charles Acton and Richard Pine, 'Brian Boydell', *Irish Times*, 17 Nov. 2000. This is a revised version by Pine of the obituary originally prepared by Acton, www.theguardian.com/news/2000/nov/17/guardianobituaries1.
2. Michael Taylor, 'An interview with Brian Boydell', in Gareth Cox, Axel Klein and Michael Taylor (eds), *The Life and Music of Brian Boydell* (Dublin: Irish Academic Press, 2004), pp 63–95, (p. 75). See also 'A reluctant slice of autobiography', in Brian Boydell, *Rebellious Ferment: A Dublin Musical Memoir and Diary*, ed. Barra Boydell (Cork: Atrium, 2018), pp 3–18, (p. 11), where Brian Boydell recounts how he was 'so very enthusiastic about his [Prokofiev's] music'.
3. See Eve O'Kelly, 'An On-going Tradition', in *New Music News* (May 1992), p. 8. (This informs n. 23 in Gareth Cox's chapter 'The musical language of Brian Boydell: Octatonic and diatonic interaction', in Cox, Klein, Taylor, *Life and Music*, p. 124).
4. See Joseph J. Ryan, 'Nationalism and Music in Ireland' (Unpublished PhD thesis, National University of Ireland, Maynooth, 1991), p. 432, available at: http://eprints.maynoothuniversity.ie/5158/1/Joesph_J_Ryan_20140707161517.pdf
5. Cox, 'The musical language of Brian Boydell', pp 25–43, (p. 28).
6. Ibid., p. 81.
7. Gareth Cox, 'Octatonicism in the string quartets of Brian Boydell', in Patrick F. Devine and Harry White (eds), *The Maynooth International Musicological Conference 1995: Selected Proceedings Part One*, Irish Musical Studies 4 (Dublin: Four Courts Press, 1996), pp 263–70.

8. See the interview with Charles Acton in *Éire-Ireland: A Journal of Irish Studies* 5:4 (Winter 1970), pp 97–111, (p. 106).
9. The programme for this recital held on 30 January 1944 included first performances of *Three Songs for Soprano and String Quartet*, op. 10, *The Feather of Death*, op. 22, and the String Trio, op. 21, as well as the Oboe Quintet, op. 11 dating from 1940. See Boydell, *Rebellious Ferment*, p. 60.
10. Taylor, 'An interview with Brian Boydell', p. 78. The comment arose from a discussion where the composer noted that his first String Quartet was the work 'that stamped me as a dangerous avant-garde'.

TWO

1. Hazel Farrell, 'Compositions by Brian Boydell', in Gareth Cox, Axel Klein and Michael Taylor (eds), *The Life and Music of Brian Boydell* (Dublin: Irish Academic Press, 2004), pp 99–111.
2. Eve O'Kelly, 'An On-going Tradition', in *New Music News* (May 1992), p. 9.
3. Charles Acton in *Éire-Ireland: A Journal of Irish Studies* 5:4 (Winter 1970), pp 97–111, (p. 105).
4. Gerry Smyth, *Music in Irish Cultural History* (Dublin: Irish Academic Press, 2009).
5. John O'Flynn, *The Irishness of Irish Music* (Farnham, Surrey: Ashgate, 2009).
6. See Mark Fitzgerald and John O'Flynn (eds), *Music and Identity in Ireland and Beyond* (Farnham, Surrey: Ashgate, 2014), notably the essays by Edmund Hunt, Fabian Huss, Mark Fitzgerald and Harry White.
7. Joseph J. Ryan, 'Nationalism and Music in Ireland' (Unpublished PhD thesis, National University of Ireland, Maynooth, 1991), p. 432, available at: http://eprints.maynoothuniversity.ie/5158/1/Joesph_J_Ryan_20140707161517.pdf
8. Ibid.
9. From Boydell's own comment in Aloys Fleischmann, 'Boydell, Brian (Patrick)', in B. Morton and P. Collins (eds), *Contemporary Composers* (Chicago and London: St James Press, 1992), p. 112.
10. Charles Acton, 'Interview with Brian Boydell', p. 104; for the concluding question and answer, see p. 105.
11. Gareth Cox, 'Boydell, Brian', in *The New Grove Dictionary of Music and Musicians* (London, Macmillan, 2001) and *Grove Music Online*; also in 'The musical language of Brian Boydell: Octatonic and diatonic interaction', in Cox, Klein, Taylor, *Life and Music*, pp 25–43, (p. 25).
12. Acton, 'Interview with Brian Boydell', pp 98, 100.
13. Cox, 'The musical language of Brian Boydell', p. 26.
14. Acton, 'Interview with Brian Boydell', p. 99.
15. Ibid., p. 98.
16. The 1945 version has apparently not been recorded by Radio Éireann. Richard Pine, in the CD-ROM appendix to his *Music and Broadcasting in Ireland* (Dublin: Four Courts Press, 2005) mentions the 1954 and 1960 recordings of the 1946 revision in the RTÉ sound archive. Pine does not mention more exact dates of these nor whether they were live or studio performances. At this time, however, these were mostly live broadcasts from the St Francis Xavier Hall, which served as both a studio and a concert hall.
17. This expansion is nowadays regarded as marking the orchestra's foundation; see Pat O'Kelly, *The National Symphony Orchestra of Ireland 1948–1998: A Selected History* (Dublin: RTÉ, 1998), and the anniversaries celebrated in 1998 and 2018.

18. 'Brian Boydell's new symphony', *Irish Times*, 31 Oct. 1945, p. 3; anonymous review, probably written by Walter Beckett.
19. The manuscript score reveals that he began the work on 31 January and completed it on 21 June 1948.
20. *Brian Boydell: Orchestral Music*, Marco Polo 8.223887 (CD, 1997), NSOI, Colman Pearce (cond.). The CD also includes the Violin Concerto, op. 36 (with Maighread McCrann, violin), *Megalithic Ritual Dances*, op. 39 and *Masai Mara*, op. 87. For another commentary on the works on this CD, see Seóirse Ó Dochartaigh, *Sunlight & Shadow: A Listener's Guide to Irish Classical Music* (Leckemy, Co. Donegal: the author, 2016), pp 56–8.
21. In an interview with Michael Taylor, Boydell said about the octatonic scale: 'I soon learnt that, just like the whole-tone scale as manipulated by Debussy, you cannot stick to it because it only has three transpositions and leads to diminished sevenths logically, which somehow have an outworn feeling'; Michael Taylor, 'An interview with Brian Boydell', in Cox, Klein, Taylor, *Life and Music*, p. 83.
22. Unsourced; reprinted in booklet text to the Marco Polo CD, see n. 20.
23. I have taken the liberty here of paraphrasing my own text about the Violin Concerto that appeared in German in my monograph *Die Musik Irlands im 20. Jahrhundert* (Hildesheim: Georg Olms Verlag, 1996), pp 225–30, slightly revised.
24. In their obituary in *The Guardian*, 17 Nov. 2000. Note that Acton had died in 1999, so this *Guardian* obituary had already been prepared by Acton and then revised by Pine.
25. Acton, 'Interview with Brian Boydell', p. 105.
26. See Denis Donoghue's review in the *Irish Times*, 'Irish Words and Music', 11 Nov. 1957.
27. For Hennessy, please see the present author, *Bird of Time: The Music of Swan Hennessy* (Mainz: Schott Music, 2019).
28. Bernhard Maier, *Lexikon der keltischen Religion und Kultur* (Stuttgart, Alfred Kröner Verlag, 1994), p. 315.
29. *Irish Times*, 8 Dec. 1954, p. 11.
30. Ibid., 3 Dec. 1956, p. 6.
31. Decca DL 9843 (with RÉSO cond. M. Horvat) and Marco Polo 8.223887 (as n. 20). In Appendix IV to Cox, Klein, Taylor, *Life and Music*, p. 119, I have erroneously dated the Decca LP as 1958; see 'An Irishman's Diary', *Irish Times*, 6 Mar. 1956, p. 6, which mentions the recording.
32. In this particular scale, there are two consecutive whole tone steps from F via G to A.
33. Philip Graydon, 'Modernism in Ireland and its Cultural Context in the Music and Writings of Frederick May, Brian Boydell, and Aloys Fleischmann' (Masters Thesis, NUI Maynooth, 1999), p. 102.
34. This has also been pointed out frequently in Cox, 'The musical language of Brian Boydell'.
35. Philip Graydon, 'Modernism in Ireland', p. 102.
36. Fleischmann, 'Boydell' (1992), p. 112; see n. 9.
37. The E pitch disturbs the pentatonic scale here, rather turning it into a D Minor motif.
38. Taylor, 'An interview with Brian Boydell', in Cox, Klein, Taylor, *Life and Music*, p. 84.
39. *Irish Times*, 13 Feb. 1956, p. 5.
40. Ó Dochartaigh, *Sunlight & Shadow*, p. 58.
41. Paraphrased from an RTÉ radio interview quoted, without date, in ibid., p. 57. Boydell's quote is in relation to the Violin Concerto.

42. In his memoir, Boydell states that Incenzo 'gave the first performance in 1956, with the Dublin String Orchestra, which had been formed by Herbert Pöche', but he confused the names of the orchestra; see Brian Boydell, *Rebellious Ferment: A Dublin Musical Memoir and Diary*, ed. Barra Boydell (Cork: Atrium, 2018), p. 93. Hazel Farrell apparently misinterpreted the broadcast performance of the *Elegy* as the first performance of the complete work; see Farrell, 'Compositions', p. 102. The March 1956 broadcast was noted as such by Boydell in one of his pocket diaries, TCD MS 11128/3/22. Thanks are due to TCD librarian Ellen O'Flaherty for her assistance in clarifying this matter.

43. *Clarinet Variations* (incl. works by Jean Françaix, Gioacchino Rossini [arr. J. Michaels], Boydell, C. V. Stanford and A. J. Potter), RTÉ lyric fm CD 124 (2009).

44. *Irish Times*, 29 Jan. 1958, p. 3.

45. Ibid., 9 Jan. 1980, p. 8.

46. Ibid., 2 Mar. 1959.

47. In a programme note, dated 28 October 1968, that precedes the score as distributed by the CMC, Dublin. It has also been used in a programme note to another performance of the work on 13 November 1987 in the National Concert Hall, Dublin, in the author's possession. Here the text says that the note was originally written for the first performance of the work at the Gaiety Theatre.

48. Ibid.

49. Graydon, 'Modernism in Ireland', p. 126; Graydon's emphasis.

50. New Irish Recording Company NIR 011 (1974), recorded in 1973 in the Aula Maxima of what is now Maynooth University.

51. Gareth Cox, 'The bar of legitimacy? Serialism in Ireland', in Gareth Cox and Julian Horton (eds), *Irish Musical Analysis*, Irish Musical Studies 11 (Dublin: Four Courts Press, 2014), pp 187–201, (p. 197).

52. Graydon, 'Modernism in Ireland', p. 126.

53. *Irish Times*, 4 Oct. 1976, p. 11.

54. Ibid., 10 Sept. 1977, p. 13.

55. Boydell quoted in O'Kelly, 'An On-going Tradition', p. 7.

56. *Irish Times*, 3 July 1989.

57. In his own programme note to the recording of this work on Marco Polo 8.223887 (CD, 1997), p. 4.

58. *Irish Times*, 3 July 1989.

59. Acton, 'Interview with Brian Boydell', p. 107.

THREE

1. The contents of the sketchbook – insofar as they can be discerned – are catalogued in the Appendix to this essay.

2. Brian Boydell's Sketchbook, Brian Boydell Archive, TCD MS 11128/6.

3. Hazel Farrell, 'Compositions by Brian Boydell', in Gareth Cox, Axel Klein and Michael Taylor (eds), *The Life and Music of Brian Boydell* (Dublin: Irish Academic Press, 2004), pp 99–113, (p. 99); Boydell, A5-sized (scribbling) diary (1947), Boydell Archive, TCD MS 11128/3/13; Boydell, Pocket diary (1947), Boydell Archive, TCD MS 11128/3/6. *Magh Sleacht* is also listed

(with first performance details) under Boydell's compositions in Bernard Harrison (ed.), *Catalogue of Contemporary Irish Music* (Dublin: Irish Composers' Centre, 1982) but it is not included in either edition of Edgar Deale (ed.), *A Catalogue of Contemporary Irish Composers* (Dublin: Music Association of Ireland, 1968; second edn, 1973).

4. Jean Martinon, *Hymne variation et rondo* (1961–68), Box 10, folder 1, Jean Martinon Papers, Northwestern University Music Library.

5. Boydell, *Magh Sleacht* final score, Boydell Archive, TCD MS 11128/6/MAGH SLEACHT/3, p. 77.

6. Ibid., p. 93.

7. Ibid., p. iii.

8. Ibid.

9. Ibid.

10. Axel Klein, 'Brian Boydell: Of man and music', in Cox, Klein, Taylor, *Life and Music*, pp 1–12, (p. 3).

11. Ibid., pp 6–7. For a discussion of Boydell's early broadcasts for RTÉ radio, see Barbara Dignam's essay elsewhere in this volume.

12. J. A. Coleman, *The Dictionary of Mythology* (Hertfordshire: Eagle Editions Ltd., 2007), p. 652.

13. Brian Boydell, *Magh Sleacht* final score, Boydell Archive, TCD MS 11128/6/MAGH SLEACHT/3, front matter.

14. Lambert McKenna, 'Some Irish Bardic Poems LIV: Mag Shamhradhain: Brian, Lord of Magh Sleacht', in *Studies: An Irish Quarterly Review* 29:114 (June 1940), pp 232–40.

15. Boydell, *Magh Sleacht* final score, Boydell Archive, TCD MS 11128/6/MAGH SLEACHT/3, front flyleaf.

16. Coleman, *The Dictionary of Mythology*, p. 200.

17. Boydell, *Magh Sleacht* final score, Boydell Archive, TCD MS 11128/6/MAGH SLEACHT/3, front matter.

18. Ibid.

19. Hubert Clifford to Brian Boydell, 21 March 1947, Boydell Archive, TCD MS 11128/2/7/3.

20. Clifford to Boydell, 1 October 1947, Boydell Archive, TCD MS 11128/2/7/4.

21. Michael Taylor, 'An interview with Brian Boydell', in Cox, Klein, Taylor, *Life and Music*, pp 63–95, (p. 78).

22. Ibid., p. 80.

23. Frederick May, 'The Composer in Ireland', in Aloys Fleischmann (ed.), *Music in Ireland: A Symposium* (Cork: Cork University Press, 1952; digital edition, 2013), pp 164–75, (p. 171).

24. Boydell, Pocket diary 1947, Boydell Archive, TCD MS 11128/3/6.

25. G. O'B., 'Radio Symphony Concert', *Irish Press*, 6 Sept. 1947, p. 7.

26. Ibid.

27. Taylor, 'An interview with Brian Boydell', p. 78.

28. Clifford to Boydell, 28 October 1947, Boydell Archive, TCD MS 11128/2/7/6.

29. Ibid.

30. Ibid., 21 January 1948, Boydell Archive, TCD MS 11128/2/7/7(1).

31. G. O'B., 'Interesting Concert', *Irish Press*, 24 Apr. 1948, p. 7.

32. Michael McMullin, 'Call for Enquiry', *Radio Review*, 9 Apr. 1948, Brian Boydell, scrapbook, Boydell Archive, TCD MS 11128/4/1.

33. Ibid., p. 7.
34. Boydell, *Magh Sleacht* final score, Boydell Archive, TCD MS 11128/6/MAGH SLEACHT/3.

FOUR

1. Kevin Rockett, Luke Gibbons and John Hill, *Cinema and Ireland* (New York: Syracuse University Press, 1988), p. 73.
2. Harvey O'Brien, *The Real Ireland: The Evolution of Ireland in Documentary Film* (Manchester: Manchester University Press, 2004), p. 82.
3. Rockett, Gibbons, Hill, *Cinema and Ireland*, p. 84.
4. Barra Boydell notes similarities between the style of Carey's shots and Boydell's photographs. Personal communication with the author, 23 March 2018.
5. Interview with Brian Boydell, Peter Canning (dir.), *Paddy Carey Filmmaker*, RTÉ (1999).
6. Barra Boydell, personal communication with the author, 23 March 2018.
7. Boydell's diaries (Brian Boydell Archive, TCD MS 11128/3) include his appointments with Sluizer when preparing the score for *Ireland* and with Carey and his team when scoring these projects.
8. Barra Boydell and Enid Chaloner both recall the composer mentioning the challenge of composing music to fit with an image to the exact second. Author interview with Enid Chaloner and Pat O'Kelly, 22 March 2018; Barra Boydell, personal communication with the author, 23 March 2018.
9. The sequence of shot numbers begins anew for each cue in *Mists of Time* in contrast with *Yeats Country* and *Errigal* where they continue across shots.
10. 'Bis' is used here in the German (or French) sense of 'repeat' or 'encore'.
11. Music for *Ireland* and incidental music, uncatalogued, Boydell Archive, TCD MS 11128.
12. Letters between Boydell and Corcoran reveal that there were difficulties in securing financial sponsorship for *Ireland*, which appears to be the principal factor in the long production period. See Boydell Archive, TCD MS 11128/6/6/21–3.
13. Boydell wrote to Corcoran to suggest that a conductor experienced in conducting film music might be selected for *Ireland* because he was concerned about his inexperience in this field (Letter dated 5 Dec. 1965, Boydell Archive, TCD MS 11128/6/6/19). Philip Martell conducted the music in the end, but Boydell seems to have been present at the recording of the score on 25 November and 2 December 1966 at the St Francis Xavier Hall (1966 Pocket Diary). Consultation of his diaries reveals that the recording session for Carey's scores was also the St Francis Xavier Hall, which was the usual recording venue for the RTÉSO, and it appears that Boydell did conduct these himself.
14. Author interview with Gillian Smith, 1 February 2018.
15. Irish Film and TV Research Online database, Trinity College Dublin, www.tcd.ie/irishfilm/showfilm.php?fid=60507, accessed 13 February 2018.
16. O'Brien, *The Real Ireland*, p. 149.
17. Rockett, Gibbons, Hill, *Cinema and Ireland*, p. 84.
18. Letter from Tom Hyde (Irish Film Institute) to Frank Aiken (Department of External Affairs), 19 March 1969, Irish Film Archive.

19. 'An Irishman's Diary', *Irish Times*, 9 Apr. 1965.
20. Ibid., 28 May 1968.
21. O'Brien, *The Real Ireland*, p. 88.
22. Axel Klein, 'No state for music', in Michael Dervan (ed.), *The Invisible Art: A Century of Music in Ireland 1916–2016* (Dublin: New Island, 2016), pp 47–68, (p. 62).
23. The melodic shape evokes the folk songs 'Maggie' and 'Down by the Sally Gardens'. Klein describes the broad distinction between composers such as Ó Gallchobhair – who argued for a regeneration of Irish art music through traditional Irish sources – and the modern, European approach of Boydell, Aloys Fleischmann and Frederick May. Klein, 'No state for music', p. 62.
24. Brian Boydell, *Rebellious Ferment: A Dublin Musical Memoir and Diary*, ed. Barra Boydell (Cork: Atrium, 2018), p. 194–5.
25. Aloys Fleischmann, in *Hibernia* 32:9 (1968) Music Supplement. Boydell's incidental music for *The Wooing of Etain*, op. 37, was composed in 1954 and subsequently arranged as two orchestral suites (*The Wooing of Etain: Suite no. 1*, op. 37a, and *Suite no. 2*, op. 37b). See also Axel Klein's essay in this present volume.
26. Niall MacMonagle (ed.), *Lifelines: New and Collected Letters from Famous People About Their Favourite Poem* (Dublin: Townhouse, 2006). Boydell selected 'He Wishes for the Cloths of Heaven'.
27. Barra Boydell, personal communication with the author, 23 March 2018.
28. Boydell's manuscript score is dated 25 March 1967.
29. Interview with Patrick Carey, *Paddy Carey Filmmaker* (1999).
30. In addition to her role of playing harpsichord and celeste, Gillian Smith recalled some of the likely performers for this project, noting that most were also playing in the RTÉ Orchestra: André Prieur (fl), Sheila Larchet Cuthbert (hp), Victor Malish (hn) and Dieter Prodöhl (cbn). Interview with author, 1 February 2018.
31. Interview with Brian Boydell, *Paddy Carey Filmmaker* (1999).
32. Fleischmann, *Hibernia*, 1968.
33. Interview with Patrick Carey, *Paddy Carey Filmmaker* (1999).
34. Michel Chion, *The Voice in Cinema*, ed. and trans. Claudia Gorbman (New York: Columbia University Press, 1999), p. 5.
35. John Corner, 'Sounds real: Music and documentary', in *Popular Music* 21:3 (2002), pp 357–66, (p. 359).
36. Holly Rogers, 'Introduction: Music, sound and the nonfiction aesthetic', in *Music and Sound in Documentary Film* (New York: Routledge, 2015), pp 1–19, (p. 3).
37. 'An Irishman's Diary', *Irish Times*, 9 Apr. 1965.
38. Barra Boydell, personal communication with the author, 23 March 2018.

FIVE

1. Typed document marked 'Transcript of EFP interview 1993' in possession of the Boydell family.
2. Michael Taylor, 'An interview with Brian Boydell', in Gareth Cox, Axel Klein and Michael Taylor (eds), *The Life and Music of Brian Boydell* (Dublin: Irish Academic Press, 2004), pp 63–95, (p. 72).

3. These six songs were performed by the author with Dearbhla Collins (piano) on 23 June 2017 at the Brian Boydell Centenary Conference in the Royal Irish Academy of Music, Dublin. I am grateful to the Contemporary Music Centre, Dublin for providing copies of the music. Songs that had been withdrawn by the composer were performed and are discussed and illustrated here by kind permission of the Boydell family.

4. Axel Klein, 'Brian Boydell: Of man and music', in Cox, Klein, Taylor, *Life and Music*, pp 1–23, (p. 2).

5. Taylor, 'An interview with Brian Boydell', p. 65.

6. Ibid., p. 67.

7. Charles Acton, 'Interview with Brian Boydell', in *Éire-Ireland: A Journal of Irish Studies* 5:4 (Winter 1970), pp 97–111, (p. 97). See also his interview with Michael Taylor in which, referring to *Wild Geese*, he commented that 'curiously enough, [it] is still alright, I think… I am still not ashamed of it' ('An interview with Brian Boydell', p. 65).

8. Taylor, 'An interview with Brian Boydell', p. 66; also see Brian Boydell, *Rebellious Ferment: A Dublin Musical Memoir and Diary*, ed. Barra Boydell (Cork: Atrium, 2018), p. 21n.

9. Boydell, *Rebellious Ferment*, p. 68. Although he goes on to comment that '[i]t has never been performed', it would subsequently receive a first performance given by the author in June 2017 (n. 3 above).

10. Barra Boydell suggests that it may indeed be precisely its quality of a parlour song, a form of which Brian Boydell would later be highly dismissive, that was the reason for its being withdrawn (private communication with the author).

11. Acton, 'Interview with Brian Boydell', p. 99.

12. Ibid., p. 101.

13. Taylor, 'An interview with Brian Boydell', p. 78.

14. Ibid., p. 79.

15. Ibid., p. 83.

16. *Cradle Song*, *A Child's Grace* and *The Bargain* were revised in 1943 as *Three Songs for Soprano and String Quartet*, op. 10.

SIX

1. Quoted in S. B. Kennedy, with an essay by Bruce Arnold, *The White Stag Group*, Exhibition Catalogue (Dublin: Irish Museum of Modern Art, 2005), p. 42.

2. For more information on the White Stag Group, see Brian Boydell, *Rebellious Ferment: A Dublin Musical Memoir and Diary*, ed. Barra Boydell (Cork: Atrium, 2018), pp 65–81. See also Kennedy, *The White Stag Group*, *passim*, and Róisín Kennedy, 'Experimentalism or Mere Chaos: The White Stag Group and the Reception of Subjective Art in Ireland', in Edwina Keown and Carol Taaffe (eds), *Irish Modernism: Origins, Contexts, Publics* (Bern: Peter Lang, 2010), pp 179–94.

3. Quoted in Peter Murray, 'A White Stag in France', in *Irish Arts Review* 22:4 (Winter 2007), pp 96–101, (p. 99).

4. See Kennedy, *The White Stag Group*, pp 33–4.

5. See Brian Fallon, 'The White Stags', in *Irish Arts Review* 22:2 (Summer 2005), pp 68–73, esp. pp 72–3.

6. Quoted in Peter Murray, 'The language of dreams: Peter Murray remembers the multi-talented artist-composer Brian Boydell', in *Irish Arts Review* 32:4 (Winter 2015), pp 524–5, (p. 524). See also Brian Boydell, *Rebellious Ferment, passim*.
7. Murray, 'The language of dreams', p. 525. On *The Lamenting* see also Aylish E. Kerrigan's essay in this volume.
8. Quoted in Murray, 'A White Stag in France', p. 100.
9. Ibid.
10. Thurloe Conolly, statement supplementing the article, Herbert Read, 'On Subjective Art', in *The Bell* 7:5 (Feb. 1944), pp 424–9, (p. 429).
11. Kennedy, 'The White Stag Group', *idem*, *The White Stag Group*, n. 1, p. 13.
12. Personal communication with the author, 11 May 2017.
13. Brian Boydell, *Rebellious Ferment*, p. 12.
14. Letter from Brian Boydell to John Haffenden, 13 July 1972, quoted in John Haffenden, *John Berryman: A Critical Commentary* (London: Macmillan, 1980), n. 30, p. 192.
15. Letter from John Berryman to his mother, 23 Feb. 1937, quoted in ibid., n. 30, p. 192.
16. See ibid., p. 71. In 'Friendless', Berryman refers to Boydell's 'expressive tenor speaking voice' (see *Rebellious Ferment*, p. 12 [n. 16]). His singing voice was bass-baritone.
17. Brian Boydell (bar), Doris Cleary (later Keogh; fl); Morris Sinclair, John MacKenzie and Betty Sullivan comprised the string trio.
18. The author is grateful to the composer's sons, Cormac and Barra, for alerting him to the existence of this transfer and for furnishing him with a copy of the latter (personal communication with the author, 31 July 2017).
19. 'The Feather of Death, op. 22 (1943)', Roland Davitt (bar), Ríona Ó Duinnín (fl), members of the ConTempo String Quartet, *Brian Boydell, The Roaring Forties: The Early Chamber Music of Brian Boydell* (CD recording made by the CMC and the Irish Museum of Modern Art (IMMA) to accompany Kennedy, *The White Stag Group* [2005]).
20. The approximate time lengths given in Boydell's hand on the front page of the score are: 3'10, 2'30 and 2'00 while the IMMA recording's track lengths are 2'06, 1'50 and 1'37, respectively.

SEVEN

1. Charles Acton, 'First-Class Chamber Music One of Festival Highlights', *Irish Times*, 29 June 1960.
2. Charles Acton, 'Recital by Prieur Ensemble', *Irish Times*, 4 Mar. 1966.
3. Ibid.
4. Recordings consulted in the CMC: radio broadcast of premiere performance by Prieur Ensemble (1960); recording of performance by Elizabeth Gaffney (fl), Caitríona Yeats (hp) and members of the Testore String Quartet (1981).
5. Brian Boydell Archive, TCD MS 11128/1/6/2/30–6.
6. Brian Boydell, 'A Pack of Fancies for a Travelling Harper' (1970), programme note by composer.
7. *Five Mosaics* for violin and piano or harp was written for Geraldine O'Grady in 1972. The score indicates that the violin and piano version was written in September 1972 and then transcribed for harp in November 1972. Boydell added an additional movement ('Impetuous

Capriccio') for violin and piano in 1978 and the piece became known in the violin and piano version as *Six Mosaics*. In the same year (1978) the music of the *Six Mosaics* was rescored for solo violin, harp and orchestra to become the *Partita Concertante* (1978). There is a note on the final score from 1983 that the solo violin part was adapted for solo flute with revisions to the orchestral wind parts. See Boydell Archive, TCD MS 11128 Box 22 for manuscript of score and parts for *Mosaics*.

8. Concert Programme, 1 February 1980, Boydell Archive, TCD MS 11128/1/6/2/24.

9. See Boydell Archive, TCD MS 11128/1/6/2/47–8 for the concert programme of 'Music Association of Ireland presents a Tribute to Brian Boydell', John Field Room, National Concert Hall, Dublin, 29 January 1986[sic]. This concert was in celebration of Brian Boydell's 70th birthday. The concert date is incorrect and should read 29 January 1987, which is verified in a National Concert Hall Calendar of Events for January 1987 (see Boydell Archive, TCD MS 11128/1/6/2/49). Note the concert programme lists 'Six Mosaics', when it should be 'Five Mosaics' for violin and harp.

10. Concert Programme, 17 Feb. 1990, Boydell Archive, TCD MS 11128/1/6/2/68 (1) and Concert Programme, 10 July 1992, Boydell Archive, TCD MS 11128/1/6/2/83.

11. 'Next week in the arts', *Irish Times*, 7 May 1983.

12. Boydell Archive, TCD MS 11128/1/6/2/30–6.

13. Boydell Archive, TCD MS 11128/1/6/2/47–9.

14. 25 March 2017, St Patrick's Cathedral, performed by Simon Harden (org), Denise Kelly (hp) and Noel Eccles (perc). Denise Kelly and Noel Eccles performed in the premiere of the work with Peter Sweeney (org) at the 1986 Dublin International Organ Festival.

15. Ian Fox, 'Music of our time', *Irish Times*, 5 Jan. 1971.

16. Brian Boydell to Una O'Donovan, 18 Sept. 1970, Boydell Archive, TCD MS 11128, Box 22.

17. Ibid.

18. Una O'Donovan to Brian Boydell, 23 Sept. [1970], Boydell Archive, TCD MS 11128/2/1.1095.

19. Boydell, 'A Pack of Fancies' (1970), programme note.

20. Brian Boydell to Teresa Lawlor, undated, Boydell Archive, TCD MS 11128/1/6/6/69.

21. Charles Acton, 'Interview with Brian Boydell', in *Éire-Ireland: A Journal of Irish Studies* 5:4 (Winter 1970), pp 97–111, (p. 100).

22. Boydell, 'A Pack of Fancies' (1970), programme note.

23. Una O'Donovan to Brian Boydell, 23 Sept. [1970], Boydell Archive, TCD MS 11128/2/1.1095.

24. Ibid.

25. Brian Boydell to Una O'Donovan, 20 Oct. 1970, Boydell Archive, TCD MS 11128/2/1.1096. Emphasis in original.

26. Derek Bell to Brian Boydell, 18 Jan. [no year], Boydell Archive, TCD MS 11128/2/1/146. The year is most likely 1972 as a postcard in response from Brian Boydell to Derek Bell is dated 25 January 1972 (Courtesy of the Derek Bell Collection, Technological University Dublin).

27. Brian Boydell to Derek Bell, 25 Jan. 1972, Derek Bell Collection, Technological University Dublin (uncatalogued).

28. Boydell, 'A Pack of Fancies' (1970), programme note.

29. Ibid.

30. *A Pack of Fancies for a Travelling Harper*, Boydell Archive, TCD MS 11128 Box 22.

31. Acton, 'Interview with Brian Boydell', p. 104.
32. Clíona Doris, Programme Notes, 27 Nov. 2003.
33. Martin Adams, 'Reviews', *Irish Times*, 29 Nov. 2003.
34. See also Gareth Cox, 'The musical language of Brian Boydell', in Gareth Cox, Axel Klein and Michael Taylor (eds), *The Life and Music of Brian Boydell* (Dublin: Irish Academic Press, 2004), pp 25–43; also, Philip Graydon, 'Modernism in Ireland and its cultural context in the music of Frederick May, Brian Boydell and Aloys Fleishmann', in Gareth Cox and Axel Klein (eds), *Irish Music in the Twentieth Century*, Irish Musical Studies 7 (Dublin: Four Courts Press, 2003), pp 56–79.
35. Boydell Archive, TCD MS 11128, Box 22.
36. Michael Dervan, 'Celebration of Composer at 80', *Irish Times*, 26 Mar. 1997.
37. Charles Acton, 'Fine harp playing by Una O'Donovan', *Irish Times*, 14 Jan. 1971.
38. Ibid., 'Una O'Donovan plays at RDS', *Irish Times*, 2 Mar. 1976.
39. Ibid., 'Reviews', *Irish Times*, 11 Nov. 1980.
40. Ibid., 'Retrospective Concert for Brian Boydell', *Irish Times*, 7 May 1981.
41. Concert Programme for 'Musik Fran Irland' [Music from Ireland] presented by Rikskonserter [Sweden] and Irish Composers Centre [Ireland], Boydell Archive, TCD MS 11128/1/6/2/39. There is no date but the logo for the European Music Year 1985 is included. Boydell Archive, TCD MS 11128/1/6/2/41 is a provisional programme for 'Irish Music in Stockholm November 1985' and lists a concert date of 27 November 1985 for the Quintet's performance. Boydell Archive, TCD MS 11128/1/6/2/40 is a concert programme for a second Stockholm concert featuring Brian Boydell's String Quartet no. 3, op. 65.
42. Charles Acton, 'Recital by Prieur Ensemble', *Irish Times*, 4 Mar. 1966.
43. Recording on RTÉ lyric fm label (release pending) featuring Quintet for Flute, Harp and String Trio, op. 49 performed by Ciaran O'Connell (fl), Clíona Doris (hp), David O'Doherty (vn), Andreea Banciu (va) and Margaret Doris (vc) recorded in June 2019 in Technological University Dublin. The recording also includes *Five Mosaics*, op. 69 (David O'Doherty, Clíona Doris), *Four Sketches for Two Irish Harps*, op. 52 (Clíona Doris, Denise Kelly McDonnell) and *A Pack of Fancies for a Travelling Harper*, op. 66 (Clíona Doris).
44. Boydell Archive, TCD MS 11128/2/1/146.
45. Brian Boydell to Derek Bell, 25 Jan. 1972.
46. Boydell Archive, TCD, The Irish Times Newspaper Database, and personal programmes.
47. Clíona Doris, *In Blue Sea or Sky* (Riverrun Records RVRCD59, 2003).
48. Andrew Achenbach, 'In Blue Sea or Sky' [Review], in *Gramophone* (September 2013), available at: www.gramophone.co.uk/review/in-blue-sea-or-sky.
49. Acton, 'Interview with Brian Boydell', p. 104.

EIGHT

1. I am indebted to Aisling Lockhart and her colleagues at the Manuscripts & Archives Research Library at Trinity College Dublin for allowing me to access material from the Brian Boydell Archive in the course of my research.
2. Composer's note on manuscript of *An Album of Pieces for the Irish Harp* (1989), Boydell Archive, TCD MS 11128/1/6/2/126(2).

3. The term 'Irish harp' is used throughout this essay to refer to the modern Irish harp, which traces its origins back to the early nineteenth-century harps designed and manufactured by John Egan in Dublin. The technique used to play these instruments is adapted from pedal harp technique but a considerable amount of its repertoire is derived from the wire-strung Irish harp tradition of the seventeenth and eighteenth centuries. The modern Irish harp is widely played internationally but is often referred to as a folk harp, Celtic harp, lever harp or non-pedal harp.

4. See Appendix at end of this essay for a complete list of Boydell's compositions and arrangements for Irish harp(s) and voice (soprano) to harp accompaniment.

5. Teresa Lawlor studied Irish harp with Máirín Ní Shé at the Dominican College Sion Hill, Dublin and was a prizewinner at the Festival Interceltique de Lorient in 1989. She played harp at Bunratty Castle and recorded two albums of harp music: *Moods* (1986) and *Strings and Things* (1989). She performed selections from *An Album of Pieces for the Irish Harp*, op. 88 on many occasions, including at recitals at the John Field Room at the National Concert Hall, Dublin and the Weill Recital Hall at Carnegie Hall, New York in 1991.

6. Letter from Brian Boydell to Teresa Lawlor, Boydell Archive, TCD MS 11128/1/6/6/(69).

7. Charles Acton, 'Interview with Brian Boydell', in *Éire-Ireland: A Journal of Irish Studies* 5:4 (Winter 1970), pp 97–111, (p. 100).

8. The standard tuning for modern Irish harps that was established with the invention of Portable Irish harps by John Egan in the early nineteenth century is E flat major when all the levers are down and E major when all the levers are raised. It should also be noted that some harp makers and harpists tune their instruments in C major or A flat major with all the levers down. Each string has a lever which, when raised or lowered, effects a change in the pitch of that particular string. Lever changes are generally manipulated by the left hand, therefore if lever changes are required during a performance, the composer must allow space to facilitate this.

9. For more information on the development of chromatic harps (with and without levers), see Anne-Marie O'Farrell, 'The chromatic development of the lever harp: Mechanism, resulting technique and repertoire', in Sandra Joyce and Helen Lawlor (eds), *Harp Studies: Perspectives on the Irish Harp* (Dublin: Four Courts Press, 2016), pp 209–38, (pp 235–8).

10. Michael Taylor, 'An interview with Brian Boydell', in Gareth Cox, Axel Klein and Michael Taylor (eds), *The Life and Music of Brian Boydell* (Dublin: Irish Academic Press, 2004), pp 63–95, (p. 80).

11. 'Transcript of Interview with Barra Boydell 10 February 2005', in Nicola Corbet, 'The Solo Harp Music of Brian Boydell' (Masters Thesis, Dublin City University, 2005), p. 40.

12. *Irish Press*, 6 Dec. 1958.

13. The appointment diaries that Boydell kept during the 1960s, 70s and 80s abound with references to social evenings spent with Michael and Gráinne Yeats, reminders to attend recitals and lectures given by Gráinne or her daughter Catríona, and details relating to Gráinne's engagements to lecture Senior Freshmen students at TCD. See, for example, Boydell Diaries, entries dated 30 October 1960, 14 November 1964, 1 January 1968, 10 November 1980 and 15 August 1988, Boydell Archive, TCD MS 11128/3/(35–60 and 61–72).

14. Michael Yeats (1921–2007) was the only son of the poet and playwright William Butler Yeats. He joined the Fianna Fáil party in the 1940s and served as a senator and as Cathaoirleach of the Seanad. He was a Member of the European Parliament from 1973–9 and served as its first Irish vice-president.

15. For more information on the Consort's repertoire and membership, see Axel Klein, 'Brian Boydell: Of man and music', in Cox, Klein, Taylor, *Life and Music*, pp 1–23, (pp 20–2); Brian Boydell, *Rebellious Ferment: A Dublin Musical Memoir and Diary*, ed. Barra Boydell (Cork: Atrium, 2018), pp 113–17; and Harry White and Barra Boydell (eds), *Encyclopaedia of Music in Ireland* (Dublin: UCD Press, 2013), i, p. 310.

16. Klein, 'Brian Boydell: Of man and music', p. 21.

17. Mary O'Hara (b. 1935) is an Irish singer/harpist, arranger and author. She enjoyed unprecedented national and international success and, during her lengthy career, she released several solo EPs to critical acclaim, performed regularly on Radio Éireann's 'Children at the Mike' Series, secured her own primetime series on BBC, and performed on the *Ed Sullivan Show* on the CBS network in the USA. Her repertoire of Irish- and English-language songs, her style of accompaniment and her arrangements significantly influenced the singer/harp tradition in Ireland and internationally in the 1950s and 60s. For more biographical information, see O'Hara, *Travels with my Harp: The Complete Autobiography* (London: Shepheard-Walwyn, 2012).

18. A performance of *Four Sketches for Two Irish Harps*, op. 52, was broadcast on Radio Éireann on 29 February 1964. Nos. 2 and 3 of the *Four Sketches* were published in Sheila Larchet Cuthbert, *The Irish Harp Book* (Cork: Mercier Press, 1975).

19. Ruth Mervyn was a composer and arranger who came to live in Ireland in 1935. She was an organist and pianist and was awarded prizes for her compositions at the Dublin Feis Ceoil and at an t-Oireachtas.

20. Thomas C. Kelly (1917–85) studied music at the National University of Ireland and was appointed head of the music department at Clongowes Wood College, Co. Kildare in 1952. His output includes orchestral and chamber works, and arrangements of Irish airs. See also White and Boydell, *Encyclopaedia of Music in Ireland*, vol. i, p. 562.

21. The programme also included performances of Edmund Rubbra's *Two Songs for Voice and Harp*, three seventeenth-century songs arranged by Arnold Dolmetsch, and arrangements by Joseph Groocock of *Scarúint na gCompánach* and *Betty O'Brien*.

22. *Irish Times*, 2 Mar. 1964. Charles Acton was referring to the British composer Raymond Warren (b. 1928) who composed operas and symphonies and was professor of composition at The Queen's University Belfast and later, professor of music at Bristol University.

23. Corbet, 'Interview with Barra Boydell', p. 41 (see n. 11).

24. No. 3 was arranged for solo Irish harp by Ank van Kampen in 1982.

25. *Irish Press*, 12 Mar. 1962.

26. *Irish Times*, 12 Mar. 1962.

27. 'Words and Music', A Lecture delivered to the Yeats International Summer School, Sligo 22 August 1969, Boydell Archive, TCD MS 11128/1/8/1/20, p. 14.

28. Boydell used 'Red Hanrahan's song about Ireland' in *A Terrible Beauty is Born*, op. 59 (1965), which was composed for RTÉ to mark the 50th anniversary of the Easter Rising. The work was premiered on 11 April 1966 at the Gaiety Theatre, Dublin.

29. Yeats recorded the *Three Yeats Songs* on the Nippon Columbia record label in 1965, and I am grateful to Catríona Yeats for allowing me to access her copy of the album for this research. Boydell transposed the piece down a tone for mezzo-soprano and Irish harp in 1992, and the work, which is available for purchase from the CMC, is now only available to the public in the transposed version. *Two Yeats Songs* for soprano or tenor and pianoforte, which included *A Drinking Song* and *Red Hanrahan's Song about Ireland*, was published in 1966.

30. For further information and an analysis of *An Album of Pieces for the Irish Harp*, see Corbet, 'Solo Harp Music', pp 21–8.
31. Composer's note on *An Album of Pieces for the Irish Harp*, Boydell Archive, TCD MS 11128/1/6/2/126(2).
32. This arrangement was published by Comunn na Clàrsaich/The Clarsach Society in Edinburgh in 1980.

NINE

1. This choir and the professorship in music were established by Provost Francis Andrews (*c*.1718–74: provost 1758–74).
2. The exact date is not entirely clear; it may be 1615 rather than 1612.
3. For a critical edition of *Holy, Lord God Almighty*, see Barra Boydell (ed.), *Music at Christ Church before 1800: Documents and Selected Anthems* (Dublin: Four Courts Press, 1999), pp 187–93.
4. Ralph Roseingrave (*c*.1695–1747) was the son of Daniel Roseingrave, who was possibly of Irish extraction and almost certainly a chorister at the Chapel Royal in London at the same time as Henry Purcell. He was successively organist of Gloucester, Winchester and Salisbury Cathedrals before moving to Dublin in 1698 where he became organist of Christ Church Cathedral, a post that he held until his death in 1727 when he was succeeded by his son Ralph. Daniel Roseingrave also held the post of organist of St Patrick's Cathedral Dublin from 1698 and was succeeded by Ralph in 1719. Ralph's older brother Daniel jr is almost certainly the 'young Roseingrave' who was appointed organist of Trinity College chapel in 1707.
5. Prout's edition of *Messiah* would be considered overly interventionist by modern editorial standards and includes 'additional accomp[animent]s largely re-written by E. Prout', (London: Novello & Co, 1902). Watkin Shaw's edition was also published in London by Novello & Co.
6. Percy Carter Buck, *The First Year at the Organ* (London: Stainer and Bell, 1912).
7. Kitson lived in Dublin during the 1916 rising. His account of the rising is preserved in the archives of the Royal College of Music, *GB-Lcm* MS 4735. This colourful narrative includes a description of his attempts to get to Christ Church to play the organ but being turned back by 'rebels'.
8. A large-scale choral cantata that looks suspiciously like a doctoral exercise survives in the archives at St Patrick's and received its premiere in the National Concert Hall in Dublin on 15 February 1998 as part of the bicentenary celebrations for Trinity College chapel.
9. Boydell was particularly critical of one of his predecessors mentioned above, Charles Kitson, with regard to his approach to teaching harmony: 'One of the things I set out to do was to try to get rid of what I think is an appalling attitude to the teaching of the fundamental theoretical aspects of the music, the old Kitson approach where you learn harmony as a series of dots on paper and are never trained to use your ear.' Michael Taylor, 'An interview with Brian Boydell', in Gareth Cox, Axel Klein and Michael Taylor (eds), *The Life and Music of Brian Boydell* (Dublin: Irish Academic Press, 2004), pp 63–95, (p. 90).
10. Boy choristers from St Patrick's who sang in the chapel at TCD were entitled to scholarships if they chose to study there in later life.
11. For more on repertoire at St Patrick's Cathedral, see Kerry Houston, 'From Marchant to Greig: A seamless thread through an uncertain terrain', in Kerry Houston and Harry White (eds), *A Musical Offering: Essays in Honour of Gerard Gillen* (Dublin: Four Courts Press, 2018),

pp 178–92, and Kerry Houston, 'Restoration and Consolidation: Music, 1865–1977', in John Crawford and Raymond Gillespie (eds), *St Patrick's Cathedral, Dublin: A History* (Dublin: Four Courts Press, 2009), pp 353–82.

12. St Patrick's Cathedral board minutes, 24 Apr. 1967, *Irl-Dpc* MS C.2.1.5.5.
13. Woodhouse was Regius professor of divinity 1963–82.
14. St Patrick's Cathedral board minutes 11 Dec. 1876, *Irl-Dpc* MS C.2.1.5.1. For more information on the Guinness Choir Scheme see Kerry Houston, 'Guinness is good for you: The contribution of a Dublin brewing family to St Patrick's cathedral and its musical establishment in the late nineteenth century', in Kerry Houston, Maria McHale and Michael Murphy (eds), *Documents of Irish Music History in the Long Nineteenth Century*, Irish Musical Studies 12 (Dublin: Four Courts Press, 2019), pp 224–38.
15. Bicycles were the main mode of transport used by the singers to relocate from TCD to St Patrick's.
16. St Patrick's Cathedral board minutes, 29 Nov. 1927, *Irl-Dpc* MS C.2.1.5.3.
17. Ibid., 23 Mar., 26 Oct. and 21 Dec. 1970, *Irl-Dpc* MS C.2.1.5.5.
18. Barra Boydell, 'Dowland Consort', in Harry White and Barra Boydell (eds), *The Encyclopaedia of Music in Ireland* (Dublin: UCD Press, 2013), p. 310.
19. Despite his very considerable contribution to the repertoire of the Anglican church, Howells was not a Christian in the orthodox sense.
20. Some of the more prominent former organ scholars include Malcolm Proud, David Milne, David Adams and Simon Harden, while former conductors include Peter Shannon and George Jackson.
21. Axel Klein, 'Brian Boydell: Of man and music' in Cox, Klein, Taylor, *Life and Music*, pp 1–23, (p. 2).
22. See also Barra Boydell, 'John Baptiste Cuvillie, Ferdinand Weber, and the Organ of Trinity College Chapel, Dublin', in *The Organ*, 72:283 (1992), pp 15–27.
23. Green's instrument was acquired by St Fintan's Church, Durrow, Co Laois in 1842.
24. Most of the pipework for this instrument was new but some of Telford's work was retained.
25. Later work by Kenneth Jones removed the four-foot principal from the swell so the principal rank on this division is now at two-foot pitch.
26. Report on the organs of Trinity College by Ian Bell (1995, p. 11). This report is held in the files of the TCD organ committee.
27. Ralph Downes, *Baroque Tricks* (Oxford: Positif Press, 1999), p. 212.
28. *Irish Times*, 1 Mar. 1969.
29. The international organ competition moved to Christ Church Cathedral following the installation of the new three-manual Kenneth Jones organ there in 1984.
30. Letter dated 15 August 1988 in the files of the TCD organ committee.
31. This 1961 rebuilding of the organ in the Public Theatre was overseen by George Hewson, Boydell's predecessor as professor of music.
32. Minutes of the organ committee meeting on 19 October 1993. In the files of the TCD organ committee.

TEN

1. Charles Acton, 'Interview with Brian Boydell', *Éire-Ireland: A Journal of Irish Studies* 5:4 (Winter 1970), pp 97–111.
2. Brian Boydell's article, 'Organs associated with Handel's visit to Dublin', in *Journal of the British Institute of Organ Studies* 119 (1995), pp 54–74, was his last publication that appeared during his lifetime. Posthumous publications included a number of articles on eighteenth- and early nineteenth-century Irish composers and musicians in Stanley Sadie (ed.), *The New Grove Dictionary of Music and Musicians* (2nd edn, London: Macmillan, 2001) and in Ludwig Finscher (ed.), *Die Musick in Geschichte und Gegenwart*, Biographical Section (rev. edn, Kassel: Metzler, 1999–2007).
3. For a full list of Brian Boydell's publications, see Gareth Cox, Axel Klein and Michael Taylor (eds), *The Life and Music of Brian Boydell* (Dublin: Irish Academic Press, 2004), pp 112–15 (compiled by Axel Klein).
4. Brian Boydell, *A Dublin Musical Calendar 1700–1760* (Dublin: Irish Academic Press, 1988), p. 7.
5. Boydell graduated from Clare College, Cambridge in 1938 with a first-class degree in natural sciences.
6. Boydell, *A Dublin Musical Calendar*, p. 7.
7. Ibid., p. 16.
8. Lady Llanover (ed.), *The Autobiography and Correspondence of Mary Granville, Mrs. Delany…* (3 vols, London: Richard Bentley, 1861), ii, p. 558: letter 22 June 1750, cited in *A Dublin Musical Calendar*, p. 11.
9. Boydell, *A Dublin Musical Calendar*, p. 80.
10. *Faulkner's Dublin Journal*, 16–20 Mar. 1742, cited in *A Dublin Musical Calendar*, p. 81.
11. Ibid., 8–11 May 1742, cited in *A Dublin Musical Calendar*, p. 13.
12. *A Dublin Musical Calendar*, p. 7.
13. Ibid., p. 81.
14. *Dublin News-letter*, 25–29 May 1742, cited in *A Dublin Musical Calendar*, p. 82.
15. *A Dublin Musical Calendar*, p. 23.
16. Brian Boydell, *Rotunda Music in Eighteenth-Century Dublin* (Dublin: Irish Academic Press, 1992), p. 11.
17. Ibid., p. 44.
18. Ibid., p. 31.
19. Ibid., p. 83.
20. Ibid., p. 98.
21. Ibid.
22. Ibid., p. 96.
23. Harry White, *The Progress of Music in Ireland* (Dublin: Four Courts Press, 2005), p. 151.

ELEVEN

1. MAI, *Prospectus* (1948), Music Association of Ireland Archive, National Library of Ireland Acc 6000.
2. Brian Boydell, *Rebellious Ferment: A Dublin Musical Memoir and Diary*, ed. Barra Boydell (Cork: Atrium, 2018), p. 84.
3. Ibid.
4. MAI, *Prospectus* (1948), MAI Archive, NLI Acc 6000.
5. The inter-party government consisted of Cumann na nGaedheal, Labour, Clann na Poblachta, Clann na Talmhan and the National Labour Party with John A. Costello as Taoiseach.
6. Brian P. Kennedy, *Dreams and Responsibilities: The State and the Arts in Independent Ireland* (Dublin: The Arts Council/An Chomhairle Ealaíon, 1990), p. 65.
7. Dermot Keogh, *Twentieth-Century Ireland: Revolution and State Building* (Dublin: Gill and Macmillan, 2005), p. 202.
8. Kennedy, *Dreams and Responsibilities*, p. 2.
9. Thomas Bodkin, *Report on the Arts in Ireland* (Dublin: Government Stationery Office, 1949).
10. Michael McMullin, 'Introduction', in *Memorandum: Music and the Nation* (unpublished), MAI Archive, NLI Acc 6000.
11. For a detailed discussion on the MAI's Memorandum, see Teresa O'Donnell, 'The Music Association of Ireland: A Cultural and Social History' (PhD dissertation, St Patrick's College (now Dublin City University), 2012), available at: http://doras.dcu.ie/22596/
12. Memorandum sent by Olive Smith, MAI honorary secretary to J. McCann (former Lord Mayor) and to An Taoiseach, Éamonn de Valera on 5 July 1951, MAI Archive, NLI Acc 6000.
13. Letter from Aloys Fleischmann, Frederick May, Brian Boydell and Michael McMullin to the Minister for Posts and Telegraphs on 28 April 1948, MAI Archive, NLI Acc 6000.
14. Richard Pine, *Music and Broadcasting in Ireland* (Dublin: Four Courts Press, 2005), p. 127.
15. Ibid., pp 127–8.
16. MAI, *1948 Honorary Secretary's Report*, MAI Archive, NLI Acc 6000.
17. Brian Boydell, 'The future of music in Ireland', in *The Bell* 16:4 (Jan. 1951), pp 21–9, (p. 21).
18. Aloys Fleischmann, 'Three views on: The future of music in Ireland', in *The Bell* 17:1 (Apr. 1951), pp 5–10, (p. 5).
19. In addressing a number of Boydell's criticisms of the standard of music in Ireland, Fleischmann listed the following positive improvements, namely: the introduction of compulsory class singing in primary schools under the supervision of four Inspectors, the Department of Education's Music Summer Schools (1946–56), the improved standard of the RÉSO and their increased performance at provincial concerts, RÉ's prizes for orchestral and chamber music compositions and the increase in the number of Irish artists performing abroad. Ibid.
20. P. J. Malone, 'Three views on: The future of music in Ireland', in *The Bell*, 17:1 (Apr. 1951), pp 10–13, (p. 11).
21. Joseph O'Neill, 'Three views on: The future of music in Ireland', ibid., pp 13–18, (p. 17).
22. Copy of the letter from MAI honorary secretary to the editor of *The Bell* on 17 January 1951,

MAI Archive, NLI Acc 6000. It is evident from drafts of the MAI's letter in its archive that Boydell assisted in the MAI's letter to the editor.
23. Ibid. One wonders how Fleischmann from Co. Cork reacted to this arbitrary statement.
24. Ibid.
25. Ibid.
26. McMullin, *Music and the Nation*, MAI Archive, NLI Acc 6000.
27. MAI, *MAI Memorandum of Association* (1948), MAI Archive, NLI Acc 6000.
28. Draft letter from MAI to Ruaidhrí Roberts (no date), MAI Archive, NLI Acc 6000.
29. Letter from Éamonn Ó Sé to Brian Boydell, MAI Archive, NLI Acc 6000.
30. Ibid.
31. Letter from Michael McMullin to Ruaidhrí Roberts, 2 October 1949, MAI Archive, NLI Acc 6000.
32. It should be noted that music lecturers were the only lecturers to receive remuneration for lectures delivered at the People's College. The fee to attend the series of lectures (in any subject) was 5/– or 2/6 for a short course. A number of unions introduced scholarships as incentives for their members. *Annual Report of the People's College Adult Education Association* (1948–9), MAI Archive, NLI Acc 6000.
33. Brian Boydell's Diary, 6 Jan. 1950, *Rebellious Ferment*, p. 125.
34. Boydell's Diary, 1 Jan. 1950, ibid., p. 123.
35. Boydell's Diary, 6 Jan. 1950, ibid., p. 125.
36. Boydell's Diary, 10 Jan. 1950, ibid., p. 129.
37. Boydell, *Rebellious Ferment*, p. 88.
38. Ibid, p. 88f.
39. 'Victory over the anthem', (no date), MAI Archive, NLI Acc 6000.
40. Boydell, 'The cantatas and orchestral works of J. S. Bach', 9 Oct. 1950, Brian Boydell Archive, TCD MS 11128/1/8/1/19.
41. Ibid.
42. Ibid.
43. Boydell, 'Topical Notes for Tuesday Review' Radio Talks, 24 Oct. 1950, Boydell Archive, TCD MS 11128/1/9/1/45/1.
44. Ibid.
45. Boydell, 'Topical Notes for Tuesday Review' Radio Talks, 4 July 1950, Boydell Archive, TCD MS 11128/1/9/1/36.
46. 'An Irishman's Diary', *Irish Times*, 29 June 1950.
47. Ibid.
48. For a photograph of Brian Boydell, Olive Smith, John Beckett and Otto Mazerath inspecting the Weber harpsichord in the National Museum of Ireland, see Boydell, *Rebellious Ferment*, p. 89.
49. MAI, *1950 Honorary Secretary's Report*, MAI Archive, NLI Acc 6000.
50. Boydell, 'The future of music in Ireland', p. 28.
51. Letter from Boydell to Minister for Finance Charles J. Haughey, 18 May 1969, Boydell Archive, TCD MS 11128/1/15/17.
52. Letter from Raymond McGrath to Boydell, 15 Apr. 1970, Boydell Archive, TCD MS 11128/1/15/16 (i).

53. Brian Boydell, 'The Future of Music in Ireland,' Mar. 1944, Boydell Archive, TCD MS 11128/1/8/1 (i).
54. Interestingly, Boydell listed any song/work from the collection with an Irish language title as 'title in Irish'.
55. Brian Boydell, 'Notes on Composers' Meetings', MAI Archive, NLI Acc 6000. Similar ideas were also expressed in a number of Boydell's lectures, for example, 'Culture and Chauvinism', Boydell Archive, TCD MS 11128/1/8/1/8.
56. Boydell, *Rebellious Ferment*, pp 97–8.
57. Ibid., p. 98.
58. Ibid.
59. Ian Fox, 'Irish Recordings', in *Counterpoint* (Dublin: MAI, Apr. 1972), p. 11, MAI Archive, NLI Acc 6000.
60. Teresa O'Donnell, 'The Music Association of Ireland: fostering a voice for Irish composers and composition', in *Journal of Music Research Online* 7 (2016), pp 1–14 (p. 8), available at: www.jmro.org.au/index.php/mca2/article/view/149.
61. The festival committee successfully engaged internationally acclaimed artists and composers such as Olivier Messiaen (1976), Witold Lutosławski (1978), Andrzej Panufnik (1978), Peter Maxwell Davies and The Fires of London (1978), Elliott Carter (1980) and Karlheinz Stockhausen (1982).
62. *Irish Times*, 30 Jan. 1987.
63. Brian Boydell, *MAI 50th Anniversary Celebration Programme*, MAI Archive, NLI Acc 6000.

TWELVE

1. 'Music and Communication', an interval talk broadcast on 3 October 1976 celebrating 50 years of Irish broadcasting, Brian Boydell Archive, TCD MS 11128/1/9/1/325/1.
2. Richard Pine, *Music and Broadcasting in Ireland* (Dublin: Four Courts Press, 2005); *2RN and the origins of Irish radio* (Dublin: Four Courts Press, 2002); P. J. Kehoe, 'The Evolution of the Radio Éireann Symphony Orchestra 1926–1954' (Unpublished PhD thesis, Dublin Institute of Technology [now Technological University Dublin], 2017), available at: https://arrow.tudublin.ie/appadoc/87/; Axel Klein, 'Brian Boydell: Of man and music', in Gareth Cox, Axel Klein and Michael Taylor (eds), *The Life and Music of Brian Boydell* (Dublin: Irish Academic Press, 2004). Teresa O'Donnell also makes mention of Boydell in this capacity in the previous essay of this volume.
3. Boydell also presented television programmes such as *Music in the Making* (1963) and *Musica Reservata* (1971) and was featured in interviews, for example John Bowman's *Witness* (1999).
4. The Boydell Archive at TCD holds scripts for Boydell's contributions to the BBC: 'A Recital to Commemorate the Centenary of Dean Swift', 14 Dec. 1967, TCD MS 11128/1/9/2/1; an introductory script for a concert by the New Irish Chamber Orchestra to be broadcast on BBC Radio 3 on 25 Sept. 1977, TCD MS 11128/1/9/2/2; and 'Mr Neale's Great Musick Hall', 1995, TCD MS 11128/1/9/2/3. He also presented a number of programmes for the CBC in Canada, see Boydell Archive, TCD MS 11128/1/9/3/1–8.
5. 'Everyone's Music, A Series of Four Arguments' (hereafter 'Everyone's Music'), No. 1, broadcast 6 June 1945, Boydell Archive, TCD MS 11128/1/9/1/334/1.

6. Brian Boydell, *Rebellious Ferment: A Dublin Musical Memoir and Diary*, ed. Barra Boydell (Cork: Atrium, 2018), p. 59.
7. From 1926 through 1939, the English composer [Henry] Walford Davies (1869–1941) presented a wide range of broadcasts on classical music for BBC radio, designed specifically for the non-specialist listener under the title 'Music and the Ordinary Listener'. Other presenters of the programme included Herbert Howells who produced six talks on 'The Modern Problem', where he spoke about new aspects of musical language in the music of Schoenberg, Berg, Bartók, Hindemith, Holst, Stravinsky and others; Constant Lambert gave talks on 'The Instruments of the Orchestra' and Percy Scholes presented on 'Modern Music', intending to illustrate for the listener the value in exploring new contemporary music.
8. Boydell, *Rebellious Ferment*, p. 59.
9. Captain Michael Bowles was appointed as director of music at RÉ in 1944, having previously been acting music director since 1941 upon the retirement of Vincent O'Brien. Bowles was also the conductor of the Radio Éireann Orchestra from 1938–44.
10. 'Everyone's Music', No. 1, 6 June 1945, Boydell Archive, TCD MS 11128/1/9/1/334/1. Capitalisation of opening word retained.
11. 'Topical Notes for Tuesday Review' (hereafter 'Topical Notes'), No. 66, 22 Jan. 1952, Boydell Archive, TCD MS 11128/1/9/1/98.
12. Conolly (1918–2016) was not only Boydell's brother-in-law but was also a fellow member of the White Stag Group. See Philip Graydon's essay elsewhere in this volume.
13. Boydell, *Rebellious Ferment*, p. 59.
14. 'Everyone's Music', No. 1, 6 June 1945, Boydell Archive, TCD MS 11128/1/9/1/334/1.
15. Ibid. Live music performances of ballads and parlour songs and concerts via the BBC had been the mainstay for the station since 1926 as the announcer's report illustrates, see RTÉ Archives Exhibition, www.rte.ie/archives/exhibitions/681-history-of-rte/682-rte-1920s/290016-2rn-announcers-report-program-schedule-1926/.
16. Brian O'Neill, 'Lifting the Veil: The arts, broadcasting and Irish society', in *Media, Culture & Society* 22 (2000), pp 763–85, (p. 779).
17. Email correspondence with Barra Boydell, 5 Feb. 2019. From 1949, when tape recording was available, Boydell would have been able to record some programmes in advance; when this occurs, he includes it atop the script.
18. Boydell, *Rebellious Ferment*, p. 61. Boydell's pocket and larger scribbling diaries also document the frequency of his visits to the studios at the GPO for rehearsals ahead of broadcasts. For pocket diaries, see Boydell Archive, TCD MS 11128/3/5-8; for scribbling diaries, see TCD MS 11128/3/11.
19. 'Everyone's Music', 6 June 1945 – 4 July 1945 (No date on No. 4 but presumably it followed on from Nos. 1–3), Boydell Archive, TCD MS 11128/1/9/1/334–7. Boydell argues for music as 'necessary for a fully-lived life', in episode No. 2, TCD MS 11128/1/9/1/335/4.
20. Ireland was still an infant country in the mid-1940s when Boydell came on air, only gaining its complete independence as a Republic in April 1949.
21. Theodor W. Adorno, 'The Radio Voice', in Robert Hullot-Kentor (ed.), *Current of Music* (Cambridge: Polity Press, 2009, English edn), pp 335–91, (p. 377). For more on the MAI, see Teresa O'Donnell's essay in this volume.
22. While there were 97 broadcasts in total, the scripts for 'Topical Notes' Nos. 26 and 27 (Feb. 1951) are unaccounted for in the archive.

23. 'Topical Notes', No. 19, 19 Dec. 1950, Boydell Archive, TCD MS 11128/1/9/1/53/1.
24. Ibid., No. 4, 25 July 1950, Boydell Archive, TCD MS 11128/1/9/1/38/2.
25. Ibid., No. 58, 6 Nov. 1951, Boydell Archive, TCD MS 11128/1/9/1/90/2; ibid., No. 35, 1 May 1951, Boydell Archive, TCD MS 11128/1/9/1/67/1. Original capitalisation retained. For further discussion, see Niall Doyle's essay in this volume.
26. 'Topical Notes', No. 6, 19 Sept. 1950, Boydell Archive, TCD MS 11128/1/9/1/40/1. Fleischmann's article outlined that, in 1951, Norway supported three professional orchestras, Denmark boasted four symphony orchestras alongside two permanent opera companies and, astoundingly, Switzerland had four state-supported opera companies, eleven professional orchestras and some fifty other orchestras. See Aloys Fleischmann, 'Three views on: The future of music in Ireland', in *The Bell* 17:1 (Apr. 1951), pp 5–10, (p. 5).
27. 'Topical Notes', No. 97, 30 Dec. 1952, Boydell Archive, TCD MS 11128/1/9/1/128/2; ibid., No. 65, 15 Jan. 1952, TCD MS 11128/1/9/1/97/1.
28. Ibid., No. 97, 30 Dec. 1952, Boydell Archive, TCD MS 11128/1/9/1/128/2; ibid., No. 48, 31 July 1951, Boydell Archive, TCD MS 11128/1/9/1/80/1; ibid., No. 19, 19 Dec. 1950, Boydell Archive, TCD MS 11128/1/9/1/53/1.
29. Ibid., No. 22, 9 Jan. 1951, Boydell Archive, TCD MS 11128/1/9/1/56/2.
30. 'Everyone's Music', No. 1, 6 June 1945, Boydell Archive, TCD MS 11128/1/9/1/334/1.
31. 'Topical Notes', No. 65, 15 Jan. 1952, Boydell Archive, TCD MS 11128/1/9/1/97/2. He did however acknowledge the dichotomous 'vicious circle', whereby the only way the public could become more cultured was if there was more performances for them to attend and financially support.
32. 'Everyone's Music', No. 1, 6 June 1945, Boydell Archive, TCD MS 11128/1/9/1/334/3.
33. Ibid. Original capitalisation retained.
34. Ibid., TCD MS 11128/1/9/1/334/1. Musical extracts played within programmes are listed on the typescripts. Boydell also inserted lists of works and topics into an index book entitled 'Broadcast Scripts Index of Subjects'; see Boydell Archive, TCD MS 11128/1/9/4. Original capitalisation retained.
35. 'Topical Notes', No. 7, 26 Sept. 1950, Boydell Archive, TCD MS 11128/1/9/1/41/1.
36. 'Everyone's Music', No. 1, 6 June 1945, Boydell Archive, TCD MS 11128/1/9/1/334/1.
37. Ibid.
38. Ibid.
39. Ibid.
40. Ibid., TCD MS 11128/1/9/1/334/4–7. Emphasis in original.
41. 'Everyone's Music', No. 2, 20 June 1945, Boydell Archive, TCD MS 11128/1/9/1/335/4.
42. Ibid., TCD MS 11128/1/9/1/335/3, and 'Everyone's Music', No. 3, 27 June 1945, Boydell Archive, TCD MS 11128/1/9/1/336/1. Original capitalisation retained.
43. 'Everyone's Music', No. 3, 27 June 1945, Boydell Archive, TCD MS 11128/1/9/1/336/3. It is assumed here that Boydell was referring to Mozart's Symphony No. 40 as opposed to the other less familiar G minor Symphony No. 25. This symphony also appears in his index book under 'M' on 6 July 1947, 26 Nov. 1950, 8 Jan. 1951, and 25 Feb. 1951. See Boydell Archive, TCD MS 11128/1/9/4.
44. 'Symphonic Music for the Young Listener' consisted of five half-hour broadcasts, on Wednesday evenings between 2 April through 24 May 1950, which centred on Beethoven's 7th Symphony. See Boydell Archive, TCD MS 11128/1/9/1/1–10.

45. 'Symphonic Music for the Young Listener', 26 Apr. 1950, Boydell Archive, TCD MS 11128/1/9/1/1/1.
46. 'The Amateur in Music' (hereafter 'The Amateur'), 15 Jan. 1955, Boydell Archive, TCD MS 11128/1/9/1/285/6 and 4. Emphasis in original.
47. 'Topical Notes', No. 65, 15 Jan. 1952, Boydell Archive, TCD MS 11128/1/9/1/97/2; ibid., No. 3, 8 July 1950, Boydell Archive, TCD MS 11128/1/9/1/37/1.
48. Ibid., No. 16, 28 Nov. 1950, Boydell Archive, TCD MS 11128/1/9/1/50/1.
49. 'The Amateur', Boydell Archive, TCD MS 11128/1/9/1/285/6.
50. Ibid., TCD MS 11128/1/9/1/285/5. He also contributed a slot on 'domestic music making' to the radio magazine 'Take a Break', n.d., Boydell Archive, TCD MS 11128/1/9/1/669/1.
51. 'The Amateur', Boydell Archive, TCD MS 11128/1/9/1/285/2. Boydell also recites for his listeners the story of the old lady who was overcome by Liszt's ability with his fists at the piano.
52. Ibid.
53. From a composer's standpoint Boydell suggests that 'this business of writing what the public IMMEDIATELY likes' has caused some contemporary western composers to retreat into obscurity while others churn out insincere 'second-hand potted sentimentality', becoming little more than 'a commercial craftsman pandering to the lowest level of intelligence'. See 'Music and Communication', 3 Oct. 1976, Boydell Archive, TCD MS 11128/1/9/1/325/7; 'Everyone's Music', No. 1, 6 June 1952, Boydell Archive TCD MS 11128/1/9/1/334/6. Original capitalisation retained.
54. 'The Amateur', Boydell Archive, TCD MS 11128/1/9/1/285/1.
55. Ibid., TCD MS 11128/1/9/1/285/6.
56. 'Topical Notes', No. 85, 30 Sept. 1952, Boydell Archive, TCD MS 11128/1/9/1/116/3.
57. Ibid., No. 20, 26 Dec. 1950, Boydell Archive, TCD MS 11128/1/9/1/54/1–2.
58. Ibid., No. 29, 13 Mar. 1951, Boydell Archive, TCD MS 11128/1/9/1/61/1.
59. Ibid., No. 53, 2 Oct. 1951, Boydell Archive, TCD MS 11128/1/9/1/85/1.
60. Ibid., No. 7, 26 Sept. 1950, Boydell Archive, TCD MS 11128/1/9/1/41/1. Born in Hungary, Francois d'Albert was a solo violinist who became an Irish citizen in 1955. He taught at the Royal Irish Academy of Music from 1952–8, was a member of the RÉSO, and a founding member of the Dublin String Quartet. In 1958 he was appointed an artist faculty member of Chicago Conservatory, two years later becoming president of the institution. Despite being a virtuoso d'Albert shared Boydell's concerns around chamber music and organised a series of chamber recitals at the Hibernian Hotel in the early 1950s.
61. Ibid., No. 12, 31 Oct. 1950, Boydell Archive, TCD MS 11128/1/9/1/46/2. Eventually, following his lobbying for concert programmes in advance, the Royal Dublin Society (RDS) concert series began to provide a programme ahead of performances. For the Autumn Series of 1950 at the RDS, for example, Boydell discusses the programme before a performance by the Griller Quartet of works by Haydn, Bloch, Schubert, Beethoven and Kodály, see TCD MS 11128/1/9/1/46/3.
62. Ibid., No. 7, 26 Sept. 1950, Boydell Archive, TCD MS 11128/1/9/1/41/1.
63. See 'From the Archive: Brian Boydell in his own words', an online exhibition by the Contemporary Music Centre Ireland, available at: www.cmc.ie/boydell-100/brian-boydell-in-his-own-words.
64. 'Topical Notes', No. 83, 23 Sept. 1952, Boydell Archive, TCD MS 11128/1/9/1/114/1.

65. Ibid., No. 7, 26 Sept. 1950, Boydell Archive, TCD MS 11128/1/9/1/41/1; ibid., No. 65, 15 Jan. 1952, TCD MS 11128/1/9/1/97/2–3.
66. Ibid., No. 79, 6 May 1952, Boydell Archive, TCD MS 11128/1/9/1/110/1.
67. 'Pianoforte Music for the Young Student', No. 3, for 'Children's Hour', 1 Mar. 1946, Boydell Archive, TCD MS 11128/1/9/1/350/1–2. Original capitalisation retained.
68. Michael Taylor, 'An interview with Brian Boydell', in Cox, Klein, Taylor, *Life and Music*, pp 63–95, (p. 68).
69. Boydell states that: 'This list could also include some information about the type of music preferred, and give some indication of the ability… This is something that the Music Association of Ireland might do – in fact I must suggest it at the next council meeting'. See 'Topical Notes', No. 79, 6 May 1952, Boydell Archive, TCD MS 11128/1/9/1/110/1.
70. Ibid., No. 82, 27 May 1952, Boydell Archive, TCD MS 11128/1/9/1/113/3. A further manifestation of Boydell's proposal was the Dublin Chamber Music Group, which evolved in the 1950s largely through members of the DOP. For more, see Barra Boydell's entry in Harry White and Barra Boydell (eds), *The Encyclopaedia of Music in Ireland* (Dublin: UCD Press, 2013), i, p. 323.
71. 'Topical Notes', No. 66, 22 Jan. 1952, Boydell Archive, TCD MS 11128/1/9/1/98/2. Also ibid., No .9, 10 Oct. 1950, Boydell Archive TCD MS 11128/1/9/1/43/1.
72. Ibid., No. 66, TCD MS 11128/1/9/1/98/2.
73. Ibid., No. 15, 21 Nov. 1951, Boydell Archive, TCD MS 11128/1/9/1/49/1.
74. Ibid., No. 6, 19 Sept. 1950, Boydell Archive, TCD MS 11128/1/9/1/40/1.
75. Ibid., No. 15, 21 Nov. 1951, Boydell Archive, TCD MS 11128/1/9/1/49/1.
76. Richard Pine, *Music and Broadcasting*, p. 331.
77. 'Topical Notes', No. 9, 10 Oct. 1950, Boydell Archive, TCD MS 11128/1/9/1/43/1.
78. Ibid., No. 81, 20 May 1952, Boydell Archive, TCD MS 11128/1/9/1/112/2.
79. 'The Music Children Like', for 'Take A Break', n.d. Boydell Archive, TCD MS 11128/1/9/1/668/2. Emphasis in original.
80. Ibid., TCD MS 11128/1/9/1/668/1–2. The concert was performed by the London String Quartet and organised by the MAI.
81. 'Music for All', No.1, 3 July 1946, Boydell Archive, TCD MS 11128/1/9/1/354/1.
82. Boydell calls these 'cases of misdirected value-judgements which can lead to a failure to appreciate the music on the level of its own terms of reference'. See 'Music and Communication', 3 Oct. 1976, Boydell Archive, TCD MS 11128/1/9/1/325/2.
83. 'Pianoforte Music for the Young Student', No. 6, 12 Apr. 1946, Boydell Archive, TCD MS 11128/1/9/1/353/3. Also see 'Music for All', 3 July 1946, Boydell Archive, TCD MS 11128/1/9/1/354.
84. 'Symphonic Music for the Young Listener', 26 Apr. 1950, Boydell Archive, TCD MS 11128/1/9/1/1–2.
85. Ibid., TCD MS 11128/1/9/1/2.
86. Ibid.
87. Boydell would hopefully be pleased to learn that a radio channel dedicated to art music, RTÉ lyric fm, has reached its 20th year and music-making in Ireland is still afire.
88. As Harry White contends, Boydell didn't like the nomenclature 'musicology'; however, in this regard, he may have been a little more content. Harry White, *The Progress of Music in Ireland* (Dublin: Four Courts Press, 2005), p. 151.

89. 'Witness' presented by John Bowman, 19 Sept. 1999.
90. 'Music and Communication', 3 Oct. 1976, Boydell Archive, TCD MS 11128/1/9/1/325/2 and TCD MS 11128/1/9/1/325/7. Emphasis in original.

THIRTEEN

1. André Lhote, *Treatise on Landscape Painting*, trans. W. J. Strachan (London: A. Zwemmer, 1950), p. 37.
2. Ibid.
3. Brian S. B. Kennedy, *Irish Art & Modernism* (Belfast: Institute of Irish Studies, The Queen's University of Belfast, 1991), pp 115–46.
4. Brian O'Doherty, 'Introductory essay', in *The Irish Imagination 1959–1971* (Hugh Lane Municipal Gallery of Modern Art, Dublin, Rosc exhibition catalogue, 1971), pp 10–11.
5. Brian Boydell, *Rebellious Ferment: A Dublin Musical Memoir and Diary*, ed. Barra Boydell (Cork: Atrium, 2018), p. 65n.
6. Ibid., p. 71n.
7. Ibid., p. 74.
8. Ibid., p. 76.
9. Author's correspondence with Thurloe Conolly, 2007. On Boydell's *The Feather of Death*, see Philip Graydon's essay elsewhere in this volume.
10. Boydell, *Rebellious Ferment*, p. 80.

FOURTEEN

1. The majority of the glass lantern slides date from the earlier twentieth century and were passed down to Brian Boydell from his father.
2. As confirmed by Barra Boydell.
3. He also visited Hong Kong as an adjudicator in the 1970s, although this is not reflected in the documents.
4. An online catalogue of many of the manuscripts and collections in the Manuscripts & Archives Research Library is accessible at: https://manuscripts.catalogue.tcd.ie/CalmView/
5. A digital copy of the catalogue of the papers is available on request from the Manuscripts & Archives Research Library. This descriptive list will be uploaded to the online catalogue once the musical scores have been both catalogued, and their descriptions added to the document.

FIFTEEN

1. Although the first professorship in music at TCD was established in 1764, at the time Brian Boydell was appointed professor in 1962 the position was part-time with no other departmental staff and the MusB music degree was only offered externally. Boydell was responsible for establishing the School of Music as a full academic department, with a staff offering full-time degree courses to students.

2. Brian Boydell, 'The future of music in Ireland', in *The Bell* 16:4 (Jan. 1951), pp 21–9, (p. 21).
3. See further, Teresa O'Donnell's essay on Brian Boydell and the MAI elsewhere in this volume.
4. Michael Taylor, 'An interview with Brian Boydell', in Gareth Cox, Axel Klein and Michael Taylor (eds), *The Life and Music of Brian Boydell* (Dublin: Irish Academic Press, 2004), pp 63–95, (p. 76).
5. National Campaign for the Arts press release, 13 Oct. 2015, see http://ncfa.ie/2015/10/13/ncfa-press-release-budget-2016/

Chronology with Cited Works

	Biography	Musical compositions cited in the text
1917	Born in Dublin, 17 March	
1930–5	Rugby School, England	
1935	Studies in Heidelberg, Germany	
1935–8	Clare College, Cambridge	
1935		*Wild Geese*, op. 1, low v, pf; *Nine Variations on the Snowy-Breasted Pearl*, op. 2, pf; *Rushlights*, op. 3, low v, pf [later withdrawn];
1936		*Cathleen, the Daughter of Hoolihan*, op. 4, low v, pf [later withdrawn]; *She Weeps over Rahoon*, op. 5, low v, pf [later withdrawn]; *Watching the Needleboats*, low v, pf, rev. 1937
1937		*Cradle Song*, s, pf, rev. 1943 as op. 10 no. 3
1938–9	Royal College of Music, London	
1938		*A Child's Grace*, s, pf, rev. 1943 as op. 10 no. 1 *The Witch*, op. 6, low v, pf [later withdrawn]
1939	Returns to Dublin at the outbreak of war	*Aurelia*, op. 7, low v, pf [later withdrawn]
1940		*The Bargain*, s, pf, rev. 1943 as op. 10 no. 2; Oboe Quintet, op. 11, ob, str qt; *An Easter Carol*, op. 12, s, t, b, ch; *Hearing of Harvests*, op. 13, bar, orch, ch
1941		*Pregaria a la Verge del Remei*, op. 14, str orch, rev. 1945; *Alone*, op. 15, low v, pf [later withdrawn]
1942	MusB degree from TCD	*The Strings are False*, op. 16, orch; *Laïsh*, op. 17, orch; *A House of Cards*, op. 18, 2 pf (incidental music); *Satirical Suite*, op. 18a, orch; *The Lamenting*, op. 19, bar, pf (str qt/orch) [later withdrawn]

Year	Event	Works
1943	Conductor of the DOP (until 1966)	*The Feather of Death*, op. 22, bar, fl, vn, va, vc; *Three Songs for Soprano and String Quartet*, op. 10
1944	January: organises concert of his compositions in the Shelbourne Hotel, Dublin. Two paintings shown in the White Stag Group's Exhibition of Subjective Art in Dublin. Teaches singing at the RIAM (until 1952)	String Trio, op. 21, vn, va, vc
1945	Commences regular radio programmes on music appreciation	*Symphony for Strings*, op. 26, rev. 1946; *Suite: Naughty Children*, op. 27, pf; *The Sleeping Leprechaun*, op. 27a, pf (retitled 2nd movement of *Suite: Naughty Children*, publ separately by Ricordi, 1959)
1946		*Five Joyce Songs*, op. 28, bar, pf; *Five Joyce Songs*, op. 28a, bar, orch
1947		*Magh Sleacht*, op. 29, orch; [*Caprice for Wind Instruments*: undeveloped sketch in TCD MS 11128/6]
1948	Founding member of the MAI	*In Memoriam Mahatma Gandhi*, op. 30, orch
1949	RÉ Chamber Music Prize for his String Quartet no. 1	String Quartet no. 1, op. 31; [*Divertimento for Clarinet, Oboe and Orchestra*: undeveloped sketch in TCD MS 11128/6]
1950		*The Buried Moon*, op. 32a (1950), orch (ballet suite)
1952		*The Owl and the Pussy Cat*, op. 34, ch
1953		Violin Concerto, op. 36, rev. 1954
1954		*The Wooing of Etain* (Suites 1 & 2), op. 37a, op. 37b, orch; *Divertimento for Three Music Makers*, op. 38, ob (fl, vn), cl (vn, va), bn (va, vc, cl)
1956		*Megalithic Ritual Dances*, op. 39, orch; *Elegy and Capriccio*, op. 42, cl, str orch
1957		*The Deer's Cry*, op. 43, bar, orch; String Quartet no. 2, op. 44
1958	Founder and director of the Dowland Consort (to 1969)	*Ceol Cas Corach*, op. 46, orch
1959	MusD degree from TCD	*Dance for an Ancient Ritual*, op. 39a, pf; *Shielmartin Suite*, op. 47, orch; *Capriccio*, op. 48, pf
1960		Quintet for Flute, Harp and String Trio, op. 49, rev 1966, 1980
1961	Commissioned to arrange the national anthem for Irish television	*Mors et vita*, op. 50, s, t, b, orch, ch; *Richards Riot*, op. 51, perc, orch

Chronology with Cited Works

	Member of the Arts Council of Ireland (to 1982)	
1962	Appointed professor of music, TCD	*Four Sketches for Two Irish Harps*, op. 52
1964		*Two Madrigals*, op. 54, ch
1965	Commissioned by RTÉ to mark the 50th anniversary of the Easter Rising (1916)	*Three Yeats Songs*, op. 56a, s, Ir hp, rev. 1992 *Musician's Song [Love is an Immoderate Thing]*, op. 56b, s, Ir hp; *Yeats Country*, op. 57, orch (film music); *Ireland*, op. 58, orch (film music); *A Terrible Beauty is Born*, op. 59, s, a, b, narr, orch, ch
1966		*Four Yeats Poems*, op. 56, s, orch (adapted from op. 56a, 56b)
1967		*Three Madrigals*, op. 60, ch; *Mists of Time*, op. 61, orch (film music)
1968		*Errigal*, op. 63, orch (film music); *Symphonic Inscapes*, op. 64, orch
1969		String Quartet no. 3, op. 65
1970		*A Pack of Fancies for a Travelling Harper*, op. 66, hp
1972		*Five Mosaics*, op. 69, vn, hp (pf), rev. 1978 as *Six Mosaics*
1973		*Three Pieces for Guitar*, op. 70, gui
1974	Honorary DMus from the NUI	*Mouth Music*, op. 72, ch
1976		*Jubilee Music*, op. 73, orch
1978		*Partita Concertante*, op. 75, vn, hp, orch [adapted from *Five Mosaics*, op. 69 and *Impetuous Capriccio*, op. 75a]; *Impetuous Capriccio*, op. 75a, vn, pf; *Six Mosaics*, vn, pf; [*Five Mosaics*, op. 69 with addition of *Impetuous Capriccio* op. 75a movement]
1980		*The Small Bell*, op. 76, fl, hp, str qt, ch
1981		*Three Geological Glees*, op. 77, ch
1982	Retires as professor of music, TCD	
1983	Commendatore della Repubblica Italiana	
1984	Elected to Aosdána (the State-sponsored affiliation of creative artists honoured for their contribution to the arts in Ireland)	*The Carlow Cantata* (or *The Female Friend*), op. 83, s, t, bar, orch (cl, str orch), ch
1986		*Confrontations in a Cathedral*, op. 84, org, hp, perc
1987		*Under No Circumstances*, op. 85, t, bar, narr, orch, ch
1988	Publishes *A Dublin Musical Calendar: 1700–1760*	*I will hear what God the Lord will speak* (Psalm 85), op. 86, ch/org; *Masai Mara*, op. 87, orch

1989		*An Album of Pieces for the Irish Harp*, op. 88
1990	Honorary Fellowship of the RIAM	
1991		*Adagio and Scherzo*, op. 89, str qt
1992	Publishes *Rotunda Music in Eighteenth-Century Dublin*	*The Maiden and the Seven Devils*, op. 90, pf
1996		*Viking Lip Music*, op. 91, br bd
1997	March: Presentation in Dublin Castle from President Mary Robinson to mark his 80th birthday	
2000	Dies in Dublin, 8 November	

Discography

Oboe Quintet, op. 11 (1940)
Síle Daly (ob), ConTempo String Quartet: IMMA & CMC, CD [insert to exhibition catalogue] 2005

The Feather of Death, op. 22 (1943)
Roland Davitt (bar), Ríonna Ó Duinnín (fl), ConTempo String Quartet: IMMA & CMC, CD [insert to exhibition catalogue] 2005

In Memoriam Mahatma Gandhi, op. 30 (1948)
NSOI, Colman Pearce (cond): Marco Polo 8.223887, CD 1997

String Quartet no. 1, op. 31 (1949)
Benthien Streichquartett: Deutsche Grammophon 32291, LP c.1955
Academica Quartet: Goasco GXX 002-4, MC 1985
ConTempo String Quartet: IMMA & CMC, CD [insert to exhibition catalogue] 2005
Carducci String Quartet: Carducci Classics CSQ 8841, CD 2009

Violin Concerto, op. 36 (1953–4)
Maighread McCrann (vn), NSOI, Colman Pearce (cond): Marco Polo 8.223887, CD 1997

Megalithic Ritual Dances, op. 39 (1956)
RÉSO, Milan Horvat (cond): Decca (USA) DL 9843, LP 1956
NSOI, Colman Pearce (cond): Marco Polo 8.223887, CD 1997

Elegy and Capriccio, op. 42 (1956)
John Finucane (cl), RTÉ National Symphony Orchestra, Robert Houlihan (cond): RTÉ lyric fm CD 124, CD 2010

Noël, op. 41 (1956)
Jennifer Kelly (rec), Alison Gillespie (rec), Michael Quinn (org), TCD Chapel Choir, Simon Harden (cond): TCDCC03, CD 2000

String Quartet no. 2, op. 44 (1957)
Vanbrugh Quartet: Chandos CHAN 9295, CD 1994
Carducci String Quartet: Carducci Classics CSQ 8841, CD 2009

Dance for an Ancient Ritual, op. 39a (1959)
Charles Lynch (pf): New Irish Recording Company NIR 001, LP 1971

Capriccio, op. 48 (1959)
Charles Lynch (pf): New Irish Recording Company NIR 001, LP 1971

Quintet for Flute, Harp and String Trio, op. 49 (1960, rev. 1966 and 1980)
Ciaran O'Connell (fl), Clíona Doris (hp), David O'Doherty (vn), Andreea Banciu (va), Margaret Doris (vc): RTÉ lyric fm CD160 (release pending)

Four Sketches for Two Irish Harps, op. 52 (1962)
Mary Louise O'Donnell, Teresa O'Donnell (Ir hps): www.teresaodonnell.com, CD 2020
Clíona Doris, Denise Kelly McDonnell (Ir hps): RTÉ lyric fm, CD160 (release pending)

Three Yeats Songs, op. 56a (1965)
Gráinne Yeats (v, Ir hp): Columbia (Japan) JX-32, LP c1972
Mary Louise O'Donnell (v, Ir hp): www.teresaodonnell.com, CD 2020

Symphonic Inscapes, op. 64 (1968)
RTÉSO, Albert Rosen (cond): New Irish Recording Company NIR 011, LP 1975

String Quartet no. 3, op. 65 (1969)
Carducci String Quartet: Carducci Classics CSQ 8841, CD 2009

A Pack of Fancies for a Travelling Harper, op. 66 (1970)
Clíona Doris (hp): Riverrun Records RVRCD59, CD 2003
Clíona Doris (hp): RTÉ lyric fm CD160 (release pending)

Five Mosaics for Violin and Harp, op. 69 (1972)
David O'Doherty (vn), Clíona Doris (hp): RTÉ lyric fm CD160 (release pending)

Three Pieces for Guitar, op. 66 (1973)
John Feeley (gui): Black Box Music BBM 1002, CD 1998

Under No Circumstances, op. 85 (1987)
Eugene O'Hagan (t), Philip O'Reilly (bar), Barra Boydell (narr), Dublin Sinfonia, University of Dublin Choral Society, Bernie Sherlock (cond): University of Dublin Choral Society UDCSCD001, CD 2004

Masai Mara, op. 87 (1988)
NSOI, Colman Pearce (cond): Marco Polo 8.223887, CD 1997

An Album of Pieces for the Irish Harp, op. 88 (1989)
Teresa O'Donnell (Ir hp): www.teresaodonnell.com, CD 2020

Adagio and Scherzo, op. 89 (1991)
Vanbrugh Quartet: CMC CD01, Promotional CD 1995
Carducci String Quartet: Carducci Classics CSQ 8841, CD 2009

Viking Lip Music, op. 91 (1996)
Royal Danish Brass: Rondo Grammofon RCD 8358, CD 1997

RECORDED BUT NEVER RELEASED:

String Quartet no. 2, op. 44 (1957)
RTÉ String Quartet: New Irish Recording Company, NIR 006, LP 1973

Three Madrigals, op. 60 (1967)
New Irish Recording Company, NIR 007, LP 1974

Bibliography

[Texts cited across multiple essays, and selected texts specific to Brian Boydell]

Acton, Charles, 'Interview with Brian Boydell', in *Éire-Ireland: A Journal of Irish Studies*, 5:4, Winter 1970, pp 97–111.
——, 'Brian Patrick Boydell', in *Irish Arts Review,* 4:4, 1987, pp 66–7.
Boydell, Brian, 'The future of music in Ireland', in *The Bell*, 16:4, Jan. 1951, pp 21–9.
——, *A Dublin Musical Calendar 1700–1760* (Dublin: Irish Academic Press, 1988).
——, *Rotunda Music in Eighteenth-Century Dublin* (Dublin: Irish Academic Press, 1992).
——, *Rebellious Ferment: A Dublin Musical Memoir and Diary*, ed. Barra Boydell (Cork: Atrium, 2018).
Corbet, Nicola, 'The Solo Harp Music of Brian Boydell' (Masters Thesis, Dublin City University, 2005).
Cox, Gareth, 'Octatonicism in the string quartets of Brian Boydell', in Patrick F. Devine and Harry White, eds, *The Maynooth International Musicological Conference 1995: Selected Proceedings Part One*, Irish Musical Studies 4 (Dublin: Four Courts Press, 1996), pp 263–70.
——, 'Boydell, Brian', in *The New Grove Dictionary of Music and Musicians* (London: Macmillan, 2001) and *Grove Music Online*.
——, 'Boydell, Brian', in Harry White and Barra Boydell, eds, *The Encyclopaedia of Music in Ireland* (Dublin: UCD Press, 2013), i, pp 115–19.
Cox, Gareth, Axel Klein and Michael Taylor, eds, *The Life and Music of Brian Boydell* (Dublin: Irish Academic Press, 2004).
Cox, Gareth, and Julian Horton, eds, *Irish Musical Analysis*, Irish Musical Studies 11 (Dublin: Four Courts Press, 2014).
Dervan, Michael, ed., *The Invisible Art: A Century of Music in Ireland 1916–2016* (Dublin: New Island, 2016).
Doyle, Niall, ed., *The Boydell Papers: Essays on Music and Music Policy in Ireland* (Dublin: Music Network, 1997).
Farrell, Hazel, 'The String Quartets of Brian Boydell' (Masters Thesis, Waterford Institute of Technology, 1996).
Fleischmann, Aloys, 'Boydell, Brian (Patrick)', in Brian Morton and Pamela Collins, eds, *Contemporary Composers* (Chicago and London: St James Press, 1992), pp 110–13.

Graydon, Philip, 'Modernism in Ireland and its Cultural Context in the Music and Writings of Frederick May, Brian Boydell, and Aloys Fleischmann' (Masters Thesis, NUI Maynooth, 1999).

——, 'Modernism in Ireland and its cultural context in the music of Frederick May, Brian Boydell and Aloys Fleishmann', in Gareth Cox and Axel Klein, eds, *Irish Music in the Twentieth Century*, Irish Musical Studies 7 (Dublin: Four Courts Press, 2003), pp 56–79.

Klein, Axel, *Die Musik Irlands im 20. Jahrhundert* (Hildesheim: Georg Olms Verlag, 1996).

——, 'Boydell, Brian (Patrick)', in L. Finscher, ed., *Die Musik in Geschichte und Gegenwart*, new edn, Biographical Section (Kassel: Bärenreiter and Stuttgart: Metzler, 2000), iii, pp 600–2.

Murray, Peter, 'The language of dreams: Peter Murray remembers the multi-talented artist-composer Brian Boydell', in *Irish Arts Review*, 32:4, Winter 2015, pp 524–5.

Pine, Richard, *Music and Broadcasting in Ireland* (Dublin: Four Courts Press, 2005).

White, Harry, '"Our musical state became refined": The musicology of Brian Boydell', in *The Progress of Music in Ireland* (Dublin: Four Courts Press, 2005), pp 151–66.

White, Harry and Barra Boydell, eds, *The Encyclopaedia of Music in Ireland* (Dublin: UCD Press, 2013).

Index

Académie Julian 186
Achenbach, Andrew 119
Acton, Charles 37–8, 46, 51, 53, 99, 109, 117–18, 124, 130, 146
    interview with Boydell 25–6, 88, 96, 112, 115, 149
Adams, Martin 115–16, 147
Adorno, Theodor W. 173
Aengus Films 77
Ahrens Burton and Koralek 185
Aiken, Frank 79
Aldrich Smith, Valerie 118
Alvarez, Javier 115
An Gúm 165
Aosdána 3, 195
Arne, Michael 153
Arts Council 1, 4, 10, 123, 135, 156, 159, 164, 201, 207
Association of Irish Composers 195
Aston, Peter 130
avant-garde 7, 15, 26–7, 33, 98, 164, 187–8

Bach, J. S. 110, 114, 145–6
    bicentenary festival 8, 159, 161–3
Bank of Ireland Arts Centre 115
Bannister, George 123, 142
Bantock, Granville 38
Barry, Tom St John 80–1
Bartók, Béla 26, 42, 182
Bateson, Thomas 139
BBC 123, 149, 170–1, 195, 197
Beckett, John 163
Beckett, Samuel 191
Beethoven, Ludwig van, string quartets 17
Bell, Derek 114, 118
Bell, Ian 146
Bell, The 100, 158–9, 174, 200
Benthien String Quartet 22

Berg, Alban 95–6, 101
Berryman, John 101–2, 191
Bloch, Ernest 26
Bodkin, Thomas 156
Bodley, Seóirse 43, 53, 65, 166
Bolger, Mercedes 108, 110, 123–4
Bonynge, Richard 206
Bord Fáilte 79
Boughton, Rutland 38
Bowles, Michael 171
Boydell, Barra 1, 81, 101, 122, 124, 143, 172
Boydell, Brian *see also under* Acton, Charles
    70th/80th birthday concerts 108, 110–11, 116, 166–7
    80th birthday ceremony 200
    activism 4, 199–201, 207
    adjudication at festivals 3, 197
    archives *see* Trinity College Dublin
    art collection 187
    and the Arts Council 1, 3, 164, 195, 201
    atheism 4, 140
    bohemian lifestyle 188–9
    broadcasts: 3, 9, 62, 169–84, 186, 201; BBC 170; CBC 170; 'Children's Hour' 182; 'Everyone's Music' 170–1, 175–6; 'Music for All' 182; 'Music and Communication' 182; 'Symphonic Music' 177, 183; 'Topical Notes for Tuesday Review' 9, 162–3, 170, 173, 178–9, 182; typescripts 172
    collaborations: 4, 6–7, 74, 108, 191, 202, 207; Carey 86; Conolly 99–100, 106, 130; Gráinne Yeats 111, 121–36
    conservatism 22, 27
    cosmopolitanism 56

diaries 79–80
dislike of light music 170
and Dowland Consort 3, 87, 123, 142–4, 186, 195, 201
and Dublin Orchestral Players 3, 22, 28, 39, 62, 180, 186, 195, 200
early life 2, 15, 186
education: 2–3, 15–16, 26, 88, 101; view of 16
Imaal, Rathfarnham 99–100, 190–2
influence of 14, 56–7, 199–200
influences on 3, 9, 16–17, 26–7, 30, 39, 42, 49, 64–5, 88, 90, 101, 112, 114, 122, 144
interests: 197; art 72; eighteenth-century music 149; literature 191; nature 9, 54, 56; organs 144–5; prehistory 56, 64; Yeats 130–1
internationalism 5, 26, 38, 64–5, 115, 120, 164
lectures: 3, 160–1; Bach 8, 162; Brahms 160; music appreciation 160; Yeats 131
and the MAI 155–68, 201
and modernism 101, 185, 191
musicology 1, 3, 8, 51, 149–54, 170, 200, 206
national identity 3–5, 8, 15–16, 24–6, 64
painting 9, 98–9, 185–92; *Abandoned Engine Works* 190–1; *Atlas Approached* 99, 107, 190; *Gunnera* 191; *Laurel Tangle* 191; *Return of the Wood* 99, 107, 190–1; *Worm Hole* 190
performer: 2, 181; conductor 3, 22, 28, 62, 74, 180, 186, 200; oboe 123, 152, 165; piano 189; singer 6, 22, 87, 104
photography 72, 197–8
professor of music, TCD 7, 18, 51, 139–48, 149, 185–6
professor of singing, RIAM 62, 185–6, 201
rebelliousness 2, 191
and Renaissance music 3, 14, 55, 123, 143
singing 22, 87, 97
sketchbooks 5, 58–62, 67–70
travels 53
views: amateur music-making 9, 171–2, 178–81, 183 (*see also* Dublin

Orchestral Players); avant-garde 26–7; chamber music 178–81; critics 47–8, 117; music appreciation 9, 175–7; music in Ireland 173–4, 200; musical education 181–3; virtuosos 18, 43, 178–9
working methods 72–3
works, literary: articles 149, 158; contributions to *Grove* 3, 149; *Dublin Musical Calendar* 8, 149–51; memoir 1, 95–6, 101, 166, 190; *Die Musik* 149; *New History of Ireland* 3, 149; *Rotunda Music* 8, 149, 152–3

works, musical:
Adagio and Scherzo 17–19
allegorical 64
Buried Moon 59, 69–70
Carlow Cantata 167
Ceol cas corach 38, 46
chromaticism 7, 49, 62, 116, 124, 130–1
Confrontations in a Cathedral 10, 109, 111
'cornerstones' 48–9
Deer's Cry 38
Divertimento 70, 165
early 6, 27–8, 87–97
Elegy and Capriccio 43–6
experimentation 72, 84
film scores: 47, 71–86; *Errigal* 71–5, 77–9, 83–6; *Ireland* 71, 73–7, 86; *Mists of Time* 71, 73–4, 81–3, 86; working methods 72–5; *Yeats Country* 71, 73–4, 79–80, 85–6
Five (Six) Mosaics 109–10, 167
for harp: 6–7, 108–9; *Album of Pieces for the Irish Harp* 109, 111–12, 121, 135; *Four Sketches* 7, 10, 109–11, 121–2, 124–30, 135; *A Pack of Fancies* 6–7, 108, 110–20; *Tighearna Mhuigheo* 135
In memoriam Mahatma Gandhi 5, 24, 32–4, 40, 59, 69
Irish subjects 38–43
Irish voice 5, 24–6, 37–8, 40, 43, 52, 56–7, 64–5, 116, 120
Jubilee Music 51–3
Magh Sleacht 5, 38, 58–70
Maiden and Seven Devils 10

Boydell, Brian {*cont.*}
   Masai Mara 53–6
   Megalithic Ritual Dances 38, 40–3, 46,
      58, 64, 81, 128, 166
   Mors et vita 46
   Mouth Music 167
   orchestral, generally 24–57
   Owl and the Pussy-Cat 70
   Partita Concertante 109–11
   Piano Album I 10
   programmatic 38–9, 54, 62, 64
   Quintet for Flute, Harp and String
      Trio 109, 111, 117–18
   recordings 6, 10–11, 40, 65, 67, 103–4,
      109, 118–19, 165–6, 169, 198
   Richard's Riot 43
   sacred 144; Psalm 85 144
   scores 198
   Shielmartin Suite 46, 123
   The Small Bell 109, 111, 167
   songs, song cycle: 6, 87–97, 100; *Aurelia*
      94; *Cathleen, the Daughter of*
      Houlihan 130; *Feather of Death* 6,
      99–107, 130, 191; *Five Joyce Songs*
      27–8, 96, 130, 165; *The Lamenting*
      95–6, 100, 189; *Musician's Song*
      109, 121, 131, 134; *Rushlights* 90–1,
      96; *Three Yeats Songs* 108–9, 121–
      2, 130–5; *Watching the*
      Needleboats 91–2, 95–6; *Wild*
      Geese 88–90, 96; *The Witch* 92–4,
      96, 130; withdrawn 6, 87, 91, 93–7
   string quartets 4, 16–23, 24, 27, 46, 53,
      59, 68–70, 165
   String Trio 96
   Symphonic Inscapes 28, 46–51, 53, 86
   Symphony for Strings 28–32, 46
   A Terrible Beauty is Born 46
   for theatre: 189: *House of Cards* 99, 189
   Three Geological Glees 167
   Two Madrigals 10
   Under No Circumstances 193
   Violin Concerto 24, 34–8, 40, 43
   Wooing of Etain 38–40, 47, 80
   Yeats Songs 7
Boydell, Eileen 14–15, 140
Boydell, James 14–15, 140
Boydell, Mary (née Jones) 123, 187, 190–3
Boydell (Conolly), Yvonne 100, 191

Boyle, Ina 28
Boyle, Peter 147
Brady, Erina 187
Brennan, Paddy 206
Buck, Percy Carter 140
Buckley, John 57
Buhler, René 190
Burton, Nigel 143–4
Butler, Thomas O'Brien 38
Byrd, William 143

Cage, John 82
Cáirde na Cruite 123
Capitol Theatre, Dublin 157
Carey, Patrick 5, 47, 71–2, 77, 79–81, 83–5
Carlow Town Hall 39
Carney, Frank 99, 189
Carolan, Turlough 108, 114, 115, 119, 122, 124
CBC (Canadian Broadcasting
   Corporation) 170
Celticism 38, 40, 56, 64
Cenn Cruaich 63
Chaloner, Enid 123
Chegwidden, Ann 72
Chewitt, Jocelyn 190
Chion, Michel 85
Choirland anthology 10
Christ Church Cathedral 139–141, 144
Clare, William 99
Clare College, Cambridge 2, 87, 101, 194
Clifford, Hubert 64–7
Clontarf Choral Society 162
Committee for the Promotion of New
   Music 165
Concorde 110
Connellan, Thomas 124
Connellan, William 124
Conolly, Thurloe 98–9, 106, 130, 171, 176–7,
   189–91
Conolly (née Boydell), Yvonne 100, 191
Consort of St Sepulchre 201
Contemporary Music Centre (CMC) 10,
   109
Cooper, Cáit 123
Cooper, Dick 123
Copland, Aaron 47
Cór Radio Éireann 162
Corcoran, Frank 57
Corcoran, Vincent 5, 71

Index

Corner, John 85
Cox, Gareth 1, 17–18, 26–7, 48
Crookshank, Anne 185
Crowe, Trevor 146, 148
Cubism 187
Cultural Relations Committee (CRC) 71, 79, 155, 159, 165
Culwick Choral Society 162
Cusack, Ralph 99, 188–90
Cutner, Solomon 2
Cuvillie [Caville], John Baptiste 145

Davidson, Lilian 186
Davies, Walford 171
Dawson, George 185
Deale, Edgar 155–7, 161–2
Decca 165
Delany, James 156
Degani Quartet 167
Dervan, Michael 53, 56, 116, 167
diatonism 23, 56, 112, 128
Dillon, Gerard 188
DIT Conservatory of Music and Drama 111
dodecaphony 26, 47
Doherty, Marion 167
Donoghue, Denis 39
Dorian mode 29, 40
Doris, Clíona 119
Dowland Consort 3, 87, 123, 142–4, 186, 201
Downes, Ralph 145–6
Dragon School, Oxford 2
Dublin Chamber Orchestra (DCO) 28, 43
Dublin Consort of Viols 201
Dublin Festival of Twentieth-Century Music 8, 27, 43, 108, 136, 166
Dublin International Organ Festival 111, 146
Dublin International Piano Competition 10
Dublin Marionette Group 191–2
Dublin Orchestral Players (DOP) 3, 22, 28, 39, 62, 180, 186, 195, 200
Dublin University Choral Society 193
Duff, Arthur 166
Dunne, Brendan 156–7, 160
Durrow, Co. Laois 147–8

Eblana Theatre, Dublin 124
Echo Club, Cambridge University 165
Eckerberg, Sixten 162
École des Beaux Arts 186

Education, Department of 157, 159
Egestorff, Paul 100, 189
Éire-Ireland 25, 115
Enchiriadis Treis Choir 167
Encyclopaedia of Music in Ireland 10, 206
Errigal 47, 71–5, 77–9, 83–6
European Union 56
Everett, James 157
External Affairs, Department of 71, 79

'Faeth Feadha' 38
Fallon, Padraic 39, 80
Farrell, Hazel 59
Farrington, Anthony 8, 158
FÁS (An Foras Áiseanna Saothair) 167
Fearon, W. R. 90
Fearon, William 100
Feis Ceoil 165
Field, John 152
Field, Robert 152
film scores 72 *see also* Boydell, Brian (works, musical)
Finucane, John 43
Fitzgerald, Mark 25
Fleischmann, Aloys 27–8, 40, 53, 56, 80, 84, 136, 155–6, 158–9, 161, 164, 174
Fleischmann, Georg 79
folk music 5, 8, 15–6, 23, 26, 79, 90, 115–16, 122, 124, 155, 164, 166 *see also* Irish traditional music
Fox, Ian 166
French, R. B. D. 75
Frost, Stella 186

Gaeltacht, Department of 79
Gaffney, Elizabeth 110
Gaiety Theatre, Dublin 39–40, 47, 51
Gandhi, Mahatma 32
Gibbons, Luke 77
Gilbert, Stephen 190
Gillen, Gerard 146, 167
Gleizes, Albert 187
Gloucester Cathedral organ 146
Goetze and Gwynn 147
Government, first inter-party 156
Gramophone 119
gramophone technology 6
Graydon, Philip 47, 49
Grayson, David 147

Green, Samuel 145
Greevy, Bernadette 167
Greig, William Sydney 140–2
Groocock, Joseph 123, 135, 155–6, 161

Hadley, Patrick 3, 16, 91
Haffenden, John 101
Hall, Kenneth 98, 190
Handel, George Frideric 150–1
harp 108–20, 121–36
    accompaniment 131–3
    Irish 85, 108, 110–11, 121–36
    pedal 6, 108–9, 116, 135
    techniques 76, 84, 110, 112, 114, 124–6
Harriet Cohen International Music
    Award 123
Harty, Sir Herbert Hamilton 5, 15, 25, 38
Harvey, Revd Canon Patrick 147–8
Haughey, Charles J. 163
Haughton, Joe 185
Heidelberg University 2, 16, 26, 88, 91, 144
Hennessy, Swan 38
Henry, Paul 186
Heseltine, Nigel 9, 95, 100, 189
Heseltine, Philip *see* Warlock, Peter
Hewson, George 140, 142–3
Hill, John 77
Hill and Son 145
Hindemith, Paul 26–7
Holohan, Michael 57
Hone, Evie 9, 99, 186–7
Hopkins, Gerard Manley 47, 56, 84
Horvat, Milan 35, 39–40, 43, 165
Houlihan, Robert 43
Houston, Kerry 143, 147
Howells, Herbert 3, 16, 92, 144
Hugh Lane Municipal Gallery of Modern
    Art 110–11
Hughes, Anthony 156
Hunt, Peter 72, 79
Hunt, Una 206

Imaal, Rathfarnham 99–100, 190–2
Incenzo, Michele 43, 166
Ingouville-Williams, Herbrand 98–9
International Society for Contemporary
    Music 165
Ireland (film) 71–7, 86

Ireland, music in 173–4, 199, 202–7
Ireland, prehistoric 64
Irish Church Hymnal 143
Irish Exhibition of Living Art (IELA) 188,
    192
Irish Film Archive 77–8
Irish Harp Book 10, 135
Irish identity, and music 24–6, 164–6
Irish mythology 5, 38–40, 58, 62–3
Irish National Teachers' Organisation
    (INTO) 159
Irish Press 65, 130
Irish Times 30, 39, 42, 53, 109, 130, 149, 174,
    191
    'An Irishman's Diary' 78–9, 85–6, 163
Irish Tourist Association 71
Irish Trade Union Congress 160
Irish traditional music 6, 25, 37, 51–2, 116 *see
    also* folk music

Jackson, George 32
Jellett, Mainie 9, 98, 186–9
Johnston, Fergus 57
Jones, Kenneth 146
Jones, Mary *see* Boydell, Mary
Jose, Leonard 123
Joyce, James 91

Keating, Seán 186, 188
Kehoe, P. J. 169
Kelly, Denise 108, 110–11, 116, 118–19
Kelly, Francis J. 161
Kelly, Jean 119
Kelly, T. C. 124, 166
Kennedy, S. B. 99
Kennedy Memorial Hall 163–4
Kerwood, Lionel 99, 190
Kinmonth, P. B. 94
Kinsella, Thomas 38
Kitson, Charles 140
Klein, Axel 1, 88, 169

Larchet, John 16, 166, 182
Larchet, Madeleine 156
Larchet, Máire 109
Larchet Cuthbert, Sheila 108–9, 111, 123,
    135
Lawlor, Teresa 108, 111–12, 121, 135

le Brocquy, Louis 188
le Brocquy, Melanie 188
Lemass, Seán 163
Lhote, André 187
Listen to Britain 85
Lord, Nancie 156, 162
Lyon, P. H. B. 88
Lyons, Cornelius 124

Macbride, Seán 71
MacGonigal, Maurice 186, 188
McGrath, Raymond 164
McGuinness, Norah 187–8
McKenna, Lambert 63
McKenna, Siobhán 80
Mac Liammóir, Micheál 80
McMullin, Michael 66, 155–8, 160–1
McQuaid, Archbishop Charles John 15
Mág Shamhradain, Brian, Lord of Magh Sléacht 63
Magahy, Cork 145
Malîr, Andreja 118–19
Malone, P. J. 158–9
Martell, Philip 75
Martinon, Jean 58, 60–1, 64–7
Masai Mara, Kenya 53
Matzerath, Otto 162
May, Frederick 17, 28, 33, 56, 155–6, 158, 161, 164, 166
May, Thomas 160
Mervyn, Ruth 124
Messiaen, Olivier 18, 27
Meulien, Maurice 109
Middleton, Colin 188
Milesians 63
Mists of Time 47, 71, 73–4, 81–3, 86
Modernism, 185–6, 189, 191
    European 6, 98, 101
Moeran, Ernest John 26, 30–2
Moffett, Margot 98–9, 190
Moffett, Noel 98, 190
Mornington, Lord (Gareth Wesley [Wellesly]) 139, 152
Morris, Hazel 123
Mosse, Bartholomew 151–2
Mostly Modern Series concerts 115
Moyse, Arthur 142
Moyslaught (Magh Sleacht), Co. Cavan 63

Music Association of Ireland (MAI) 8–9, 110, 155–68, 173, 201
    Archive 160
    Composers' Group 155, 164–8
    establishment 155–7
    golden jubilee 167
    initiatives 157–64
    policy 157–60
Music Generation 202
Music Network 200
Music World 180
'My Gentle Harp' recital, Eblana Theatre 124

na gCopaleen, Myles 191
national anthem 162
National Campaign for the Arts 204
National College of Art 188
National Concert Hall, Dublin (NCH) 108, 110, 135, 166–7, 201–2
National Film Institute of Ireland 79
National Gallery of Ireland 19, 110
National Music Association *see* Music Association of Ireland
National Opera Company 202
New Irish Chamber Orchestra 43
New Music Dublin 8
Ní Chathailriabhaigh, Eibhlín 167
Ní hÉigeartaigh, Gráinne *see* Yeats, Gráinne
Nicholls, Nick 188, 190
Nichols, Robert 94
Northwestern University 60

O'Brien, Harvey 77
Ó Broin, Leon 157–8
O'Conghaile, Caoimhín 63–4, 67
O'Connor, Terry 156
O'Conor, John 167
octatonism 18–19, 27, 33, 35, 40, 54, 104, 126
Ó Dochartaigh, Seoirse 42–3
O'Doherty, Brian 188
O'Doherty, Geraldine 119
'O'Donnell Abú' 52
O'Donovan, Una 108, 111–14, 117–18
O'Dwyer, Robert 38
O'Farrell, Anne-Marie 10
O'Flaherty, Ellen 59

O'Flynn, John 25
O'Flynn, Philip 75
Ó Gallchobhair, Éamonn 79–80
O'Grady, Sheila 110
O'Hara, Mary 124
O'Huiginn, Tadhg Dall 63
Ó Laoghaire, Liam 160
Oldham, Edward 100, 189
Olympia Theatre 9
O'Neill, Brian 171
O'Neill, Joseph 156, 158–9
opera 202–7
Ord, Boris 140
O'Rourke, Brian 43
Ó Sé, Éamonn 160
Ó Súilleabháin, Tomás 123
O'Sullivan, Eilís 123
Otway Ruthven, Jocelyn 185

Paganini, Niccolò 178
Pasquali, Niccolo 152
Patrickson, Thomas 144
'Patsy Mack' 52
Pearce, Colman 51
Pease, Lancelot 144–5
People's College 8, 160–1
Petit, Maurice 91
Phoenix Hall, Dublin 65–6
Pine, Richard 8, 38, 158, 169
Pipeworks 146
Pöche, Herbert 28, 43
Poppen, Meinhard 144
Posts and Telegraphs, Department of 157
Potter, A. J. 53, 135, 165–6
Poulsen, Valdemar 104
prepared piano 82–4
Prieur, André 109
Prieur Ensemble 109
Prokofiev, Sergei 16
Prout, Ebenezer 139–40
psychotherapy 98, 100

Quidnunc 163

Radio Éireann (RÉ) 8–9, 58, 62, 157–8, 171, 183
    'Children's Hour' 170, 182
    Schools Concerts 182
Radio Éireann Orchestra 28

Radio Éireann Symphony Orchestra (RÉSO) 3, 28, 32, 35, 39–40, 43, 58, 65–6, 157, 165–6
Radio Review 66
Rady, Simon 165–6
Rákóczi, Basil 98, 100, 190
Rathfarnham Academy of Surrealist Art 100, 191–2
Read, Herbert 100, 190
recording technology 104
Reford, Tony 189
Reid, Nano 188
Renaissance music 3, 14, 55, 123, 143
Richards, Sheila 189
Roberts, Hilda 186
Roberts, Ruaidhrí 160
Robinson, Mary 200
Rockett, Kevin 77
Rogers, Holly 85
Rondel, Georgette 190
Roseingrave, Ralph 139
Rosen, Albert 47, 51
Rotunda Hospital 151–3
Roughton, Roger 190
Royal College of Music, London 2–3, 92
Royal College of Organists 140
Royal Dublin Society (RDS) 117, 161
Royal Hibernian Academy (RHA) 186, 188
Royal Irish Academy of Music (RIAM) 3, 16, 62, 87, 185–6
RTÉ 71, 79, 87, 110–11, 130–1, 183
    Archive 169
RTÉ Concert Orchestra 43
RTÉ National Symphony Orchestra 32, 43
RTÉ Singers 111
RTÉ String Quartet 19
RTÉ Symphony Orchestra (RTÉSO) 32, 43, 47, 51, 75, 135, 162, 201
Rugby School 2, 15–16
Ryan, Joseph J. 25

St Columba's College 186
St Fintan's Church, Durrow, Co. Laois 147–8
St Francis Xavier Hall, Dublin 51, 134
St Patrick's Cathedral, Dublin 111, 140–2, 144–5
    Guinness Choir Scheme 142

Index

Scott, Patrick 187–8
Seafort, Frederick 152
Seaton, Philip 189
serialism 26, 47–8
Shaw, George Bernard 160
Shelbourne Hotel, Dublin 22, 99, 190–1
Sheridan, John D. 79
Sheridan, Mary 134–5
Sheridan, Thomas 152
Sibelius, Jean 26, 115
Sleator, James 186
Sluizer, George 71–3
Smale, Alan 110
Smith, Gillian 74
Smith, John 139
Smith, Olive 8, 156, 158, 161, 163
Smyth, Gerry 25
Society for Creative Psychology 98
Society of Dublin Painters 186, 188
Stanford, Charles 5, 15, 25, 38
Stewart, Robert 139
Stokes, Dorothy 156
Strauss, Richard 88
Stravinsky, Igor 40, 42
Stubbs, Kenneth 2, 88
Subjective art 99, 100, 190
Sullivan, Arthur 143
Surrealism 9, 98–9
Swanzy, Mary 186

Takemitsu, Tōru 115
tárogató 153
Taylor, Michael 1, 17, 42, 64, 66, 88, 96, 201–2
Telford, William 145
tenor recorder 54–6
Testore String Quartet 110
'Tochmarc Étaíne' 39
Trenton, Louise 87, 92
Trimble, Joan 135
Trinity College Dublin (TCD) 18, 165
   archives: Brian Boydell archive 9–10, 67–70, 116, 169–70, 193–8; Manuscripts & Archives Research Library 58–9, 193–4
   art collection 185
   chapel: 7, 139–48; organ 144–8
   Choral Society 123
   Committee of Taste 185
   Historical Society 123
   School of Music 3
   TCD Miscellany 90

UNESCO International Rostrum of Composers 130
University College Dublin 16, 140

Vanaček, Jaroslav 35, 109
Vanston, Doreen 188
Verwoerd, Melanie 15
Victory, Gerard 53, 158, 166
Vocational Education Scheme 161
voice-overs 71, 85–6

Wagner, Richard 26, 88
Walsh, Basil 206
Walsh, Derek 206
Warlock, Peter (Philip Heseltine) 9, 95, 189
The Curlew 101–2, 104
Watt, William F. 156
Watts, William 147
Weber, Ferdinand 163
Wertheim, Lucy 98, 187
Wesley [Wellesly], Gareth (Lord Mornington) 139, 152
Whelan, Peter 206
White, Harry 3, 8, 153–4
White Stag Group 3, 6, 9, 72, 98–100, 187–8, 190
Exhibition of Subjective Art (1944) 99, 190
Williamson, Bruce 99
Wilson, James 135
Woodhouse, Hugh Frederic 141–2
'Wooing of Étain' 39
Workers' Educational Organisation 160
World Harp Congress, Ninth (Dublin) 119

Yeats, Anne 99, 189
Yeats, Caitríona 108, 110–11, 117–18
Yeats, Gráinne (née Ní hÉigeartaigh) 6–7, 110–11, 121–36
Yeats, Jack 191
Yeats, Michael 123
Yeats, W. B. 7, 23, 92, 101, 130–1
Yeats, W. B. – A Tribute 79
Yeats Country 47, 71, 73–4, 77–81, 85–6
Yeats International Summer School 131